The FBI's Obscene File

THE FBI'S OBSCENE FILE

J. Edgar Hoover and the Bureau's Crusade against Smut

Douglas M. Charles

University Press of Kansas

Published by the University Press of Kansas (Lawrence, Kansas 66045), which was organized by the Kansas Board of Regents and is operated and funded by Emporia State University, Fort Hays State University, Kansas State University, Pittsburg State University, the University of Kansas, and Wichita State University

Library of Congress Cataloging-in-Publication Data

Charles, Douglas M.
The FBI's obscene file : J. Edgar Hoover and the Bureau's crusade against smut / Douglas M. Charles.
  p. cm.
Includes bibliographical references and index.
ISBN 978-0-7006-1825-5 (cloth : alk. paper)
1. Hoover, J. Edgar (John Edgar), 1895–1972. 2. United States. Federal Bureau of Investigation—History. 3. Pornography—United States—History—20th century. 4. Obscenity (Law)—United States—History—20th century. 5. United States—Moral conditions—History—20th century. I. Title.
HV8144.F43C427 2012
363.25'97409730904—dc23

2012000590

British Library Cataloguing-in-Publication Data is available.

Printed in the United States of America

10 9 8 7 6 5 4 3 2 1

The paper used in this publication is recycled and contains 30 percent postconsumer waste. It is acid free and meets the minimum requirements of the American National Standard for Permanence of Paper for Printed Library Materials Z39.48-1992.

For my academic mentors,

Rhodri Jeffreys-Jones

Athan Theoharis

John Paul Rossi

Robert Szymczak

CONTENTS

It's fascinating to me how one comes to write about a particular subject. For instance, my first book originated from my long interest in history, beginning in the seventh grade when I first learned about Charles Lindbergh in Mr. Wilson Holbein's class. Later, in college, I learned of the FBI's interest in Lindbergh. But I did not sit down one day resolved to write a book about the FBI and obscenity. I came to this topic by way of my research interest in the FBI and homosexuality. During inquiries for that project, I learned that the FBI had targeted early gay rights groups using anti-obscenity law. As an FBI scholar, I was aware of the existence of the FBI's Obscene File through the work of Athan Theoharis; however, given the dearth of research about it, I, like everyone else, knew very little. I believed the Obscene File had to contain information that would help me better understand the FBI's interest in homosexuality. But I feared that it would be impossible to gain access to the file, either because it no longer existed or because the costs of obtaining what I assumed to be a huge amount of material through the Freedom of Information Act (FOIA) would be prohibitive (at ten cents per page). I decided to take a shot in the dark, submitted my FOIA request, and was surprised to receive in the mail the reasonably sized administrative portion of the FBI's Obscene File. While reading through it, I realized that it did indeed contain information about the FBI and homosexuality, but it also revealed much about the FBI and obscenity—a topic no scholar had examined in depth and one that was innately interesting. I thought the topic was important enough to warrant its own study, and because it informed my research on the FBI and homosexuality, I decided to pursue it before completing that project. Hence, this book.

There are countless people who helped me put this book together in one way or another—too many to acknowledge in this short space. I must thank my history colleagues, whose advice, comments, friendship, and willingness to share their expertise were invaluable. They include Athan Theoharis, Robert Justin Goldstein, Rhodri Jeffreys-Jones, Robert Mason, John Paul Rossi, Robert Szymczak, and Aaron Stockham. Dave Brown, of Marietta College, helped me compile FBI data into the graph in chapter 3, a skill sadly lost on me. My friend Ryan Graziani has a keen eye for political news and pointed out obscure and recent obscenity news that I would have missed. Dr. Kurt Torell released me from my courses so that I could complete most of the writing of this book, for which I am grateful.

Numerous archivists, librarians, and government employees were invaluable in locating materials. Kimberli Morris, a reference librarian at Penn State's law library, located information that I could not. Hannah August of the Justice Department's Office of Public Affairs kindly sent me data on recent obscenity cases, and the department's FOIA staff helped me determine whether certain case files were accessible or lost. The archivists of the Nixon Presidential Materials kindly located documents scattered in different files, even after I left College Park. The FBI's FOIA staff was particularly helpful in narrowing down my requests and keeping me posted on their progress.

I'd also like to thank Michael Briggs, editor in chief at the University Press of Kansas, for shepherding this project through and kindly answering my multiple questions, as well as the entire staff at the press for making the book preparation process easier than it normally would have been.

Finally, I'd like to thank my family for their unending support (including parrot sitting) through many research trips and research projects, including this one. I am fortunate to have them.

The FBI's Obscene File

Beginning in the 1910s, officials of the Federal Bureau of Investigation (FBI) began to develop an interest in something that had concerned law enforcement for centuries: obscenity. FBI agents uncovered obscenity by way of investigating prostitution rings, but it would take several developments before FBI officials made the decision to target and investigate obscenity in a systematic fashion. Those developments were rooted in evolving perceptions of obscenity as the twentieth century unfolded, as well as two specific traumatic events—the First and Second World Wars— that caused public and governmental concern for the welfare of America's impressionable youth to bubble to the surface. The aftermath of the First World War led FBI officials to develop special procedures for the collection of obscenity during a period of traumatic social change, and the FBI created its centralized and sensitive Obscene File after the Second World War. From that point forward, FBI officials would make obscenity, pornography, and the politics of morality one of their primary concerns, and this concern would constantly evolve as the country entered and exited various troubled periods in its history.

The issues of obscenity and pornography in American history have evolved in numerous ways over multiple decades, if not centuries. Even the definition of what is and is not obscene has changed seemingly countless times, clouding the issue not only for moralists and law enforcement officials from various historical periods but also for historians trying to make sense of a complex and nebulous topic. Nevertheless, numerous studies have been undertaken, with many of the earlier works focusing on censorship, legal history, and Supreme Court decisions.[1] Others have focused on nineteenth-century moral crusader Anthony Comstock,[2] and more recently, scholars have examined obscenity and its intersection with gender history and sexuality.[3] Some scholars have focused on American cities, significantly New York City,[4] while others have looked to right-wing politics to understand this elusive topic.[5] What is missing from the historiography is the role played by the FBI, the federal government's chief law enforcement arm, housed in the Justice Department. This is surprising, given that the FBI has existed since 1908 and has involved itself with the issue of obscenity from at least 1910 and continues to do so today. A glaring example of the lacuna in the literature is the fact that my search produced just a single scholarly article on a specific and narrow topic involving obscenity and the FBI.[6] Beyond this, there are only brief mentions in FBI historiography—by a single scholar—of the existence of an FBI Obscene File,[7] the nature of which scholars have never fully understood. Otherwise, the FBI's significant and evolving role in targeting obscenity, and later pornography, has gone unexamined.

One explanation for this oversight has to do with the relative newness of histories of the FBI. True scholarly works examining the FBI have existed only since the mid-1970s, when, after various FBI abuses became public, scholars won access to FBI files as primary sources via the Freedom of Information Act (FOIA). Previous studies were either journalistic or FBI-sanctioned "official" histories. Additionally, FBI scholars have been most interested in issues of political surveillance and abuses of authority rather than muddled social issues such as obscenity. Obscenity scholars have not examined the FBI because primary sources were difficult to come by and because the FBI and its history constitute a complex and specialized field of study.

An examination of the FBI and its interest in obscenity and pornography not only fills a gap in the histories of obscenity regulation and the FBI; it also informs our larger understanding of how obscenity targeting and regulation have evolved from the American colonial period to the present. More specifically, as the existing literature on obscenity and the FBI's long history make apparent, obscenity targeting is influenced by and responsive to significant changes in American social values, culture, and politics over time. Changes in obscenity regulation have flowed, historically, from sociocultural shifts, which can be either cultural or political, or from cataclysmic events—namely, wars—that dramatically call into question society's moral state, raise questions about how the country became involved in such traumatic times, or focus public scrutiny on gender and the influences on American youth, especially those headed into the maelstrom of combat.[8] Obscenity regulation has also changed in response to technological developments affecting the obscenity and pornography industry. Similarly, innovations in the distribution of obscenity and pornography have made such materials more available and more accessible, leading to upswings in obscenity regulation.

The FBI's unique role is determined in large measure by the nature of the beast. The FBI is, to a significant degree, responsive to the interests of policy makers and to the influences of social pressures, especially when it comes to popular and controversial subjects like obscenity. Therefore, when the country experienced a sociocultural shift, prompting a response from policy makers, FBI officials invariably acceded to the desires of their political overseers or to intense public pressure, when warranted. Public pressure and politics raise another important historiographical issue regarding the Nixon administration. Of all the studies of Richard Nixon, only three touch on the obscenity issue as one of his domestic political concerns,[9] and even these three mention it only briefly. But as I show here, the FBI provided significant assistance to Nixon in this area— one that both the administration and the bureau considered important and in which they were deeply involved. Moreover, evidence indicates that the Nixon administration sought to curtail the influence of obscenity in the country rather than simply exploiting the issue for rhetorical and political purposes, which is the traditional historical interpretation. Last, FBI officials had to respond to changes in the law; especially after 1957, the U.S. Supreme Court repeatedly refined legal definitions of obscenity and what could and could not be targeted for prosecution.

The FBI's role in obscenity cases was further and significantly influenced by the views, priorities, and backgrounds of its various directors. Given the long tenure of J. Edgar Hoover (1924–1972), one can view the totality of the FBI's history with regard to obscenity issues as consisting of two broad and distinct periods: the Hoover era and the post-Hoover era. The FBI's formal role in obscenity regulation began in 1925 under Hoover's stewardship, and it reflected his own priorities—that is, this stalwart bureaucrat sought to use anti-obscenity law to protect American culture from the influences of what he perceived as un-American forces. Hoover also used the issue and the means by which FBI agents collected data on obscenity to advance his own particular bureaucratic and political objectives. Hoover was able to accomplish this because, under his direction, the FBI grew from a small, relatively insignificant agency into a large, influential, and highly respected one. In 1936, under Hoover, the FBI's priority shifted from criminal investigations and prosecutions to national security and the collection of intelligence (i.e., noncriminal information); in addition, under Hoover, the bureau undertook both overt and covert efforts to shape public opinion. At the heart of both these developments was Hoover's strong sense of anti-communism and morality. Therefore, during the Hoover era, obscenity was very much a primary concern of the director's and hence the bureau's, and it is an aspect of FBI history that historians have mostly ignored.

Following Hoover's death and public revelations of the FBI's abuse of authority, which were followed by more stringent efforts at congressional oversight, subsequent FBI directors redirected the bureau's priorities. They sought, first, to restore the FBI's public image and public sense of respectability. Second, they actively refocused FBI efforts in obscenity cases away from cultural containment and back to a primarily law enforcement role. Anti-obscenity efforts by post-Hoover era FBI directors reflected their own particular priorities, whether these involved the means by which FBI agents collected data, the particular targets they focused on, or responses to technological advances or other innovations used by the purveyors of smut. But these FBI directors and their anti-obscenity plans always had to correspond with the political and policy interests of their superiors in the Justice Department and the White House.

This book does not profess to be a definitive or comprehensive study of the FBI and obscenity. Rather, given the enormity of the topic—which spans nearly a century—and the dearth of scholarly examinations of the issue, this book serves as a primer. The primary documentary basis for this book is the administrative portion of the FBI's Obscene File, which was originally composed of both a massive physical file of collected obscene samples (magazines, pictures, films, and the like), which was incinerated in the early 1990s, and an (incomplete) administrative file of memoranda, reports, and other documents. The administrative portion of the Obscene File, as a bureau policy file, provides information about FBI officials' policy decisions regarding obscenity and pornography targeting and about creating and maintaining the sensitive and centralized Obscene File itself. Ideally, historians would also like to have access to all FBI case files on individuals and organizations targeted under federal anti-obscenity law; however, given the realities of research into FBI records—requests must be made under the FOIA, and it typically takes years to process a request and win access to a single file—gaining access to every case file is simply not feasible. Additionally, scholars lack access to a centralized index of obscenity targets, so identifying specific files for FOIA requests is extremely difficult.

The National Archives surveyed the contents of FBI records[10]— records that, except for some popular files, have not been deposited in the National Archives—and found that obscenity- and pornography-related FBI case files number over 100,000. For example, the FBI's file classification 145 (Interstate Transportation of Obscene Matter) included 6,087 bureau headquarters case files and 37,631 field office case files; FBI file classification 71 (Bills of Lading) included 6,175 headquarters case files and 17,894 field office case files; FBI file classification 178 (Interstate Obscene or Harassing Telephone Calls) included 297 headquarters files and examples from all 59 FBI field offices, with some records having been destroyed; FBI file classification 36 (Mail Fraud) included 2,776 headquarters files and no field office files; and FBI file classification 183 (Racketeer-Influenced and Corrupt Organizations), which FBI officials used to target organized crime and its links to pornography, included 4,464 headquarters files and 35,000 field office case files.[11] Since it is not feasible to gain access to these voluminous records, any examination into the FBI's role in obscenity and pornography issues must rely on the FBI's policy file about obscenity and identifiable and accessible case files. This book takes that approach.

Finally, this study examines the topic of the FBI and obscenity based on its institutional and bureaucratic history and the impact of politics and pressures stemming from changes in American culture and society. The FBI's priorities and foci have shifted over the decades of its 100-plus years of existence. This book does not analyze FBI officials' interests in obscenity through the lens of gender or sexuality—a significant focus of obscenity scholarship today—although those issues are touched on at appropriate points. Studies of the FBI are many, and scholarly works in the field of obscenity are wide ranging, but next to nobody has examined the two together. This book is merely a start and will, I hope, spark further scholarship.

CHAPTER ONE

The Evolution of American Obscenity Regulation and the FBI

The 1830s to 1932

For centuries, Americans from all walks of life have been fascinated with obscenity. In the eighteenth century, sexually themed literature was something that either appealed to or concerned many Americans. The locus of this literature was America's colonial port cities—New York City, Philadelphia, and Boston—where a significant amount of titillating print was imported from Europe and sold by American merchants, to the delight of colonial readers. These books included English works of fiction that were laced with sexual overtones, the various and explicit writings of the French philosophes, eighteenth-century sex manuals, anti-masturbation books, and even the published transcripts of European criminal trials that involved the gentry class and their sordid sex scandals.[1] Yet irrespective of the significant interest in and sale of items that some Americans might have regarded as obscene and therefore inimical to the mores of society, there were few if any prosecutions involving such literature. One reason for this was that prosecution relied on private citizens filing complaints rather than the blanket enforcement of laws—obscenity law at this time was common law—which would not, and did not, lead to any serious anti-obscenity targeting. Not until the 1820s did some American states, mainly in the Northeast, begin to enact anti-obscenity laws to clamp down on the pervasiveness of lurid literature, and federal law enforcement efforts were not seriously considered until midcentury.[2]

Immediately prior to these mid-nineteenth-century efforts to restrict obscenity, a uniquely American—that is, not imported—sexually themed literature was born. These publications originated in New York City in the 1830s and 1840s, and readership extended beyond the upper classes, which had previously been the almost exclusive buyers of sexually themed books. The best example of this class shift in the interest in obscenity can be seen in the city newspapers and especially in the development of the penny press and the flash weeklies. The penny press consisted of newspapers costing only one cent—allowing people of lesser means to buy them. These newspapers targeted a largely working-class audience and focused their reporting on the illicit activities of city brothels, various lurid sexual escapades, and local sporting events. The flash weeklies covered topics that were outside respectable society (i.e., they were flashy or flamboyant), including sexually themed topics, which they scrutinized even more closely than the penny press did. Newspapers were not the only publications reporting on the city's brothels; some even reviewed them for the urban American citizenry. The most famous example was the pamphlet *Prostitution Exposed,* in which the author ranked the various houses of degradation in a half-mocking way, as if he were reviewing the city's restaurants. In short, sexually themed literature in America evolved from an imported product to a domestic and commercialized product.[3]

How did American authorities respond to this social and legal problem? The vast majority of nineteenth-century Americans viewed law enforcement in strictly states' rights terms. They did not believe the federal government should be involved in law enforcement in any significant way and fervently believed that this was the responsibility of local and state governments. In pursuing obscenity, local and state officials had legal precedent with which to prosecute those involved in anything that, in their opinion, was obscene. American jurisprudence was still evolving during the 1800s, so law enforcement officials looked to legal precedents from English common law, as well as various legal opinions rendered in the states of New York, Pennsylvania, and Massachusetts. Those three states had effectively affirmed the efficacy of English common law in the embryonic U.S. judicial system. Yet prosecutors chose not to focus on the publication of obscene materials; instead, they prosecuted individuals for their wayward personal conduct—such as publishers of flash weeklies who regularly blackmailed well-to-do individuals with the lurid information they collected. But even these prosecutions did not extend much beyond the 1840s. Dating from the 1820s and 1830s, state legislatures—such as those in Vermont, Connecticut, and Massachusetts—had begun to pass their own anti-obscenity statutes rather than relying on English common law. This pattern continued, and by the time of the Civil War era, a total of sixteen states had enacted their own anti-obscenity statutes.[4]

With these new state laws on the books, prosecutions began to shift away from individual personal conduct and started to target the production or distribution of obscene products. Despite the dominance of an anti-statist philosophy of government, a legal precedent in 1842 set the stage for the later federal crackdown on obscene literature and materials. That year Congress quietly, and without public explanation, amended the Tariff Act explicitly to prohibit the importation of any "obscene or immoral" publications or images. Although we do not know exactly why Congress took this action, it likely had to do with the Whig Party's frustration with President John Tyler. Tyler wanted to limit the tariff rates, while the Whig Party wanted high protective ones. Whigs probably included obscenity in an attempt to get what they could from a president who was constantly frustrating their efforts during an election year in which the tariff was a major issue (the tariff was the party's one accomplishment at the time). In addition, prohibiting the importation of obscenity undoubtedly had to do with the fact that the Whigs were champions of moral reform. In any event, the law empowered the Bureau of Customs and its agents to seize anything regarded as obscene or that violated their own perceptions of American morality. Because lawmakers did not clarify what was and was not obscene, such distinctions were largely made by federal customs agents.[5]

During the 1850s, as the United States began to witness the gathering storm that would become the Civil War, Congress again expanded the Tariff Act's anti-obscenity provisions to include more obscene items and specifically photographs. As the technology of photography advanced—such as the advent of less expensive types of photography and the development of the stereoscope box, which offered three-dimensional views of photographic images—the production of obscene materials became easier, and American lawmakers included this medium in their anti-obscenity efforts. Also of increasing concern was obscenity purveyors' recent innovation of using the U.S. mail to disseminate their materials across the country. Whereas obscenity prosecution was strictly a local affair, and selling obscenity was sometimes banned in places such as New York City, there was no federal law against selling it by mail order or mailing it between states. Concurrently, the rapid development of railroads enabled the quick distribution of mail—and therefore obscenity—nationwide. These innovations would give rise to a new national and federal effort to clamp down on obscenity, thereby defining a federal role in law enforcement. Trumping these important developments, however, was a more pressing concern that arose during the Civil War and prompted Congress to specifically target obscenity and crack down on obscene items sent through the U.S. mail.[6]

Smut dealers began to focus their business efforts on Union soldiers by advertising mail-order erotica in flash weeklies. The widespread distribution of obscenity among soldiers led one man to comment that his compatriots, whether religiously oriented or not, "have taken to reading flimsy publications, obscene books, and the worst species of yellow-covered literature."[7] (Yellow referred to the wrapping around obscene publications that was meant to attract customers.) Even so, it was not until 1865, the final year of the Civil War, that Postmaster General William Dennison discovered that a large number of obscene books and pictures were being sent through the mail to Union soldiers. Perceiving this to be only the tip of the iceberg and a problem that required immediate attention, Dennison championed the enactment of legislation that would give him the power both to seize any obscene matter from the mail and to seek prosecution of those who dared to send it. After a short debate, on 3 March 1865 Congress declared "that no obscene book, pamphlet, picture, print, or other publication of a vulgar and indecent character shall be admitted into the mails." Furthermore, the law held that anyone who knowingly mailed such items would be guilty of a misdemeanor and subject to a $500 fine, one year in jail, or both. Significantly, lawmakers again failed to offer a clear definition of what qualified as obscene, which meant that federal bureaucrats would continue to make such determinations and therefore exercise a great degree of latitude in whom they targeted.[8]

Within the next decade American jurisprudence would be expanded even more, all in an effort to clamp down on the prevalence of obscenity. At the heart of this expansion was Anthony Comstock, a moralist crusader from New York City. Comstock had an unusual personal interest and background in tracking down peddlers of smut and distributors of mail-order obscenity; he had a parallel interest in pursuing those who violated the narrowly prescribed gender roles of the nineteenth century. Following the Civil War, Comstock worked as an investigator for the Young Men's Christian Association's (YMCA's) Committee for the Suppression of Vice and later for the New York Society for the Suppression of

Vice, whose charter mandated the assistance of the New York City police. While targeting obscenity locally, Comstock came to realize that it had become a serious national problem for which local laws were inadequate. So in 1873, the YMCA sent the twenty-eight-year-old Comstock to Washington to lobby hard for a new federal law that covered not just obscene publications and images but also information about contraception, abortion, and anything else related to sex, whether intended for educational or lascivious purposes. In his Manichaean outlook, Comstock regarded the broad category of obscenity in the mail as a "hydra headed monster" that needed to be slain.[9]

Comstock and his cohorts pushed hard in their lobbying efforts. He made use of the obscenity examples he had collected over the years and put them on display for shocked congressmen, while making the argument that the U.S. mail had helped this particular business not only grow but also thrive. Comstock achieved success when, in March 1873, Congress passed a new and stronger federal anti-obscenity law and named it after the New York crusader. Specifically, the law outlawed sending through the mail anything that could be construed as "obscene, lewd, lascivious, indecent, filthy, or vile," including all foreign obscene materials and, specifically, information about contraception. Yet once again, legislators made no attempt to define obscenity. As in the past, this gave customs agents and postal inspectors a tremendous amount of latitude in deciding what was obscene and therefore a violation of the law. They would retain such discretion for decades to come.[10]

Passage of the Comstock Act did not end Comstock's crusade. He won a federal appointment as a postal inspector and assumed a lead role in enforcing the law that carried his name. Prior to his appointment, postal inspectors sought few prosecutions—only seven between 1865 and 1872. Over the next seven years, Comstock was personally responsible for the government's pursuit of more than a hundred anti-obscenity prosecutions. His method of going after smut peddlers was to order erotica through their advertising and then use it as evidence against them in court. What's more, Comstock won the support of federal prosecutors and sympathetic Justice Department officials (the department itself was only two years old, having been established in 1870), and he made use of rural jurisdictions, where views about obscenity were more conservative, to ensure successful prosecutions. This last tactic would be replicated in the twenty-first century when the FBI resumed its targeting of what officials called "adult obscenity."[11]

Irrespective of the latitude granted to customs agents and postal inspectors, the overall scope of federal prosecutions in the late nineteenth century was still limited. Traditionally, dating from the founding of the nation, law enforcement in the United States had reflected the governmental philosophy of laissez-faire. The federal government's responsibilities were limited, and law enforcement was traditionally reserved as a matter for state and local governments. The anti-obscenity movement, moreover, was led by anti-vice societies in American cities that pushed for local law enforcement rather than a federal effort. The first significant change in this area came after the Civil War, during Reconstruction, when in 1870 the Republican Congress created the Department of Justice to be headed by the attorney general. Previously, the attorney general's role had been limited to representing the federal government in court and advising the president in matters of law. As such, and unlike his fellow Cabinet members, the attorney general had not overseen an executive department like the Departments of State, Treasury, or War. But when it became clear that local and state governments in the South could not be counted on to enforce the new Fourteenth and Fifteenth Amendments to the U.S. Constitution—ensuring equal protection under the law and the freed slaves' right to vote, respectively—or to protect African Americans and their champions from violent intimidation and white terrorism at the hands of groups such as the Ku Klux Klan and Knights of the White Camellia, Congress responded.

The Republican Congress passed three Enforcement Acts in 1870 and 1871 to criminalize interference with a citizen's right to vote, to permit federal supervision of elections, and to allow the federal government to crush white terrorist organizations—the last referred to as the Ku Klux Klan Act. This was a watershed moment for the federal government: for the first time, it assumed a significant role in law enforcement and intruded on what had once been the exclusive role of state and local governments. For a time the federal government, armed with this new legislation and the Department of Justice to prosecute violators, was fairly successful, but only in specific locations—South Carolina, for instance— and only during the early 1870s. Moreover, the Justice Department did not have its own professional investigative force; instead, it relied on private detectives and federal marshals. Though valiant, the effort did not last, and when Reconstruction ultimately foreclosed with the Compromise of 1877, the federal government's role in enforcing civil rights laws went with it.[12]

With the advent of industrialization and the rise of behemoth corporations, which some perceived as detrimental to fundamental American liberties and individualistic values, Congress created legislation to address potential problems. The Interstate Commerce Act of 1877 and the Sherman Anti-Trust Act of 1890 were enacted to regulate railroad rates (railroads were the first American big business) and to prevent the abuses of monopoly. Despite concerns about huge corporations, the idea of laissez-faire remained strong, and the Justice Department's efforts in regulating big business were limited. The reality was that although lawmakers recognized the problems with monopoly, they responded with only lip service. Because regulatory efforts were minimal at best, there was no perceived need for an investigative unit in the Justice Department to look into violations of federal law. If need be, U.S. attorneys would investigate law violations themselves, hire Pinkerton detectives, or borrow Secret Service agents from the Treasury Department. The Comstock Act also fit into this reality, as there was no significant federal law enforcement effort to clamp down on obscenity after Comstock himself exited the scene. That, in fact, would come only with the advent of the FBI in the twentieth century.

All this changed, significantly, with the rise of Theodore Roosevelt as president of the United States and the advent of the Progressive Era dating from 1901. Over the last three decades of the nineteenth century, the United States industrialized at a rapid pace. Such rapid industrialization was made possible by the development of new technologies, the expansion of the country's railroad network, and special legal advantages that permitted various entrepreneurs—such as John D. Rockefeller, Andrew Carnegie, and J. P. Morgan—to create giant national corporations that quickly monopolized the oil, steel, and railroad industries (among others) and significantly altered the American landscape. These entrepreneurs had the benefit, for example, of a federal government that fervently believed in laissez-faire and a Congress that passed laws to bolster entrepreneurial experimentation and to protect businessmen who experienced failure; it was also a government that rarely regulated and did not tax big corporations.

By the start of the twentieth century, America saw the birth of its first billion-dollar corporation—J. P. Morgan's United States Steel—and Americans began to fully appreciate the excesses of these large and powerful businesses. Significantly, this included the observation that the traditional American ideal of the righteousness of the individual was being subsumed by the corporation. As a result, the federal government finally began to assert itself. This was especially so after the Progressive Roosevelt became president following the assassination of William McKinley in 1901. The energetic Roosevelt regarded wholly unrestrained corporations as inimical to American capitalism. As such, he sought to rein in only those corporations that, in his view, were "bad trusts" and hence were restraining competition and hurting American capitalism as he saw it.

Roosevelt would attempt to bring order to the corporate world by breathing life into the Sherman Anti-Trust Act of 1890, which had been passed with bipartisan support but with no serious attempt at enforcement. He would also make use of the Interstate Commerce Act of 1877 to regulate railroad freight rates. Roosevelt's problem was that the Department of Justice lacked its own investigative agency to enforce these statutes, and its reliance on private detectives or Secret Service agents was curtailed in 1892 and 1908, respectively, after two serious incidents. In 1892, a bloody gun battle between striking Homestead Steel workers and Pinkerton detectives acting as strikebreakers caused Congress, fearing a public backlash, to outlaw federal agencies from hiring private detectives. Then, in 1908, when President Roosevelt sought funds from Congress to establish a professional investigative force within the Justice Department to make the regulation of corporations more efficient, Congress refused to vote on extending the funding. Instead, after a congressman and a senator from Oregon were convicted of defrauding the U.S. government—their crimes had been uncovered through the Justice Department's use of Secret Service agents—Congress amended an appropriations bill to ban the loaning of Secret Service agents to other federal departments. At the time of Roosevelt's funding request, Congress had become consumed by the fear of a national secret police forming, citing the tsarist Russian secret police as an example.

Frustrated by Congress's inaction, Roosevelt used his executive authority to create the Bureau of Investigation (renamed the Federal Bureau of Investigation in 1935) while Congress was adjourned over the summer of 1908. He paid for it using the Justice Department's miscellaneous expense fund. When Congress reconvened, it demanded that the attorney general explain the president's unilateral action. Testifying before Congress, Attorney General Charles Bonaparte assured legislators that their fears about the development of a tsarist-like secret police force were unfounded. The attorney general was able to convince legislators of the efficacy of the Bureau of Investigation by appealing to Progressive Era beliefs that through professionalism, efficiency, and rationality one could solve complex problems and ensure that no abuses occurred. He told them that bureau agents would not, in fact, engage in extralegal investigations because only professional investigators would be hired, and they would be overseen, personally, by the attorney general. Bonaparte assured them that the only way to regulate corporate capitalism efficiently was through the development of a professional investigative unit within the Justice Department, and he argued that this was the only logical solution to the department's problems. Satisfied, Congress approved funds for Roosevelt's Bureau of Investigation.

For the first two years of its existence, the bureau's mission was limited to enforcing interstate commerce and anti-trust laws. But by 1910, with passage of the White Slave Traffic Act—dubbed the Mann Act, after its congressional sponsor James Robert Mann—the bureau's law enforcement responsibilities began to grow and it began to move, albeit indirectly, into the field of obscenity. The Mann Act, which in vague language outlawed the transportation of women across state lines for "immoral purposes," was in many ways a product of the Progressive Era. Between 1907 and 1914 the United States experienced the traumatic effects of rapid industrialization and urbanization, compounded by tens of millions of non-Anglo-Saxon immigrants flooding the country from eastern and southern Europe. A widespread panic ensued, a product of the belief that these so-called new immigrants were responsible for importing a variety of social problems, especially to urban areas. Among these problems were a perceived increase in crime, a so-called papal conspiracy, disease, and prostitution. Concerned Americans believed that these immigrants were organizing prostitution rings in America's rapidly developing cities and hunting for and singling out young, naïve American women who were moving into the cities, away from parental and religious oversight, to become unwilling members of these prostitution enterprises. The Mann Act targeted these prostitution rings.[13]

With the Mann Act now federal law, and with the public in a panic over white slave traffic, the bureau's responsibilities increased beyond the regulation of the corporate economy. To enforce the Mann Act adequately, bureau agents needed to be stationed in the field, across the country. This contributed to the development of the bureau's various field offices and helped make it a truly national police force. Serving as the first director of the Bureau of Investigation (until 1912) was Stanley Finch, a man who had built his career on targeting prostitution rings and who would later serve in the Justice Department and focus on white slave trafficking cases. As director, Finch created a special file-card index of identified prostitutes, and he epitomized the bureau's move into the realm of anti-obscenity work. In 1913, for instance, he contributed a chapter to a sex manual, *Self Knowledge and Guide to Sex Instruction: Vital Facts of Life for All Ages,* in which he advocated expansion of the Mann Act to make it a crime "to communicate by mail, telegraph, or in any other manner from one State or territory to another, or to any foreign country, for the purpose of inducing or persuading any woman or girl . . . [into] prostitution or debauchery, or for any other immoral purpose."[14] Finch believed white slavery to be so pernicious and "evil" that it could "not be successfully dealt with by local authorities."[15] Because of the Mann Act's vague wording, however, investigators and prosecutors used it to target not only prostitution but also widely perceived immorality among the public. Individual Americans could be (and were) arrested, prosecuted, and sent to jail simply for crossing state lines with their girlfriends if authorities believed it was their "intent" to engage in sexual relations. Moreover, law enforcers targeted specific groups such as gangsters, confidence men, African Americans—including heavyweight boxing champion Jack Johnson, who had wantonly violated the separation of the races—and anyone advocating political positions contrary to the status quo. In terms of the FBI's later interest in obscenity, the Mann Act significantly increased the collection of obscene items by FBI agents because, as one FBI official observed, obscene literature was inevitably found in the course of investigating white slave trafficking cases.[16]

The bureau's particular interest in white slave trafficking was confined to the period between 1910 and 1914, during which time it focused intensely on prostitution rings and the alleged immoral activities of individuals. Afterward, the bureau did not abandon its new role as one of America's moral overseers. FBI officials shifted their focus to issues of obscenity, whether in published form or in the various activities of Americans, both common and prominent. But it was not until the 1920s that bureau activity in this area became formalized.

In the meantime, with the rise of the First World War and imperial Germany's efforts to spy in America and sabotage munitions depots, the bureau concentrated on internal security. After the war ended and progressivism declined in favor of the New Era of the 1920s, reflecting a far more conservative politics and more negative reactions to perceived threats, the bureau was involved in several scandals. The first was the Red Scare of 1919–1920, during which the Bureau of Investigation, in cooperation with the Immigration Bureau, rounded up thousands of suspected aliens to deport them. Russia had gone communist in the midst of civil war, and when some 3,600 labor strikes took place in the United States in 1919, involving 4 million workers, Americans widely believed that Bolsheviks were afoot, fomenting revolution. Playing on these popular fears, management deliberately attributed these strikes to the work of communists, going so far as to take out full-page newspaper ads saying as much. In the end, the bureau's efforts resulted in the arrest and detention of 10,000 suspects—aliens and American citizens alike—in woefully inadequate facilities, making this one of the most glaring examples of civil liberties abuses in American history. Senior officials in the Labor Department—where the Immigration Bureau was housed—undercut the attempted deportation scheme by reviewing the arrest records and releasing most of those being detained for possible deportation (some 3,500 individuals). In the end, only 556 were actually deported.[17]

Deeply involved in the so-called Red raids was a young J. Edgar Hoover. Attorney General A. Mitchell Palmer had appointed Hoover to head the Justice Department's Radical Bureau—later renamed the General Intelligence Division. It was Hoover who intimately cooperated with the Immigration Bureau in the dragnet raids; it was Hoover who directed the efforts via telephone from his office in Washington, D.C.; and it was Hoover who used telegraphic warrants—warrants issued without an individual's name—to assist agents in their mass arrests. Yet when this scandal was investigated by the Senate, Hoover emerged relatively unscathed.

The Red Scare was not the only scandal to hit the bureau in the 1920s. During the presidency of the affable, if oafish, Warren G. Harding, the bureau found itself front and center in the Teapot Dome scandal. Harding's corrupt interior secretary, Albert Fall, had control over the navy's emergency oil reserves at Teapot Dome, Wyoming, and Elk Hills, California. Instead of ensuring the security of these reserves, Fall signed no-bid contracts with two oil companies to allow them to tap the government's oil reserves. In exchange, the oil companies gave Fall (who had lost his own personal fortune) some $400,000 in what Fall described as "loans" but were, in reality, kickbacks. When Senators Burton Wheeler and Thomas Walsh investigated this scandal in 1923, Harding's corrupt attorney general, Harry Daugherty, and his corrupt Bureau of Investigation director, William J. Burns, attempted to discredit the senators by unearthing derogatory information about them. To do so, they tapped the senators' telephones, broke into their offices, and intercepted their mail. In the end, this nefarious activity was exposed, leading the Coolidge administration (upon Harding's death) to clean house.

First, Coolidge appointed a new, reformist attorney general to replace the disgraced Daugherty. Harlan Fiske Stone, the former dean of Columbia University's law school, sought men of high moral and professional standards to staff the troubled Justice Department. Ironically, however, Stone's choice to assume the directorship of the Bureau of Investigation was J. Edgar Hoover. Since Daugherty and Burns had taken the rap for the abuses involving the bureau, Hoover was regarded as an underling who had simply obeyed the orders of his superiors. With the support of esteemed Secretary of Commerce Herbert Hoover (no relation), Stone appointed J. Edgar Hoover to the job in 1924.

As bureau director, Hoover would involve his agency in even more matters involving obscenity. Explaining Hoover's interest, in part, was his background. Born in 1895 to civil-servant parents in Washington, D.C., Hoover was raised during the Progressive Era, and the conservative values of middle-class, Anglo-Saxon, Protestant America were instilled in him by his parents, his church, and his schools. Among these values was a resistance to change. When millions of eastern and southern European immigrants arrived, seeking work in the country's urban factories, they brought cultural traits that clashed with traditional American customs. It was widely believed, moreover, that these non-Anglo-Saxon, largely Catholic immigrants, who spoke strange and alien languages, were responsible for various social, economic, and political problems, including the infusion of radical beliefs such as Bolshevism and anarchism.

Repulsed by anything he regarded as un-American, Hoover would use his new position as bureau director to protect his country from these perceived threats, including obscenity.[18]

Hoover's appointment as director only partially explains the bureau's renewed efforts against obscenity. The nature of the 1920s—a decade variously referred to as the New Era, the Roaring Twenties, the Jazz Age, the ballyhoo years, the era of excess, and the aspirin age—also played a part. The First World War profoundly affected the worldview and personal values of people around the globe, including millions of Americans. The stark realities of industrialized warfare, which led to the gruesome deaths of more than 13 million people, shocked the American conscience. Americans were disillusioned, and this led some to question their own values, which had seemingly led to this carnage. Moreover, people raised in an Anglo-Saxon culture instilled with Victorian manners and values began to break away from many of those beliefs. Indeed, this had been a major concern among some in the Woodrow Wilson administration at the start of America's involvement in the war. For instance, in 1917 Secretary of War Newton Baker had banned alcohol from military training camps and initiated a program designed to protect the morality of America's vulnerable soldier boys. He warned: "These boys are going to France; they are going to face conditions we do not like to talk about, that we do not like to think about. . . . I want them to have an armor made up of a set of social habits replacing those of their homes and communities . . . a moral and intellectual armor for their protection overseas."[19] While stationed "over there," but especially when visiting Paris on leave, millions of young American soldiers had been exposed to a much looser social culture, which they helped transplant in formerly Victorian America. This shift in young people's attitudes was reflected in the lyrics of the popular postwar song "How Ya Gonna Keep 'Em Down on the Farm? (After They've Seen Paree)":

How ya gonna keep 'em down on the farm
After they've seen Paree
How ya gonna keep 'em away from Broadway
Jazzin' around and paintin' the town
How ya gonna keep 'em away from harm, that's a mystery
Imagine Reuben when he meets his Pa
He'll kiss his cheek and holler "OO-LA-LA!"

How ya gonna keep 'em down on the farm
After they've seen Paree?

What was developing was a more cosmopolitan and more sophisticated America, with a so-called new morality. But there was also a severe backlash to these new ideals.

Buttressing the new morality were the effects of Prohibition. Since the late nineteenth century, women's groups had been advocating for the prohibition of alcohol. Indeed, it had been a Progressive Era issue within the social justice movement, even though no national law was passed during that time. It took the confluence of wartime sacrifice, anti-German sentiment (manifested in the idea that German beer brewers were bad), and the necessity of using grain for food rather than for distillation to make national Prohibition—in the form of the Eighteenth Amendment (1919)—palatable. By the 1920s, however, many people were flouting the moralistic anti-drink attitudes and the law. Women, who had previously been unwelcome in bars—which were considered men's preserves, where drinking was a masculine endeavor—now drank and even smoked in public, to the shock of those with old guard values. What's more, women, known as "flappers," wore scandalous dresses that ended at the knees, along with rolled stockings and red lipstick, and they bobbed their hair, as if to give themselves a boyish appearance. These same women could be seen shimmy dancing with men at illegal bars and clubs—called speakeasies and roadhouses—where they might be wearing hip flasks to conceal their equally illegal drink. Even those who did not patronize illegal drinking establishments probably attended cocktail parties, where they could just as easily flout the Victorian values they were rebelling against while drinking martinis.

Many of these same people were enamored by the published works of the father of psychoanalysis, Dr. Sigmund Freud. Although they did not fully appreciate or understand the concepts of libido, repression, sublimation, or the Oedipus complex, Americans were lured to this and other reading material that discussed sex openly, which led to issues of obscenity and law enforcement. To Victorians, the topic of sex had been strictly taboo—with some going so far as to publish premarital tracts warning of the moral dangers of spooning.[20] These attitudes began to shift in the 1920s. As Frederick Lewis Allen pointed out in *Only Yesterday* (1931), "a bumper crop of sex magazines, confession magazines, and lurid motion pictures" offered a titillating look into a previously concealed segment of American life. In addition, many book publishers abandoned their reserved attitudes of the past to embrace new and younger authors whose work flew in the face of convention. This led to the creation of vice societies to counter their efforts. Partly as a result of the apparent explosion of obscene literature and films and the resultant crackdown on the same, the federal Customs Court evolved to handle obscenity cases. The court, established in 1926, was originally designed to arbitrate disputes over the value of commodities in matters related to federal taxation. However, with a surge in obscene imports and prosecutions, its focus shifted to obscenity cases, imposing blanket bans rather than having disparate local customs agents make decisions.[21]

It was within this social context of increased interest in sexual matters and a virtual explosion of obscene items—many of which bureau agents encountered during Mann Act investigations—that J. Edgar Hoover established his agency's obscene materials filing and mailing procedure on 24 March 1925. It was no accident that this new bureau procedure was developed at the height of the so-called Clean Books crusade of 1923–1925, a major reactionary book censorship drive. The bureau's specialized procedure would evolve over the next seventeen years to became one of the FBI's most sensitive centralized files—the Obscene File—by 1942. But in 1925 Hoover's primary interest was to ensure the security of all obscene materials collected by special agents in charge (SACs) and either sent through the mail or filed in their respective field offices. Hoover ordered his SACs to take anything that was "properly . . . classified as obscene or improper" and seal it "in a separate envelope or package" with the word "OBSCENE" written on the package in large, uppercase letters. Hoover ordered "strict compliance" with this new procedure.[22]

Despite Hoover's new procedure, and despite the seeming proliferation of obscene literature, images, and films nationwide, few SACs forwarded obscene material to FBI headquarters during the 1920s. The FBI itself characterized such transmissions as occurring only "from time to time." This is not surprising. The FBI's role as a national police force was still limited in the 1920s. It was limited because anti-statist Republicans dominated the federal government, as reflected in President Calvin Coolidge's famous quip: "Four-fifths of our troubles would disappear if we would sit down and keep still." Historically, the FBI did not lead the effort in prosecuting the purveyors of obscenity. Anti-obscenity efforts were largely a matter for postal inspectors and customs officers—as reflected in the Customs Court—and for municipal and state vice societies. Even the influence of the vice societies began to wane after 1925 and the end of the Clean Books crusade. All this helps explain why there was little FBI activity with regard to obscenity during the late 1920s.

Nevertheless, the bureau moved closer to assuming a role in prosecuting obscenity, albeit at a snail's pace. The first significant step in this regard, after the establishment of the obscene materials filing and mailing procedure, was the bureau's increased anti-crime work during the Great Depression. The advent of the Depression and its cataclysmic effects—with countless men becoming jobless, then homeless, then desperately resorting to petty crime—led to the perception among many Americans that crime rates were on the rise. This seeming breakdown in law and order was compounded by the activities of a variety of celebrity criminals. But reality did not fit this perception. In truth, by the 1930s the United States was experiencing the *end* of a crime wave, not the start of one.

Between 1925 and 1932 the United States indeed experienced a crime wave, but one restricted to the Midwest between the states of Texas and Minnesota—the so-called Crime Corridor. Moreover, the celebrated criminals operating in this region were making good use of new technologies. They used the Thompson submachine gun—capable of firing 800 rounds a minute—to outgun the local police, and they used automobiles with the new V-8 engine to outrun the local police, who were still driving old Model A Fords fitted with hand-cranked engines. As a result, a perception emerged in the early 1930s that a federal law enforcement entity was badly needed because local and state police lacked the technology, resources, and jurisdiction to deal with these sophisticated interstate criminals. As a man purporting to be John Dillinger wrote to Henry Ford: "[Thank you] for building the Ford V-8 as fast and as sturdy a car as you did, otherwise I would not have gotten away from the coppers in that Wisconsin, Minnesota case."[23]

Attorney General Homer Cummings used the perception of a rise in crime to increase the federal government's national policing role. Ultimately, his efforts ended in a series of crime bills during 1934 that significantly expanded the FBI's jurisdiction, arrest powers, and ability to carry weapons; it was given the authority to apprehend interstate escaped felons, enter kidnapping cases after seven days, and participate in bank robbery cases if the bank was a member of the Federal Reserve. This increase in federal anti-crime efforts had an effect on anti-obscenity prosecutions. In 1932, to assist in crime detection, Hoover created the FBI's vaunted crime laboratory. With the assistance of scientific policing methods, the FBI would be able to pursue and arrest mobile, sophisticated criminals. But the FBI's crime lab was also being used to identify purveyors of obscene literature and images. After 1932 FBI officials began to recognize the existence of "a substantial collection of obscene materials," thanks to the bureau's obscene materials filing and mailing procedure. Although these obscene materials had been forwarded from field offices to the crime lab for examination, they "had never been compiled, classified or embodied in a central file." Yet, similar to the post office's foray into anti-obscenity efforts at the end of the Civil War in 1865, not until the United States entered the Second World War would the FBI create a centralized file for use in clamping down on purveyors of obscenity.[24]

CHAPTER TWO

The Development of a Centralized Obscene File

The 1940s

The creation of the FBI's filing and mailing procedure for obscene materials was largely a function of the development of and reaction against the so-called New Morality, the 1920s cultural phenomenon among American youth that challenged the traditional and stolid Victorian-era values system. Even so, enforcement of anti-obscenity law was still strictly a local and state affair or it was handled on the federal level by postal inspectors or customs officers. Effectively, the FBI's role in investigating and prosecuting obscenity cases was minimal at best. This explains why FBI officials did not recognize that they had collected a substantial amount of obscene materials until after the creation of the FBI crime laboratory in the 1930s and the bureau's concomitant transformation into a national police force. Still, FBI officials did little with these materials. Not until the United States entered the Second World War did bureau officials organize and centralize a formal obscene file in a proactive effort to limit the pervasiveness of obscenity.

The United States was a late entrant into the war. By the mid to late 1930s, as President Roosevelt's New Deal lost momentum, the administration and the country increasingly turned their attention to perilous events transpiring around the world. The Japanese were on the march in China, Nazi Germany had rearmed itself and occupied the Rhineland, Spain had descended into a three-year civil war that saw the victory of quasi-fascist forces, the Rome-Berlin Axis had formed, and Hitler had annexed his home country of Austria into the greater German Reich. Disillusionment over American involvement in the First World War—during which tens of millions of young men died and nearly a whole generation of Europe's youth was wiped out in the first truly industrialized war—characterized the American response to this new conflict. Americans were worried that, just as in 1916, another president would lead them into a devastating war. As a result, beginning in 1934 Congress reasserted itself in foreign policy issues. In the forefront of this effort was Senator Gerald Nye of North Dakota, who formed a special committee to examine the extent to which international bankers and munitions manufacturers had influenced President Wilson to involve the country in the First World War. During this investigation, which continued until 1936, Nye helped foster a virulent anti-interventionist attitude among many Americans that led to passage of the Neutrality Acts (1935–1937). These laws were designed to avert U.S. involvement in another world war by restricting the sale of weapons, banning the extension of loans, and preventing American merchant ships from being attacked.

During this time, the FBI's responsibilities in the domestic security field increased, which explains why there was little effort against obscenity during these years. In 1934 President Roosevelt asked the FBI to monitor domestic fascists and Nazis. In 1936 he verbally authorized the FBI to engage in intelligence investigations; this involved collecting a wide variety of information not for prosecution but to monitor domestic fascists and communists to ascertain how they might influence the country both economically and politically. This was a watershed moment for the bureau, after which its primary focus became not law enforcement but intelligence collection and domestic security. When the Nazis invaded Poland in 1939, Roosevelt declared the United States to be neutral, but he also told Americans that he could not ask them to be neutral in their sympathies. Subsequently, Roosevelt's foreign policy moved the United States incrementally closer to the Allied side, while still avoiding involvement in anything that might lead the country directly into the war. In the meantime, in addition to monitoring domestic fascists and communists, FBI agents began to monitor the president's increasingly vocal and active anti-interventionist foreign policy critics, whose dissent they regarded as somehow subversive.[1]

By the time of the attack on Pearl Harbor, the FBI was not only the dominant American domestic security agency but also the unofficial intelligence arm of the White House. FBI director Hoover, ever the pragmatist, clearly knew how to navigate the treacherous political waters of Washington to the benefit of both himself and his FBI. Though he was a conservative, Hoover managed to cultivate a close relationship with the president and catered to his political wishes, proving his worth while expanding the FBI's power and influence. After the United States entered the war, Hoover used his FBI less in an effort to crack down on crime and more to target leftists, shape public policy and attitudes, and resist certain changes in American society. The way the FBI handled matters of obscenity fell perfectly within this paradigm.

Ironically, the FBI entered into anti-obscenity work as a result of public pressure—not unlike the popular pressure exerted at the end of the Civil War that had prompted Congress to authorize the postmaster general to seize obscene material and prosecute those who had mailed it. With the United States now a member of the Allies, and with millions of young men being drafted into the armed forces, some Americans feared that certain influences would be brought to bear on these boys, many of whom were only teenagers. In May 1942 the New York Society for the Suppression of Vice mounted a publicity campaign, claiming that the war made its work more important than ever. The society's executive secretary and Comstock's successor, John Sumner, claimed that "countless young people will not enjoy the same degree of parental and other helpful influences as in ordinary times." He warned, "there will be many who will be thrown into strange environments and who will be subjected to previously unknown temptations." The group's president, Francis Bertram Elgas, observed, "reports have come to us of the presence near army encampments of dealers driven from New York by our activities." The following year, Sumner stressed that wartime mobilization of not only the military but also the civilian population created conditions "conducive to laxity in ethical standards, vicious practices and spiritual decay." He continued that anti-obscenity work was vital "for the salvation of youth."[2]

The FBI responded to this public pressure in late 1942. By that time, a variety of civic and religious organizations had voiced their concerns about the prevalence of obscenity and had written numerous letters to the FBI encouraging a crackdown. Among these organizations were not only the New York Society for the Suppression of Vice but also the National Council of Catholic Men of Washington, D.C.; the Episcopal Committee of Obscene Literature of Fort Wayne, Indiana; and the Illinois Vigilance Association of Chicago.[3] In addition to this public pressure, local and state police forces began to submit seized pornographic items to the FBI crime lab in the hope that bureau technicians could ascertain the locations of the distributors. These submissions increased during the war, "especially in connection with efforts to protect Army cantonments from commercialized vice." The end result of FBI agents' "intensive efforts" to investigate the interstate distribution of obscenity was a marked growth in the FBI's collection of obscene materials.[4]

Given the number of obscene submissions and the public pressure to pursue the purveyors of obscenity, FBI officials decided to create a special unit within the Document Section of the crime lab to focus on this work. The idea was to compare obscene samples "from different geographical areas and various jurisdictional sources" to ascertain information that might identify manufacturing and distribution centers. Technicians classified each submission by the way it was manufactured, and incorporated this information into the FBI's Obscene File. Comparing submissions from entirely different obscenity cases led to the discovery that these items were, most often, "part of the same conspiracy to distribute the products of the same printer."[5]

Responding to public concerns about the susceptibility of American youth, FBI officials focused on an obscenity case based in New York City—historically a hub for obscene activity—that involved the distribution of cartoon booklets to teenagers. The FBI laboratory was at the forefront in this effort, along with a valuable FBI confidential informant who had assisted the bureau in another obscenity case in 1939. Reporting to Hoover, an FBI official claimed that the investigation in New York was "proceeding vigorously," and he believed that "a successful solution of the case will probably go a long way toward curtailing the dissemination of obscene literature in this country," alluding to the fact that this case extended beyond New York to include Cleveland, Detroit, and Baltimore. The official also described the FBI's recently centralized Obscene File to Hoover, noting that it had been formed from old and new case files and included an index with segregated files of cartoons, pamphlets, playing cards, movies, books, and typeset readers. An assistant laboratory examiner had been assigned to oversee the file. Hoover, however, was not overly impressed. He responded by writing on the memo: "I fear we have been just dallying along with no doubt voluminous reports but no results. Let us get down to business & do something."[6]

With stern prompting from Hoover and after several months of investigating, FBI agents finally broke up the obscenity ring based in New York. They raided a print shop in the Bronx, arrested five men, and seized vast quantities of "finished cartoons, fiction naratives [*sic*], photographs, original drawings and manuscripts, line engravings and half-tone plates for the manufacture of such material." According to the *New York Times,* FBI agents seized "8,000,000 cartoon booklets, showing crude imitations of various comic book characters in lewd poses," which the distributors sold for twenty-five or fifty cents. They also took possession of playing cards with "filthy pictures" on them. The arrests were publicly hailed as a success in preventing the national distribution of "tons of obscene printed matter to children in their teens." Obscene material was also seized in Akron, Baltimore, Indianapolis, Detroit, Cleveland, and Pittsburgh. According to FBI estimates, somewhere between 20,000 and 25,000 obscene exhibits were seized, and 10,391 of them were sent to the FBI's laboratory for examination. FBI laboratory technicians used the Obscene File to determine that 80 percent of all the cartoon booklets, 85 percent of all the narrative booklets, and 75 percent of all the obscene playing cards had originated in the New York obscenity ring.[7]

The sheer volume of obscene items seized in the New York raid convinced FBI officials that their newly centralized Obscene File was beneficial. One FBI official suggested that a special room be designated where evidence could "be properly mounted and kept for examination." Indeed, this particular raid was so important that FBI officials thought future seizures would inevitably be linked to the New York obscenity ring. One even commented that the FBI would have "one of the largest and most comprehensive [obscene exhibits] ever collected." FBI agents could use this collection, they believed, to ensure "the quick disposition of new operations in this field provided the laws concerning prosecution are adequate." One FBI official even seemed to suggest that bureau officials were in a position to influence the shape of future anti-obscenity laws.[8]

The FBI's initial 1942 effort to clamp down on the interstate transportation of obscene materials (ITOM, in FBI parlance) was markedly successful, if fleeting. Between the creation of the centralized Obscene File in September 1942 and August 1944, FBI laboratory technicians examined some 80 percent of all obscene submissions and determined that a single source was likely behind their distribution. That source, of course, was the target of the FBI's New York City raid.[9] Eventually, by early March 1943, FBI officials recognized that the laboratory's obscenity work had become "rather specialized," leading them to establish an administrative file "for reports and memoranda" related to the Obscene File, which was composed of the actual magazines, photographs, and other obscene submissions. This file was assigned the file number 80–662.[10] By the spring of 1943, however, after the New York ring had been busted, wartime priorities for the FBI laboratory switched to national defense cases, and FBI officials decided to defer the examination of obscene materials except when doing so was "absolutely essential" for prosecuting a case. Effectively, with criminal cases on the decline in favor of national security issues, obscene submissions to FBI headquarters dwindled.[11]

In the meantime, a question arose over maintenance of the bureau's Obscene File. Edmund Coffey, assistant director of the FBI's Laboratory Division, believed that even though "the frequency of cases is not great," the file was "useful," leading him to recommend that it be kept in good order and not closed. This was possible, he argued, since the chief of the Document Section, Inspector Harbo, had reported that the backlog of obscene submissions was "not urgent" and acknowledged that the FBI laboratory had more pressing matters to attend to.[12]

In a side note, this decision irritated Hoover. When he learned that Coffey and Harbo had come to these conclusions without conferring with other individuals, Hoover scrawled on Coffey's report: "I am amazed at this. I don't see how any intelligent recommendation can be made by inspectors if they don't secure the views of interested and informed parties. I hope this is the exception." In reply, the assistant director of the Training and Inspection Division, Hugh Clegg, advised Hoover that Harbo had not conferred with Coffey; in fact, he had talked with the one technician assigned to maintain the Obscene File. Clegg reassured Hoover that the Obscene File could be kept in order with minimal attention, or "approximately 30 man days' work."[13]

Despite the belief that the file could be maintained with little effort, in just one month's time "a large back-log of specimens to be added to this File was accumulated." But the war was still raging, and FBI personnel had other priorities. The solution to this problem was a simple but efficient one. FBI personnel were given just one week to add to the file those specimens "believed to be of value" and incinerate the remainder—somewhere between 10,000 and 20,000 exhibits—by 22 August 1944. After this was done, Coffey concluded that since some 1,300 specimens in the Obscene File had been classified and the backlog burned, further maintenance of the file would now require only "two man days per month."[14]

Coffey deemed the Obscene File to be "a valuable and helpful reference file." In his recommendation to Assistant Director Edward Tamm to keep the file, Coffey offered a useful insider's description of it. He referred to it, broadly, as "a central depository for all types of obscene material" used by the laboratory to "furnish upon demand a wide variety of general and special information" about obscenity. He described the file's "primary function" as allowing "inter-comparisons to be made which in turn in most instances show a definite interstate angle of the cases involved." He stressed that it might be problematic for the laboratory to prove interstate transportation—a violation of federal law—but it might be able to show, at least, what he called "interstate movement." He therefore recommended maintaining the Obscene File in its current state.[15]

Another unidentified FBI official described the Obscene File's "value . . . as an investigative aid" to Alex Rosen, assistant director of the Investigative Division. He began with the "significant" observation that "obscene literature is characteristically obtained" by FBI agents as they investigate violations of the Mann Act, a law designed to target prostitution rings. This official recognized that "salacious materials have been found to be the working partner of the prostitute." Reflecting the dominant racism of the time, when many believed African Americans were more sexually driven and more easily influenced than whites, he bolstered his reasoning by pointing out that "responsible police authorities" have argued that "circulation of pornographic materials have contributed to racial agitation and juvenile delinquency." As evidence, this FBI official cited the opinion of Los Angeles police chief C. B. Horrall, who, upon learning about an allegedly obscene film target by the FBI, concluded: "the obscene motion picture film circulated no doubt has a direct bearing on the juvenile delinquency and the large number of sex crimes prevalent in this area." Concerning this case, FBI officials believed "that obscene motion picture films are being distributed on the West Coast depicting juveniles as young as eleven and fourteen years of age as engaging in immoral activities with adults while other films involved negroes and whites in lascivious positions."[16]

Beyond the bureau's bigoted perception of the Obscene File's value in curtailing racial and juvenile problems, this senior FBI official cited six examples of its "practical value." First, it could prove that obscene items had been transported across state lines, something that FBI field offices could not establish on their own. Second, it could identify the individuals depicted in obscene photographs and films. Third, it could identify the cartoonists who had created obscene booklets because each artist exhibited "individual peculiarities" in drawing his subjects. Fourth, the file could advise senior FBI officials and field offices about innovations in the creation of obscene items, whether in the origin of obscene playing cards or the development of obscene films with sound and color. Fifth, it could facilitate wartime propaganda efforts (described later in this book). And sixth, the file could help local and state police departments locate the purveyors of smut.[17]

This FBI official also reiterated for his superiors the prosecutorial achievements stemming from agents' use of the Obscene File. He noted that two of the largest "national obscene lottery syndicates ever identified were smashed." Eight individuals had been convicted in another case (probably the New York case), and he noted that if federal law covered the use of automobiles in the interstate transport of obscene material, another seven individuals might have been convicted. During 1943, ten additional convictions were obtained—involving sentences of at least ten years and $15,000 in fines—and FBI agents also apprehended fourteen fugitives. During 1944, FBI officials secured twelve convictions and captured two fugitives, and a comparable number of convictions were obtained on federal reservations.[18] Given these facts and figures, Assistant Director Coffey recommended that the FBI retain the Obscene File,[19] and in October 1944 the FBI's Executive Conference—a regular meeting of the bureau's assistant directors—decided unanimously, and with Hoover's approval, to reactivate Obscene File submissions and searches because the file "had a very definite value."[20]

A case from this era illustrates the bureau's interest in race, juvenile delinquency, and obscenity. It involved the first novel written by anti-segregationist and leftist writer Lillian Smith. The novel, titled *Strange Fruit,* was published in 1944. By 1940s standards, Smith's story was quite controversial. It involved an interracial relationship between a highly intelligent young black woman and the well-to-do son of a white southern physician. In May 1944 various elements in Detroit attempted to blacklist Smith's novel because its content, they claimed, was obscene. But when librarians and bookstore owners refused to voluntarily remove the novel from their shelves, local law enforcement officials attempted to develop an obscenity case against Smith. It was at this juncture that the FBI became interested. The concern among public authorities in Detroit was that Smith's novel contained language about its characters' interracial relationship that could "aggravate a serious juvenile delinquency problem which is of utmost interest at the present time." Their overarching concern was wartime unity and a fear that the controversial book might cause racial problems among the youth of Detroit.[21]

The special agent in charge in Detroit sent Hoover portions of the novel that were allegedly obscene. Hoover was apparently not impressed and suggested that the book was not a good case for prosecution because it was similar to other popular novels, such as *The Grapes of Wrath*. The FBI director advised the SAC to seek the opinion of the U.S. attorney in Detroit about the advisability of prosecution. In October the U.S. attorney notified the Detroit field office that he considered passages in the book to be obscene and believed that, due to the book's wide popularity and national distribution, FBI officials should ask the Justice Department for an official opinion as to prosecution. Hoover requested such an opinion from his superiors, but they declined to prosecute. Nevertheless, the case illustrates FBI officials' concern when obscenity intersected with race.[22]

Hoover and other FBI officials did not limit their interest in obscenity to shutting down the transportation of obscene items across state lines. They proactively leaked information to trusted recipients in an attempt to shape public opinion. One such recipient was the ardently anti-communist Catholic priest Francis Cardinal Spellman. Spellman was eventually placed on the FBI's Special Correspondents List, a compilation of those individuals FBI officials trusted to receive leaked information for the purpose of influencing public opinion or for any other purpose that might be in the bureau's best interest.

Hoover's relationship with Spellman began in June 1942, when they began a long-term correspondence. Hoover wrote to Spellman to compliment him on his recent book *The Road to Victory*. In that book, Spellman stressed that victory in war could not be attained unless America adhered to the Ten Commandments and renewed its faith in God. According to an FBI reviewer, Spellman "speaks violently against moral degradation and paganism which has engulfed not only America but the entire world."[23] Hoover agreed with Spellman and reiterated to him that victory indeed depended on "the protection of internal America, our faith in God, and our morality at home, as [much as] our winning of battles on foreign fields."[24] In response, the cardinal wrote that he had read Hoover's various speeches with great interest and felt "we could pinch hit for each other as we seem to have similar appraisals on various matters."[25]

Shortly thereafter Spellman wrote to congratulate Hoover on his twenty-five years of government service. Hoover replied to thank Spellman and added, "I hope we will always be able to work together in the same spirit of mutual accord."[26] And when it came to the controversial issue of obscenity, they did just that. In the spring of 1944 Hoover sent Spellman copies of two speeches he had delivered on the topic of juvenile delinquency. It is unknown which speeches Hoover forwarded, but according to the *New York Times,* Hoover gave three speeches on the subject between January and May 1944. In one, commenting on the sudden increase in crime among seventeen-year-olds in 1943, Hoover blamed "broken homes and irresponsible parents." In another, he called juvenile crime a "third front" during wartime, and in yet another speech he warned that communists were proactively seeking to influence American youth.[27] Spellman filed these speeches away and told the FBI director that, if he had the time, he intended to write on the topic of juvenile delinquency and noted that Hoover's "observations [on the subject] will be very helpful to me."[28] In 1946 an FBI agent who visited with Spellman reported that the cardinal "spoke very highly of the Director . . . and particularly mentioned his recent public references to the deterring effect that the Catholic Church has had upon Juvenile Delinquency." Indeed, in 1946 Spellman awarded Hoover the Club of Champions Award of the New York Catholic Youth Organization "because of his energetic campaign against the causes of juvenile delinquency." Hoover stated in his acceptance speech that Americans, in the face of growing crime, needed to "return to fundamentals." He noted that the Catholic Youth Organization, among others, was doing this, and he warned that if groups such as American Youth for Democracy, which "conceals the evils and corruption of American Communism," had their way, they "would convert our haven of liberty into a godless, totalitarian state where the adversaries of democracy can do as they please."[29]

With interstate obscenity rings being targeted nationwide, with certain "obscene" literature being cited by the FBI for contributing to juvenile delinquency or racial difficulties, and with information about obscenity being leaked to trusted recipients in an attempt to influence public opinion, it is probably no surprise that by 1944 FBI officials sought to supplement the Obscene File. The special agent in charge of the Miami field office proposed a way to do this in June 1944 after meeting with the customs control officer of Miami. The SAC learned from this customs official that obscene materials entering the country were seized and forwarded to the Bureau of Customs in Washington, D.C., where they were inspected and then returned to the office that had seized them. Upon their return, these materials were destroyed. The SAC suggested that an arrangement be made between the FBI and the Bureau of Customs whereby the FBI would be permitted to either examine this material or take possession of it and add it to the Obscene File.[30]

Hoover liked this suggestion and delegated it to Guy Hottel, the SAC of the Washington, D.C., field office, who was charged with contacting the Bureau of Customs. On 27 July, Hottel talked with E. E. Mattern, the customs official in charge of obscene materials, and explained the FBI's interest. Mattern "saw no reason why such a liaison could not be effectively established," and about a month later he forwarded the proposal to his assistant deputy commissioner, who needed time to consider it.[31]

It took the head of the Customs Bureau a little over two months to make a decision on this liaison with the FBI, mainly because the relevant correspondence had inadvertently been filed away. In February 1945 the Customs Bureau chief denied the FBI's request because, he argued, it would not be "practicable or desirable." Customs Commissioner W. R. Johnson argued that the provisions of the 1930 Tariff Act mandated the destruction of "obscene and immoral matter"; in addition, he doubted the effort would be worthwhile because the Customs Bureau had "very few cases." This would not be the FBI's last attempt at liaison.[32]

The FBI might have failed to strike a deal with the Bureau of Customs, but during that same period it was successful in establishing a different institutional liaison. During 1944, FBI officials made their massive Obscene File available to the Office of Strategic Services (OSS)—not to apprehend purveyors of smut or to break up obscenity rings but "for propaganda purposes."[33] The origins of the OSS date to July 1941, when, after a bureaucratic battle over intelligence coordination, President Roosevelt ordered the creation of an office called the Coordinator of Information. Within five months the United States was at war, and by the summer of 1942 the Coordinator of Information was reconfigured into the OSS, which not only coordinated foreign intelligence but also was responsible for special operations. Among the various special operations undertaken by the OSS was overseas propaganda.[34]

In June 1944 an OSS official contacted the FBI, seeking its help in countering a Japanese propaganda operation in Asia. The Japanese government had been disseminating obscene images of American women throughout Asia in an attempt to turn the indigenous populations against the United States on the basis of Americans' low standards of morality. The OSS wanted to turn the tables on the Japanese and asked for access to the FBI's large collection of obscene materials—specifically, "certain obscene prints depicting Japanese individuals in lascivious poses."[35] Hoover was advised by his subordinates that the Obscene File contained twenty-five or thirty images of Japanese individuals, and he authorized their release to the OSS for the propaganda operation.[36]

By November, OSS officers had made use of some of the FBI's material. They returned "two negatives and prints" of the images they wanted to distribute. On those prints, OSS personnel had placed captions in Japanese, which they translated for the FBI (there is no indication in FBI records what the captions were). FBI officials then placed this material in the Obscene File "for future reference and comparison purposes."[37]

Contributions to the Obscene File did not come only from FBI agents investigating the interstate transportation of obscene materials. Much of it originated from local authorities—local police and sheriff's departments, town marshals, district attorney's offices, military authorities, or even morally conscious citizens (some of whom chose to remain anonymous). The expanding physical component of the FBI's Obscene File came from a wide variety of sources.[38]

By the time the FBI reactivated the Obscene File in 1944, the bureau had trained enough personnel to keep the file "up-to-date and active"; they could also efficiently search the file to make comparisons with obscene materials seized in the field. FBI officials also developed special policies to govern the details of submitting obscene materials. To avoid duplication of exhibits, FBI agents were instructed to inform FBI laboratory personnel whether the obscene materials they submitted should be destroyed after examination or returned to the submitting field office (this remained FBI policy through the 1990s).[39] Given the fact that obscene submissions originated from such a wide array of sources, it was probably inevitable that FBI officials would identify some "improper handling of obscene exhibits and investigative reports by Agents in the Field on numerous accessions."[40]

Accordingly, in July 1945 the Executive Conference issued a bureau bulletin to reiterate the FBI's policy on submitting both obscene materials and FBI reports containing "indecent language." FBI agents were admonished to submit these items quickly—"at the earliest possible moment"—even before presenting them to a U.S. attorney for an opinion about prosecution. FBI agents were given four reasons for this action: to determine whether the item was indeed obscene, to compare it with the Obscene File to determine its source, to compare it with the file to determine whether the item had crossed state lines, and to determine whether the submission should be made a permanent part of the Obscene File itself.[41]

FBI agents were instructed to submit all obscene items and reports "under obscene cover" (as per the bureau's original 1925 instructions) and directed to the attention of the FBI laboratory. The cover letter was to include instructions relative to the disposition of the submitted material—in essence, whether it should be destroyed or returned. FBI agents were also given clear instructions about which materials they should target—that is, anything that depicted or described "activities which are clearly lewd, lascivious and licentious." FBI agents were given examples of "unquestionable obscene exhibits": stag films (with or without sound, in either color or black and white), pamphlets, drawings, cartoons, novels, playing cards, and photographs. Effectively, though, as had been standard practice in the United States for the last hundred years, it was really up to the individual FBI agent to determine whether an item was or was not obscene.[42]

FBI officials also warned agents about avoiding potential embarrassment to the bureau in obscenity cases. They cited a case in which the Post Office Department attempted to revoke the mailing permit of *Esquire* magazine, only to be rebuked by the courts for trying to impose its own "moral standards relating to material admittedly not obscene." Hoover therefore ordered SACs at FBI field offices to closely monitor all obscenity cases "to insure that criticism does not result from the Bureau's investigation of cases which involve such items as pin-up pictures, art poses, nudist photographs or magazines, parlor novelties, or other exhibits obviously not obscene or which are of highly questionably [sic] obscenity." Hoover advised agents to take a "common-sense view" in obscenity cases and "not a prudish one."[43]

Hoover also recognized that obscenity cases had "potential publicity value." Again, SACs were ordered to closely follow such cases but to notify headquarters before any arrests or arraignments were carried out. FBI agents were also ordered to comply strictly with all search and seizure rules when it came to obscene items to avoid embarrassment by defense attorneys. But underscoring it all, Hoover told agents that obscenity cases must be successfully prosecuted because obscenity encouraged juvenile delinquency and led to increases in local crime, and "in some instances racial agitation is inflamed."[44]

FBI officials sought to limit the number of exhibits placed in the Obscene File by incinerating duplicate samples, yet they were always seeking to expand the file and sometimes hesitated to discard certain items. One such example involved exhibits the Investigative Division had marked "miscellaneous." This particular collection, which was not described in any detail, had been purchased at "considerable expense," and because it was deemed to have "potential investigative value" and could not be duplicated, it was maintained in the Obscene File in a "No. 5 manila envelope" inside a red folder.[45] (It was not unusual for FBI officials to purchase obscene material. In 1948 they "paid in full" for a 16mm film submitted from Los Angeles.) Whether to destroy this particular submission was repeatedly raised over subsequent years. In 1947 the assistant director of the Investigative Division, Alex Rosen, ordered this expensive material retained even though no one was certain of its origin. He believed it still held some investigative value and refused to allow his subordinates to burn it.[46] Thereafter, on an annual basis, persistent FBI supervisors argued that the "red folder" had no investigative value and should be destroyed, but each time, Rosen vetoed their recommendations. He finally relented in August 1952, when he stated he had no "further need for it."[47]

In their efforts to secure obscene materials for the file, monitor the movement of obscene material, and analyze the effects of obscene material on juvenile delinquency, FBI officials even scrutinized Hollywood celebrities Bud Abbott and Lou Costello. Over different decades, both comedic actors were reputed to be significant connoisseurs of pornography.

The two had serendipitously teamed up in 1929 at a Brooklyn theater after Costello's "straight man" partner became ill. They performed on the burlesque and vaudeville circuits for nearly ten years before achieving real success, and they became especially famous after appearing in Hollywood films such as *Ride 'Em Cowboy* (1942), *Abbott and Costello Meet Frankenstein* (1948), and *Abbott and Costello in the Foreign Legion* (1950).

First to come under FBI scrutiny was Lou Costello. In October 1944, while FBI agents were investigating allegations of an obscene movie ring operating in Hollywood, an informant claimed that Costello was one of the "best known customers" for these obscene films. Admitting that the informant had a tendency to exaggerate, an FBI agent nevertheless described Costello as having "the largest library of obscene films in Hollywood." He had so many films, in fact, that the informant described them as "running out of his ears."[48]

Through one of the bureau's white slave trafficking cases, FBI agents learned that in 1946, while Costello was visiting Portland, Oregon, to attend a film premiere, an acquaintance of his had allegedly paid two prostitutes $50 each to "put on a lewd performance" for the actor. This apparently confirmed to FBI officials that Costello was heavily involved in obscene activities of various kinds.[49]

Also besmirching Costello's character was his admiration for Charlie Chaplin, an actor who had drawn FBI interest because of his leftist sympathies. Costello was also alleged to have ties to organized crime. In one case he reportedly made arrangements with a New Jersey mafioso to physically intimidate an individual in Los Angeles who was causing him trouble. That incident led Hoover to comment about Costello: "What a tie-up to the underworld." FBI officials also learned that, despite his interest in obscenity, Costello had toured the country to raise money to combat juvenile delinquency. The totality of this information, whether true or not, convinced FBI officials not to permit Costello to participate in the FBI radio program "This Is Your FBI" as part of his fund-raising efforts.[50]

By 1958 the FBI turned its attention to Costello's former partner, Bud Abbott, who was reputed to be "a collector of pornography and allegedly has 1,500 reels of obscene motion pictures which he shows in his home where he has a projector of his own." FBI officials learned about Abbott's pornography collection from an officer in the Los Angeles police department's vice squad. That officer, in turn, picked up the information from an informant who claimed to have been approached by Abbott to secure "girls for a private party." The vice squad planned to raid the party if it ever transpired. But FBI officials were interested in this information for a different reason. Even though they freely admitted there was no "allegation of interstate transportation of this matter," which meant they had no jurisdiction, they opened a case on Abbott "as a control file to follow and report to the Bureau information coming to the attention of this office though police liaison with Ad Vice, LAPD." Moreover, as the FBI's SAC in Los Angeles observed, the LAPD "is well aware of the Bureau's interest in this category [obscenity] and any films obtained will be submitted to the FBI Lab for examination and comparison purposes."[51]

With the Second World War ending in victory and the subsequent rise of the Cold War to contain international communist influences, some in the United States saw a similar threat to the conformist postwar American culture. In an effort to contain the various perceived threats to the American home front, FBI officials began to use the Obscene File to regulate public morality, as they saw it.

CHAPTER 3

The Postwar Obscene File
and Social Regulation

The Late 1940s and 1950s

After the conclusion of the Second World War, FBI officials' use of the Obscene File changed in significant ways. Increasingly, FBI agents submitted more specimens to the FBI laboratory for identification and comparison to ascertain the sources and distributors of obscene publications and other items. The hope was to increase prosecutions for violation of federal anti-obscenity law. Although the number of Obscene File searches multiplied, the number of successful identifications made via those searches steadily decreased over time—with the exception of a few periods when obscenity became a great public focus. This failure to positively identify obscene specimens led FBI officials—in the midst of the traumatic social, political, and national security upheaval of postwar America—to begin using the Obscene File for alternative purposes. During the Hoover years, FBI agents began to target not only purveyors of obscenity but also those who violated the postwar culture of conformity that some Americans regarded as coming under attack from different segments of society. Concurrently, Hoover continued to educate the public about the obscenity issue, much as he did with communism, as part of his efforts to protect American culture from what he perceived as un-American influences.

Among the first nonconformist targets singled out by the FBI were African American musicians. Beginning in the late 1940s, as so-called race music moved beyond the confines of African American culture and began to rise in popularity as a part of the broader postwar culture, FBI officials made a concerted effort to contain it. In these efforts, they employed the Obscene File. FBI officials were concerned by race music's lyrics, which reverberated with a combination of sexual innuendo and religious energy—in stark contrast to contemporary hits such as "How Much Is that Doggy in the Window?" This particular musical innovation led FBI officials, who were exclusively Caucasian, to regard race music as obscene. Contributing to this perception was the popularly held notion that African Americans were more sexually driven and influenced more readily by obscenity than were whites. Indeed, it was this very notion that had led to FBI officials' earlier concern that obscenity might spark racial agitation and juvenile delinquency. But despite this prejudice, race music became a popular phenomenon across postwar, segregated America. In fact, it became so popular that in 1949 *Billboard* magazine renamed race music "rhythm and blues" to make it more appealing to a white audience.[1]

It was the transcendence of race music from an almost exclusively African American audience to a wider white audience that led FBI officials to recognize it as something obscene and therefore dangerous to the postwar conformist society. This concern was not limited to white law enforcement officials; it was something black musicians themselves recognized. Historian William Ferris discovered that dating from at least 1936, African American blues musicians regularly employed slightly different musical repertoires for black audiences and white audiences. For blacks, blues musicians freely used lyrics with suggestive sexual and racial overtones as a means of protesting the social plight of African Americans; these suggestive lyrics were more or less a code that an African American audience would easily comprehend and sympathize with. For white audiences, African American blues musicians purposefully concealed their so-called racial repertoires, knowing full well that whites would neither understand nor appreciate the lyrics and would perceive them as obscene. But as African American music entered into the dominant white culture by the late 1940s (thanks in large part to the new vinyl microgroove recording technology that helped expand the music industry), these neatly defined audience-specific musical repertoires broke down. The suggestive lyrics entered the larger culture, where white law enforcement officials took special note of them. African American musicians and their record labels were thereby targeted as purveyors of obscenity because their music—and their growing interstate record sales—ran counter to the conformist and dominant national white culture.[2]

FBI officials began their anti–race music efforts during the spring of 1948, when a sergeant in the Boston police department approached the FBI's Boston field office seeking a list of obscene phonograph records. He wanted the list so that his department could locate such items more easily. Citing this sergeant's successful record of prosecutions—notwithstanding judicial rulings as to whether the selling of phonograph records was in fact an interstate matter for the FBI—the SAC in Boston requested the list from Hoover.[3] Hoover agreed to supply the list, provided the SAC inform the sergeant that "the question of obscenity of any of the records is not decided by the bureau" but by the U.S. attorney's office or the Justice Department's Criminal Division—and, though Hoover did not say so, ultimately by the courts. Hoover also ordered that the sergeant be told that some of the records might best be described as "suggestive rather than obscene." Irrespective of this differentiation, Hoover offered up a list of 128 records that the Justice Department had already declared to be obscene under Section 396 of U.S. Code Title 18. The Boston SAC then quietly provided the police officer with this information, which originated from the FBI's Obscene File. It is unknown whether the Boston police ever used this information successfully.[4]

By the fall of 1948, FBI agents had developed enough evidence of their own to warrant, in their view, the prosecution of five separate cases involving the interstate transportation of "obscene [African American–recorded] phonograph records." Four of these cases were centered on the West Coast, and one was prosecuted in Topeka, Kansas. Extant FBI records are heavily redacted, making it impossible to ascertain all five targets, but two of them were the Columbia Music Company and Ted's Radio Shop of San Francisco. Both had allegedly mailed across state lines phonograph records that contained, according to one FBI official, "lewd and licentious acts in obscene and foul language." Assistant Director Rosen, head of the FBI's Criminal Division, suggested presenting the evidence to U.S. attorneys and authorizing simultaneous raids at all five locations because "considerable interest has been evidenced in the interstate transportation of these records."[5]

Given the redacted FBI files and the difficulty of obtaining information about these prosecutions from the Justice Department, the ultimate disposition of these cases remains unclear. Nevertheless, beginning in mid-1948, FBI agents began to achieve success in other cases involving the interstate transportation of obscene phonograph records. The key to their success was the Obscene File, which permitted them to identify obscene materials by comparing them with other items gathered from various geographic locations. FBI officials claimed success in reducing the prevalence of allegedly obscene records; dating from mid-1949, they noted a "marked decrease" in the number of such records in the public sphere. They attributed this decrease to their many successful prosecutions over the previous two years. Nevertheless, FBI officials expected a new peak in obscenity prosecutions during 1950 owing to a particular case the FBI and Justice Department had successfully prosecuted in San Francisco that subsequently made its way to the U.S. Supreme Court.

In 1948 a man named Alexander Alpers was convicted of mailing obscene phonograph records from San Francisco to Olympia, Washington, and Dallas, Texas, using the Railway Express Agency. (Although it is impossible to confirm because of redactions, Alpers was likely one of the four West Coast targets mentioned earlier.) Federal prosecutors regarded Alpers's action as a violation of the interstate transportation of obscene materials law. Alpers appealed his conviction in California and won, making the argument that the law's language did not specifically single out phonograph records as it did other items such as books, magazines, films, and photographs. But in February 1950 the U.S. Supreme Court, in a five-to-three decision, overturned the appeals court ruling and handed down a new decision that affirmed, definitively, that regardless of the law's imprecise language, phonograph records were covered by the anti-obscenity statute. Because the Supreme Court's decision was split and because the appeals court had decided the matter differently, Congress amended the law in May 1950 to specifically include phonograph records and similar items. In the view of FBI officials, this ruling and amendment to federal law would have the effect of resurrecting previously quiescent cases, and the FBI's crackdown on African American musicians and recording companies would continue. Still, because it is hard to gain access to relevant records, the exact scope of this effort remains unclear.[6]

With the advent of the Cold War and the rise of McCarthyism by 1950, FBI officials adapted the Obscene File for new purposes. Senator Joseph McCarthy, the little-known junior senator from Wisconsin, claimed to have a list of 202 "known Communists" in the State Department. He thus unwittingly supplied a convincing explanation of why the United States seemed to be losing the Cold War to the Russians: it was a matter of subversion. In the context of the 1948 Smith Act prosecutions of Communist Party USA leaders, the Alger Hiss case, the apparent "loss" of China to communists, and the Soviet development of an atomic bomb in 1949, the subversion rationale resonated well with many Americans. Yet in reality, it was difficult, if not impossible, to root out and identify communists or communist sympathizers. What did they look like? How did they carry themselves? What commonalities did they share? None of these things was clear, so just about anyone could have been a so-called Red. There was, however, a more successful anti-subversive avenue for national security bureaucrats and advocates. What became far more successful than the hunt for communists in government and society was a parallel hunt for gays and an effort to purge them from government service and beyond. One reason for this switch in focus was that, based on 1950s stereotypes of homosexuals, these targets could seemingly be easily identified.

This hunt for gays in government service is known today as the Lavender Scare. Although the FBI had been monitoring gays since 1937, the public and popular political focus on them was rooted in McCarthy's anti-communist politics. But the Lavender Scare was, in fact, a unique event, singling out gays not only as a threat to national security (because, like alcoholics or adulterers, gays could allegedly be blackmailed by communist agents) but also as a threat to the conformist, overtly moralistic, and gender role–oriented culture of 1950s America. FBI officials' use of the Obscene File during this decade continued to reflect not so much a concern with eliminating obscenity rings but larger concerns about social and cultural influences and Hoover's attempts to contain these influences and educate the public about morality. The bureau's focus on gays was one such concern.[7]

With the federal government's increasing focus on gays as moral and security risks, Hoover instituted a formal "sex deviates" program in 1951 to furnish officials in the executive, legislative, and judicial branches and even other government offices, such as the Library of Congress, with information that could be used to purge homosexuals from federal employment. The program eventually expanded beyond the government to include George Washington University and New York University, as well as various local and state police forces.[8] Interestingly, the Obscene File confirms that the bureau's Sex Deviates File was maintained by the FBI's Special Projects Unit of the Crime Records Division (see chapter 4).

This was the section of the FBI that liaised with Congress and the media; therefore, this was also the section that leaked information to those bodies. For Hoover and senior FBI officials, leaking information about suspected homosexuals to various government agencies (especially the Civil Service Commission) was the most efficient way to ensure their termination.[9]

Interestingly, some information about gays was transmitted quietly to FBI headquarters via the filing procedure for obscene materials. FBI agents used the Obscene File in this way for a very specific reason: obscene submissions were sealed in an envelope, specially marked, and forwarded directly to specific locations—most notably the Crime Records Division—enabling FBI officials to collect sensitive information without fear that it might fall into the wrong hands and with the assurance that only a limited number of personnel would actually handle the information. The first extant example of this usage of the Obscene File dates to 1947, when two army military intelligence officers in San Antonio, Texas, responded to a complaint about a gay bar called Angie's Place, took photographs of the establishment, and then shared them with a local FBI agent. The agent, well aware of the FBI's interest in this type of information, forwarded the photos to FBI headquarters, where they were incorporated into the Obscene File.[10]

Depositing the photos from San Antonio in the Obscene File was not an isolated event. In March 1964 a detective in the Oak Park, Michigan, police department forwarded fourteen obscene photographs—two of which depicted homosexuals—to the FBI laboratory. Technicians were unable to identify any of the photos, but they added those showing same-sex couples to the Obscene File; equally revealing, they filed an unrecorded copy of the original memorandum about the photos from Michigan in the FBI's Sex Deviates File. The inclusion of the Michigan and Texas photos in the Obscene File reveals that FBI officials had motives other than prosecuting ITOM cases or other criminal matters. The FBI was concerned that the photos might be used to identify and purge suspected homosexuals from military service, government employment, or elsewhere. And with the photos safely stored in the FBI's Obscene File, unauthorized persons would not have access to these sensitive items.[11]

In their continuing hunt for gays and lesbians during the Cold War, FBI officials did not restrict themselves to using the Obscene File to transmit and store information and photographs. During the 1950s, FBI officials sought to use anti-obscenity laws to silence the first significant gay rights group in the United States, the Mattachine Society, and the first significant group to publish a nonpornographic gay magazine, ONE, Inc.

Formed in 1950 in Los Angeles by three former members of the Communist Party, the Mattachine Society had several goals. It devoted itself to uniting gays together and with the dominant heterosexual society; educating the public about homosexuals; and, reflecting its founders' backgrounds, engaging in activist politics. Harry Hay, Chuck Rowland, and Bob Hull, the three founders of Mattachine, used the template of the Communist Party as a guide. Because of the negative views of gays in the 1950s, they believed the secretive cell structure of the communists would serve their new organization well. Mattachine members would remain largely anonymous through the use of pseudonyms; the larger organization would be divided into five separate "orders," with the founding members constituting the anonymous Fifth Order. Even the name of the organization reflected the desire for anonymity for the sake of protection. Hay decided to name the group after an obscure medieval French performance group called the *Société Mattachine,* whose members wore masks that enabled them to satirize the French aristocracy without retribution.

Ironically, it was the confluence of Mattachine's secretive nature and the rise of McCarthyism that led to public scrutiny falling on the group in 1953. In 1952 a prominent member of Mattachine was caught up in a police entrapment scheme while visiting a public restroom in Los Angeles and was arrested. At trial, the jury was unable to reach a unanimous verdict, and the prosecutor refused to retry the case. Mattachine claimed this as a victory for gay rights and, feeling invigorated, publicized its win in an attempt to raise funds to support other victims of police entrapment. But, given the rise of McCarthyism and the fear of secretive, subversive influences in American society, this publicity campaign caught the eye of a reporter for the *Los Angeles Mirror,* who questioned whether subversives could gain control of Mattachine and turn it "into a dangerous political weapon."[12]

After the publication of this story, two parallel developments took place. First, members of Mattachine began to question who their leaders were. Because of the anonymous nature of the group and the secretive cell structure, most members had no idea who was leading the organization, and in light of the *Los Angeles Mirror* story and the rise of McCarthyism, many members feared attracting public and government attention. As a result, a movement developed within Mattachine, led mainly by insurgents from the San Francisco area, to purge communist influences from its ranks. At the same time, because of the *Mirror*'s public questioning of Mattachine's potential to become a subversive group, the FBI began to investigate. In addition, a separate group with loose ties to Mattachine (it had been founded by former, disenchanted members) published a story in its eponymous magazine, *ONE,* claiming that FBI agents had investigated a West Coast airline to determine whether it harbored gays. The result was an FBI probe into both groups, which FBI agents regarded as one and the same.[13]

In an attempt to ascertain the extent of communist influence in the group, FBI agents were dispatched, and they questioned multiple sources, including post office officials, local police, informers, and staff at the Los Angeles county clerk's office, to determine exactly who was behind Mattachine. Most significant in this effort was the use of informers from within the organization. One informer in the San Francisco area reported on the size of weekly Mattachine meetings and noted that its members rarely accomplished much because they inevitably ended up immersed in discussions of their own personal problems. Another reported the presence of a coastguardsman and a marine at a Mattachine meeting; although these individuals' identities were not confirmed, FBI officials forwarded this information to military authorities. Still other informers provided the FBI with Mattachine's constitution and schedule of events, and they reported that some members of Mattachine were attempting to purge suspected communists from its ranks. Indeed, it was this last bit of information that ultimately led the FBI to conclude that Mattachine (and, by extension, ONE) was neither dangerous nor subversive. At this juncture, FBI officials apparently did not fully appreciate that Mattachine had been founded by three former members of the Communist Party. All things being equal, this would (or should) have been enough reason for the FBI to pursue the group relentlessly, but in this instance, the reliance on information obtained from Mattachine members led the FBI to call off its probes. Indeed, these informers—who came from the insurgent, anti-communist faction from San Francisco—actively courted city government, the police, and the FBI to convince them their group was not subversive, all in an effort to avoid trouble.[14]

Although this strategy was effective initially, it did not keep FBI agents at bay for very long. Eventually, the FBI (and the U.S. Post Office) resumed its interest in the Mattachine Society and ONE, but this time the goal was to destroy them, using anti-obscenity law as the weapon. Two events sparked this renewed focus on Mattachine and ONE. In April 1954 the senior senator from Wisconsin, Alexander Wiley, received a copy of *ONE* magazine in the mail. He was so upset that he complained to the post office and the FBI (which filed the information in its Sex Deviates File) that he had been sent obscene material. Then, in 1956, *ONE* published an article stating that homosexuals could be found everywhere in society—working, for example, at *Time* magazine, the *New Yorker*, or the State Department; in the business community; or even at the FBI.[15]

Given McCarthyism's efforts to root out subversive elements in society and the parallel effort to root out gays in government service, the charge made by *ONE* could not be allowed to stand by the very agency responsible for rooting out subversives, whether they be communist or homosexual. The result was a renewed effort by FBI officials to silence the rabble-rousing magazine. Indeed, given the popular rumors about the FBI director's sexuality, it is no surprise that the bureau took great interest in cracking down not only on ONE but also on Mattachine, which had its own magazine at this point. And the best avenue of attack was to use anti-obscenity statutes because both groups used the postal service to mail their magazines, containing their subversive articles, to the public at large.

By the time the FBI moved to investigate the two groups' violations of anti-obscenity statutes, the U.S. Post Office had already initiated proceedings to shut down *ONE* magazine. Postal inspectors found that *ONE*'s October 1954 issue contained a story of a lesbian love affair, a risqué poem about a British homosexual sex scandal, and a suggestive advertisement for see-through pajama bottoms. Postal inspectors sought to revoke *ONE*'s mailing permit unless the publishers could demonstrate that their magazine was mailable under postal laws. *ONE* responded by going to court in an attempt to prevent the government from revoking its mailing permit. Meanwhile, postal authorities agreed to review, per the FBI's request, *ONE*'s November 1955 issue to determine whether it too violated anti-obscenity law.[16]

In the meantime, *ONE* fought its legal battle. In January 1956 the case was heard by the district court in Los Angeles, and in April, Judge Thurmond Clarke issued a ruling that sided with the post office, declaring *ONE* magazine to be obscene. *ONE* appealed the decision to the Ninth Circuit Court of Appeals. As the appeal was moving forward, FBI officials decided to seek an opinion from the Department of Justice as to whether specific issues of *ONE* magazine were obscene, planning additional obscenity prosecutions if the department concurred; they also planned to confront *ONE* about its slanderous statements regarding the FBI. Further, they hoped to mount a prosecution for the international transportation of obscene material because issues of *ONE* had reportedly been mailed to Denmark.[17]

By May 1956, Assistant Attorney General Warren Olney informed FBI officials that the alleged obscenity of specific issues of *ONE* was not clear cut; moreover, the department would not proceed until *ONE*'s appeal had been settled. Thereafter, although FBI officials continued to monitor *ONE*'s legal battle, they placed their investigation of the magazine in "pending inactive status."[18]

This effectively ended the FBI's investigation of *ONE* and, by proxy, Mattachine's magazine as well. Although *ONE* lost its appeal in the Ninth Circuit Court, it appealed that decision to the U.S. Supreme Court in July 1957. In January 1958, without hearing oral arguments and with no elaboration on why it did so, the Court reversed the lower courts' rulings to affirm, definitively, ONE's right to mail its magazine. With this legal victory, the FBI's plan to silence ONE and Mattachine through anti-obscenity statutes was destroyed, and gay and lesbian groups won a major battle. This setback in no way ended the FBI's interest in gay and lesbian groups or individuals, but it did, for all intents and purposes, end the FBI's intensive targeting of both ONE and Mattachine.[19]

With McCarthyism and the Lavender Scare in full force by 1951, FBI officials ordered a review and evaluation of the Obscene File. This became an annual event, and collectively, these reviews reveal how the FBI's Obscene File evolved and was used over time. The 1951 review showed that the physical file was composed of various sections: one indexed section was reserved for phonograph records (which were kept in a three-drawer file cabinet), books were carefully alphabetized and indexed, and films were segregated into "nude art" films and obscene films. Motion picture films were indexed alphabetically by title, file number, film size (16mm or 8mm), and "identifications." Furthermore, 400 separate fourteen-by-fourteen-inch still photographs had been taken of the films for comparison and identification purposes. These stills were arranged by race and then further divided by gender and sexual preference: all male or all female (i.e., gay) films, or those containing both. One last category involved films "in which some of the subjects use a form of disguise."[20]

The annual review indicated that the Obscene File also contained an indexed cartoon booklet section, an indexed "narrative reader books" section, a "partially arranged" (by subject) section of obscene photographs, an obscene playing cards section, a section for "miscellaneous Obscene Novelties," and the aforementioned red folder (see chapter 2). An interesting part of the 1951 review included a list "of various types of obscene items and booklets" that were kept in "a special drawer"; these select items were described for use "only" in "special tours." The review's author did not find the "physical arrangement of the obscene file" as aesthetically pleasing as that of the other files in the Document Section. Because FBI tours passed by the Document Section, FBI officials considered physically tidying up the file, but since the information was confidential and accessed by so few, they decided not to do so.[21]

After reviewing the Obscene File, one unidentified FBI official described it as being in good condition and up to date. He even offered a candid description of how the Obscene File was being used—at least officially—at the time, noting that it functioned as "a central clearing house for the Bureau in connection with obscene matters." In terms of the efficacy of working with the Obscene File, this FBI official estimated that the addition and examination of new materials would use only 25 percent of an examiner's time, while yielding "many identifications." (Over the years, the amount of time an examiner expended increased, and the identifications decreased.) Commenting on the nature of obscene submissions to the file, this FBI official recognized that items were added selectively, and only one copy was retained on a permanent basis. Significantly, however, and in line with other FBI policies regarding the destruction of records, a "great volume of [obscene] material submitted by the field is incinerated when the investigation has been completed and the proper authority obtained for its destruction."[22]

In addition to its own internal evaluation, in May 1951 the FBI permitted two Central Intelligence Agency (CIA) officers—with an FBI escort—to examine the Obscene File. The reason for the CIA's interest in the file was not recorded, but the event was not unprecedented, given the special access extended to the OSS during the Second World War. Ultimately, however, a tangentially related incident led Hoover to restrict external access to the file except when "specifically authorized" by the top two FBI officials: Hoover and Associate FBI Director Clyde Tolson. The incident involved Joseph Bryan III, one of the CIA officers granted access to the Obscene File. Bryan commented privately about the bureau maintaining an Obscene File and about Hoover's alleged homosexuality, seeming to suggest that the two were related. Hoover, who was well connected throughout the federal government, was told about Bryan's comments, and he ordered that access to the Obscene File be restricted. Hoover also spent the next four years actively working to discredit Bryan.[23]

For the remainder of the 1950s, FBI agents continued to submit obscene items to headquarters in the hope of obtaining positive identifications. A survey of the annual reviews, however, illustrates the increasingly unsatisfactory results of this undertaking over time, even though the file itself grew steadily, requiring ever-increasing bureau resources to maintain it (see table 3.1 and figure 3.1).[24]

The January 1952 review shows that the Obscene File was composed of seven sections—films, phonograph records, cartoons, books, playing cards, photographs, and novelties—and searching the file required, by bureau estimates, 25 percent of an individual examiner's time. (Out of an unknown total number of searches, 1,077 of them successfully identified obscene materials in 1951.) But due to problems ascertaining the original source of obscene films and still photos, because both were easily copied and recopied, and problems determining whether they had been transported across state lines, an FBI supervisor recommended eliminating the photograph section of the file. Assistant Director Rosen rejected this recommendation, however.[25]

By January 1953, maintenance of the Obscene File and the examination of evidence still required only 25 percent of an individual examiner's time. What's more, except for 1944 (when 16 of 18 searches yielded identifications), the year 1952 stood as the high point in successful Obscene File searches and identifications. During that fruitful year, FBI agents identified 65 percent of obscene submissions, or 1,815 identifications out of 2,794 individual searches. Given this overwhelming success, an FBI supervisor recommended that the file be maintained as it was.[26]

The very next year, however, saw a precipitous drop in obscene identifications—to 47 percent. Despite this decline, the Obscene File was physically expanded in 1953. A new section was added—captioned "Obscene

Table 3.1. Successful Identifications of Obscene Materials, 1944, 1952–1981

Year	Total Number of Searches	Number (%) of Identifications
1944	18	16 (88.9)
1952	2,794	1,815 (65.0)
1953	1,729	817 (47.3)
1954	1,859	823 (44.3)
1955	4,609	1,904 (41.3)
1956	4,077	2,322 (57.0)
1957	2,657	1,155 (43.5)
1958	3,684	1,462 (39.7)
1959	2,366	1,193 (50.4)
1960	1,994	937 (47.0)
1961	2,731	1,361 (49.8)
1962	1,992	677 (34.0)
1963	2,076	1,019 (49.1)
1964	3,552	1,158 (32.6)
1965	3,154	1,171 (37.1)
1966	10,458	5,431 (51.9)
1967	3,318	1,462 (44.1)
1968	6,365	3,557 (55.9)
1969	7,634	4,027 (52.8)
1970	7,145	2,082 (29.1)
1971	4,239	1,560 (36.8)
1972	8,160	4,502 (55.2)
1973	5,543	2,476 (44.7)
1974	3,415	998 (29.2)
1975	1,404	553 (39.4)
1976	1,855	671 (36.2)
1977	1,513	696 (46.0)
1978	2,604	1,055 (40.5)
1979	2,011	574 (28.5)
1980	1,334	484 (36.3)
1981	13,098	334 (2.6)

Readers and Pamphlets"—and others were expanded; "nudist publications," for example, were added to the obscene books section, and "obscene cartoons" and "printed matter" were added to the novelties section. Over the next two years, identifications dropped even further—a mere 44 percent in 1954 and 41 percent in 1955. Yet it was also during this two-year period that the number of obscene searches spiked, leaping from 1,859 to 4,609 (see table 3.1). As a result of this spike, examiners needed more time to conduct their work, increasing from 25 percent of an examiner's overall work time in 1954 to 50 percent in 1955. In short, the Obscene File was requiring more and more working hours while yielding fewer and fewer positive results, a statistical trend that would continue throughout the life of the Obscene File.[27]

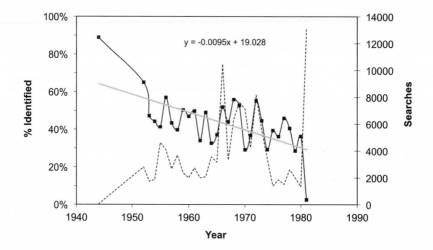

Figure 3.1. Successful Identifications of Obscene Materials, 1944, 1952–1981

The rise in obscene submissions can be explained. Dating from 1948, there developed a significant concern among the American public over the issues of juvenile delinquency, violence, and sex in the mass media. Public pressure mounted and was significant enough to result not only in FBI agents increasing their obscene submissions and searches but also in the convening of a Senate subcommittee on juvenile delinquency in 1953. By 1955 the committee had conducted public hearings and issued a report focusing on the influence of crime-themed comic books; this ultimately resulted in thirteen states enacting laws that banned comic books. The committee, chaired by Tennessee senator Estes Kefauver after 1954, then expanded its work to investigate the influence of sex and violence in film and on television. The committee concluded that moral decay in American society had resulted in increased levels of juvenile delinquency, and it recommended self-censorship in the media.[28]

Hoover took advantage of these popular concerns about juvenile delinquency to push his interest in educating the public on the roots of the problem. In 1955 Hoover blamed the rise in overall crime, but especially juvenile delinquency, on apathy and the failure of parents to instill in their children a proper sense of morality. This, he argued, played into the hands of communists who sought to discredit the American judicial system. The following year, 1956, Hoover blamed juvenile delinquency on parents' failure to provide "moral training and discipline in the home."

Finally, in a newspaper interview in 1957, Hoover was asked to identify the causes of juvenile delinquency. He answered that church and Sunday school were good bulwarks against delinquency, but they could not be found everywhere. Continuing his answer, he asked: "Do adults stand by while temptations are placed in the path of youngsters by persons who deal in printed filth, provide intoxicants to minors, encourage children to spend their lunch money on punchboards and slot machines, or otherwise attempt to undermine their morals?" His answer was yes. He cited "high rates of delinquency [as] a clear indication of moral deterioration and adult disinterest in the community."[29]

The Kefauver Committee also prompted senior FBI officials to review their policy regarding the FBI laboratory's destruction of evidence. The concern stemmed from the committee's 1955 request for bureau testimony in a perjury matter involving committee witnesses and "a very common" obscene film obtained by bureau agents from the Connecticut State Police and later destroyed (unfortunately, redactions in FBI documents conceal the title of the film in question). In July 1955 three men from New York—Eddie Mishkin, Abraham Rubin, and Irving Klaw—were cited by the Kefauver Committee for improperly invoking their Fifth Amendment rights. According to Kefauver, the three had "deprived the subcommittee of necessary and pertinent testimony" about the distribution of pornographic materials to underage youth. FBI officials were concerned that a prominent pornographic film that became pertinent to a congressional committee's investigations had been in their possession and destroyed when perhaps it should not have been. In reviewing the handling of evidence, the FBI Executive Conference noted that, except for firearms and obscene materials, all other evidence examined in the FBI laboratory was returned to the field offices. The reason for the laboratory taking responsibility for destroying firearms and obscene items was "the obvious need for controlling their disposition and to avoid the embarrassment" should it become public knowledge that such items were "at one time in the Bureau's possession." This protocol resulted in "approximately eight legal-size file cabinet drawers" of obscene material being destroyed each year, according to FBI officials, to save valuable storage space and to avoid inadvertent embarrassment.[30]

During this period, FBI agents used the procedure for filing and mailing obscene materials to quietly transmit to headquarters information concerning the alleged sexual indiscretions of prominent politicians, including President Dwight D. Eisenhower. One incident occurred in 1954 when a wiretap of mafioso John Vital revealed his interest in finding and hiring an influential Washington lawyer. The man he found was Herbert Hyde, who was rumored to have an unusual degree of influence in government circles because Eisenhower had allegedly tried to have sex with Hyde's wife and Hyde knew about it. This sensitive information about the president, irrespective of its veracity, was forwarded from the St. Louis field office to Hoover using the obscene materials filing and mailing procedure; the information was then safely filed in Assistant Director Nichols's secret office file. Having such explosive information clearly gave Hoover political leverage, and it illustrates his interest in collecting lurid innuendo involving prominent personalities, regardless of whether it was true. It also shows that FBI agents used a secure procedure to forward sensitive or embarrassing political information to their superiors.[31]

The year 1956 saw even further physical growth of the Obscene File, to the point where FBI personnel began to note space limitations at FBI headquarters. The Obscene File expanded from nine file cabinets to eleven, and two examiners plus their aides were required to maintain and search it. The time required to examine obscene submissions also increased to 70 percent of one examiner's time. Interestingly, there was also a marked increase in the identification of obscene materials that year: 57 percent of all searches yielded a successful identification. This success was not sustained, because identifications dropped to 43 percent the next year and 39 percent the year after that. The Obscene File now contained not only an index to all sections but also an index of the "models" who appeared in obscene photographs. (The following year saw the advent of a new section for obscene advertisements.) Given the increase in obscene submissions and a concomitant increase in requests for rulings on whether "borderline" materials were indeed obscene, the FBI laboratory began to maintain a close liaison with the bureau's Investigative Division in an attempt to streamline conclusions as to the efficacy of obscenity cases. Concurrently, FBI officials created a separate section of the Obscene File to organize these requests.[32]

By the summer of 1957, FBI officials identified yet another potential source to supplement their Obscene File: the Kinsey Sex Research Institute at Indiana University. Professor Alfred Kinsey's interest in human sexuality led to an extensive collection of erotica (in 1948 Kinsey spent $35,237 of his funding on erotica and pornographic collections).

After a shipment of obscene items en route to the Kinsey Institute was intercepted by Indiana police, the special agent in charge of the FBI's Indianapolis field office informed Hoover and requested the director's permission to interview officials at the institute. Hoover assented, hoping to win their cooperation in supplementing the FBI's information about the "sources and suppliers of obscene material." (Kinsey himself was deceased by this point, having died in 1956 of heart disease.)[33]

An FBI agent interviewed both the director and the field director of the Kinsey Institute, only to learn that, in his view, they had "very limited knowledge" of obscene matter and that the size of the institute's obscenity collection "has been greatly exaggerated." Tables were turned in 1959 when officials of the Kinsey Institute requested access to the FBI's obscenity collection. Undaunted, FBI Assistant Director William Sullivan recommended that the opportunity be used "to exploit the contact from the viewpoint of investigative interest in pornographic matters," and he eventually recommended that the bureau approve the institute's request for samples from the Obscene File. After several months of negotiation between Sullivan and the institute's lawyer, a frustrated and concerned Hoover foreclosed any possibility of sharing sensitive items: "In so far as any material which FBI has it is *not* going to be made available to this outfit."[34]

Although FBI officials sought to expand the Obscene File in 1957, that year also witnessed an event that had the potential to end its use altogether. Late in 1957 Attorney General Herbert Brownell issued orders that the Justice Department, and hence the FBI, comply with the classification restrictions of President Eisenhower's Executive Order 10501 and the Atomic Energy Act of 1954. Eisenhower's executive order limited the classification of national defense information to three categories: top secret, secret, and confidential. The Atomic Energy Act set restrictions on the classification of nuclear-related information. Under the executive order, FBI agents were no longer permitted to mark any bureau document with their previously unique restrictive phrases—such as "Personal and Confidential," "Strictly Confidential," or "For Official Use Only." The order also affected the FBI's "June mail" procedure, which was used to report information obtained from illegal surveillance methods (e.g., microphones). Both procedures relied on agents marking envelopes and documents either "OBSCENE" or "JUNE" to ensure that they were not filed in the FBI's central records system but were maintained separately, and safely, elsewhere. The new order seemingly banned the use of such special markings.[35]

FBI Director Hoover—ever the master bureaucrat—finessed the problem by ordering all SACs to continue to mark envelopes and documents with the words "OBSCENE" and "JUNE," noting that "these words are regarded as descriptive of the material rather than a classification." In fact, the words were not merely descriptive; they were special classifications created by Hoover to ensure the safe transmission and filing of sensitive information. But nobody except bureau agents and officials would recognize their true significance, unlike the obvious phrase "Strictly Confidential." By coyly manipulating a bureaucratic procedure, Hoover ensured the continued autonomy, and thereby the power and influence, of his bureau while ignoring an executive order. Yet Hoover and his FBI would continue to encounter difficulties when it came to the issue of obscenity, not from the executive branch of the federal government but from the judicial branch. These problems would lead to further changes in how FBI officials both investigated obscenity cases and made use of the Obscene File.[36]

CHAPTER 4

Changing Judicial Views on Obscenity, the Nixon Administration, and the FBI

1957 to the Early 1970s

A major problem for FBI officials beginning in the late 1950s, especially with regard to maintaining and utilizing the Obscene File, was the ever-changing legal criteria that defined precisely what was and was not obscene and therefore a legitimate interest for FBI agents. Over ten years (1957–1967) the Warren Court confronted a number of obscenity cases, and each of its rulings confirmed that sex had become more acceptable to the public and was therefore no longer appropriately prosecuted under the obscenity statutes. In short, the Warren Court segregated sex from obscenity, and although the Court never declared obscenity to be protected under the First Amendment, it increasingly liberalized the legal definition of what was, in fact, obscene. Taken together, the various rulings proved to be a boon for the blossoming pornography industry, and they changed the way FBI officials used the Obscene File.

Prior to 1957, when government officials detected obscenity and then prosecuted it easily and simply, the courts had few legal precedents to guide them in determining exactly what was or was not, in a legal sense, obscene. American law, in fact, offered virtually no legal criteria for defining obscenity. Instead, judges and juries used a model devised in 1868 by the British legal system known as the *Hicklin* test. The *Hicklin* case involved the publication of an anti-Catholic work that was part of a political effort to keep Catholics out of the British Parliament. The judge in the case needed to render a definition of what was obscene, and he devised what was, at best, an ambiguous standard. In Lord Chief Justice Cockburn's definition, "the tendency of the matter charged as obscenity is to deprave and corrupt those whose minds are open to immoral influences, and into whose hands a publication of this sort may fall." When American lawmakers confronted obscenity, they tended to model their legislation after *Hicklin,* and American courts based their decisions on *Hicklin*'s definitional standard of obscenity, with little consideration of its ambiguity. The upshot was that, before 1957, law enforcement officials and prosecutors were largely free to define what was obscene, which meant that nearly anything they personally deemed to be obscene was subject to prosecution. In court, judges and juries would then use *Hicklin* as a guide.[1]

The U.S. Supreme Court ended the use of the *Hicklin* test in 1957. The case involved an Austrian immigrant named Samuel Roth. Roth attended Columbia University and then opened a bookstore in New York, where he sold magazines, books, and photographs. Roth was an astute businessman, so after repeatedly experiencing trouble with authorities for selling controversial and "obscene" (at the time) books such as *Ulysses* and *Lady Chatterley's Lover,* Roth mailed circulars nationwide to increase his store's business. He was arrested in 1955 and charged with twenty-six counts of violating federal anti-obscenity law, but he was convicted on only four counts of mailing obscene material across state lines, including two magazines that contained nude photographs and erotic stories, nude photographs, a book titled *American Aphrodite,* and the advertising for these products.[2]

Roth appealed his conviction, which made its way through the appellate system and eventually reached the U.S. Supreme Court. The Court bundled Roth's federal case with two others—a California obscenity case (David Alberts) and a New York case involving an allegedly obscene comic book (Kingsley Books). In their deliberations, many of the justices suggested that although Roth was indeed guilty of violating federal obscenity law, they were concerned by the law's ambiguous definition of obscenity. In conference, Justice William O. Douglas rhetorically posed three questions: "(1) Is the definition of *obscene* adequate, and what does it mean? Is there an adequate standard? (2) How is it applied? . . . (3) How do you charge the jury?" Justice Potter Stewart found the justices' deliberations "most amazing" but warned that those who sought to uphold the lower courts' decisions "never mentioned once what the standard for obscenity is, or what standard would (and would not) be compatible with the First Amendment." Justice Felix Frankfurter disagreed, arguing that the "idea that these laws are no good because you can't frame a definition of 'obscene' to meet all notions of people's varying tastes, etc., is nonsense. Obscenity is an adequate phrase." Frankfurter went on to compare ambiguous obscenity law with the Fourteenth Amendment, which, he argued, was similarly vague yet acceptable.[3]

In its ruling, the Court upheld Roth's conviction and found that obscenity was not protected by the First Amendment. The justices cited the fact that since the eighteenth century many of the states had restricted speech, and especially obscenity; therefore, the founders did not intend the First Amendment to be unconditional. But the Court also noted that "sex and obscenity are not synonymous." Rendering its first legal definition of obscenity, the Court described it as something "appealing to prurient interest." The Court rejected the *Hicklin* test for obscenity, which permitted authorities to focus on isolated passages of allegedly obscene material, and affirmed that a determination of obscenity depended on "whether, to the average person applying contemporary community standards, the dominant theme of the material, taken as a whole appeals to prurient interest." Over the next decade the Court heard additional obscenity cases involving magazines, books, pornography, and homosexual publications, and in each instance it further refined, bit by bit, what it regarded as "prurient interest." For the first time, American law was attempting to define obscenity.[4]

Following on the heels of *Roth* and subsequent Supreme Court decisions on obscenity, the American pornography industry—consisting of books, magazines, and films—began to flourish. Even mainstream media began to loosen up and portray sex somewhat more openly with the advent of the 1960s and sexual liberation.[5] Not surprisingly, the pornography boom quickly affected the FBI's long-standing interest in obscenity issues. In July 1959 FBI officials began to recognize that agents were compiling "an ever increasing amount of material on pornography," but particularly information alluding to its social effects, its relationship to law enforcement, and, more generally, the "various side lights on this many-sided 'monster'" (interestingly, FBI officials here used words very similar to Anthony Comstock's description of obscenity as a "hydra headed monster"). In response to this evaluation, one FBI official recommended creating a special collection of pornographic materials that "would be of benefit to the Director, in the event he would like to inform the American people on this subject, as he has in the past." Unlike the Obscene File, this special collection was not intended to be a compilation of pornographic exhibits to be used to identify purveyors of smut. Instead, it would be a subunit of the Obscene File comprising only "narrative accounts" to be maintained securely as "research material" in the "Special Projects Unit, Crime Research Section, [of the] Crime Records Division."[6]

The creation of this subunit reveals much about FBI filing procedures, special files, and dissemination activities. FBI officials realized the multifaceted value of their collecting large amounts of pornographic material because of their maintenance of "research material on Parole and Probation and Sex Offender[s]." By collecting information on repeat offenders and so-called sex offenders (homosexuals were routinely lumped into this category)—information Hoover routinely used to educate the public about these threats—FBI agents had realized that the pornography issue similarly involved "many informative facets." An FBI official therefore suggested creating "a carefully kept set of material" on pornography "such as [is] presently kept under the subjects of Parole and Probation and Sex Offender material." He noted that this pornography file could be created "by the persons now maintaining the Parole and Probation and Sex Offender material"—that is, the aforementioned Special Projects Unit of the Crime Research Section of the Crimes Records Division.[7]

What is so revealing about the documents in the Obscene File, however, is the mention of the "Parole and Probation and Sex Offender" information and who maintained it. In 1951 Hoover created a Sex Deviates File to disseminate information about gay federal employees to ensure their termination; the program was then expanded to include nongovernmental employers. What the Obscene File reveals, for the first time, is that the Crime Records Division, in addition to maintaining pornographic research material, also maintained the Sex Deviates File. The Sex Deviates File was, in reality, a fusion of three separate files: one covered "sex perverts in government," another was a bureau policy file covering "Sex Degenerates and Sex Offenders," and the third and oldest (dating to 1937) covered "sex offenders." What's more, during the Hoover years, the Crime Records Division was the branch of the FBI that liaised with Congress and the media to leak information to trusted recipients. The fact that the "sex offenders" material was maintained by Crime Records reveals that this information was held for dissemination, just as the pornography material of the Obscene File was disseminated in an effort to shape public opinion on the topic. In other words, Hoover wanted to protect American culture by containing the spread and influence of pornography by educating the public as best he could.[8]

The constantly changing legal definition of obscenity after 1957 was a serious problem for FBI officials. If FBI agents were to pursue obscenity cases, they needed guidelines about what was and was not prosecutable. One consequence of these legal difficulties was the inclusion of a new type of information in the Obscene File. After 1957 FBI officials began to compile information pertaining to the development of state anti-obscenity and anti-pornography laws. Although the FBI's jurisdiction was limited to cases involving violations of federal law, the bureau often used the Obscene File to assist local law enforcement. FBI officials likely viewed anti-obscenity statutes in the states as foreshadowing the evolution of federal anti-obscenity law. Hoover therefore ordered FBI agents to monitor state legislatures but admonished them to be "discreet" in their probes. Hoover elaborated that he did not want "the Bureau's interest in these matters [to] become known." In other words, Hoover knew that FBI monitoring of state politics would be viewed, rightly, in a negative light.[9]

Extant records in the Obscene File reveal that FBI agents submitted to headquarters—using the obscene materials filing and mailing procedure and sent via the Crime Records Division and, later, the Training Division—the text of anti-obscenity statutes from Florida (twice), Maryland, Wisconsin, Maine, New Hampshire, Massachusetts, Louisiana, Pennsylvania, and Kansas. With this varied information, FBI officials could quietly monitor the changing legislative interpretations of obscenity to determine how best to deal with or even influence the shape of future anti-obscenity law, something they had noted even back in the 1940s.[10]

Given the *Roth* decision and the fluid definition of obscenity, Hoover ordered his SACs at the bureau's field offices to carefully monitor obscenity investigations and cases. He was concerned that the FBI might be publicly embarrassed should it become known that an agent had collected, for prosecution, obscene materials that did not fall within the standards laid out by the Supreme Court. As always, Hoover demanded that his personnel take great care and remain discreet.[11]

Irrespective of Hoover's concerns about the proper collection of evidence, he ordered SACs to continue to submit obscene items, "regardless of source," to FBI headquarters, especially items from local police forces. Because these items were not to be used for prosecution, Hoover had less fear of public embarrassment, and he believed they were of value. However, Hoover was concerned that such items might "arouse the curiosity of employees" and lead to embarrassing leaks. To prevent this possibility, Hoovered ordered the SACs to store their obscene specimens "in either the gun vault or the SACs safe"; at "no time" should obscene material be kept in an accessible location where it might cause "undue curiosity about such filth."[12]

Hoover's guidelines for securing obscene material and keeping FBI personnel away from these items were a failure, according to former assistant director William Sullivan. In his 1979 memoir, published eight years after Hoover fired him for openly criticizing the FBI director and seven years after Hoover's death, Sullivan wrote that "within hours a file with compromising photographs would be opened and closed [by FBI agents] so many times that the tape would lose all its adhesiveness." Moreover, Sullivan recalled an incident that took place in 1970, when FBI agents were pursuing Angela Davis—a prominent black activist associated with the Black Panthers who had gone underground when a gun registered in her name was used to murder a judge. While searching her apartment, agents discovered photographs of Davis having sex with her boyfriend. Nobody informed Hoover of the photos' discovery, and when he heard about it indirectly from the New York SAC, he was reportedly livid. He demanded to see the photographs and then delayed the promotion of the agent who had the photos in his possession. Hoover also placed "a scorching letter of censure" in the agent's personnel file.[13]

Alternatively, FBI agents could receive extraordinary praise for their work in obscenity cases. One case in point is a letter an FBI supervisor wrote, recommending that two agents receive commendations for their anti-obscenity work:

> In the year since 1968, [the subject] continued his pornographic operations, distributing his libidinous wares in great volume to the voyeur and to the depraved, at their expense, but to his own financial reward. However, as [the subject] became more bold and lascivious, [the agents] became more dauntless in their investigative pursuits to ferret out an Interstate Transportation of Obscene Matter violation. . . . The very nature of this violation is not for the faint-hearted and prudish but rather, it is for those individuals who possess an outstanding character and moral fortitude. . . . As a result of their flawless grand jury presentation [the subject] was indicted. . . . Because of

the righteous adversity inflicted upon [him], his pornographic empire collapsed and his financial woes will plague him for years. . . . Thus after five years of continuous and imaginative investigations by [the agents], [the subject's] pornographic operations are removed from the community which he tended to subvert through the prurient interest of young and old alike. The moral fiber of the community has well been served through the efforts of [the agents].[14]

Clearly, the potential for embarrassment greatly concerned the FBI director, leading him to take special steps to ensure the confidentiality and security of obscenity matters. But irrespective of his own prudishness, Hoover was a skilled bureaucrat who recognized the "potential publicity value" of obscenity investigations. Whereas leaks of obscene materials could be terribly embarrassing for the FBI, carefully publicized cases could promote the FBI's image.[15] In this effort, Hoover continued an old bureau policy and ordered SACs to review all obscenity investigations, not just to ensure they were being handled properly but also to single out special cases that might be used to promote the FBI's image as a protector of American values devoted to shielding Americans from the insidious influence of smut. At the same time, Hoover kept tight control over the use and release of any bureau information, fearing the consequences if anything embarrassing were leaked. Hoover made sure that all public statements on obscenity cases remained in the hands of FBI headquarters alone.[16]

One ITOM case that had the potential to generate publicity involved the popular 1960s song "Louie, Louie," written by African American musician Richard Berry in 1955 and performed by the group the Kingsmen. The interest in the song probably reflected the common assumption at the time that African Americans were more promiscuous than whites. The FBI's interest began in February 1964 when someone complained to the Tampa, Florida, field office after the song became popular among high school students in Sarasota, where it was commonly played on local radio stations. The complainant claimed the lyrics were obscene and provided a copy of what he believed them to be, which he had ascertained by slowing down the speed of a record player (because the words were difficult to understand at normal speed) and writing them down.[17] Hoover directed the Tampa office to discover who the complainant was and then work with the appropriate U.S. attorney to determine whether the song and those behind it were prosecutable under federal law. Hoover advised the Tampa SAC, however, that the Justice Department had recently considered the song's lyrics and had been unable to determine whether they were obscene.[18] Finally, on 4 March, the FBI laboratory reported back to Tampa that it was unable to "definitely determine" the song's lyrics.[19]

The Tampa complaint was not the only one the FBI received about "Louie, Louie." A little more than a week after the FBI laboratory sent its report to Florida, Assistant Attorney General Herbert Miller forwarded to Hoover a complaint from Indiana that Attorney General Robert Kennedy had received several days prior. Miller wanted a report from Hoover about the status of the Florida complaint, and he wanted the author of the letter from Indiana interviewed so that he could decide how to proceed. The Indiana father wrote that his daughter had purchased the record and brought it home, which shocked him because he had read that the song had been banned from the radio because of its suggestive lyrics. He demanded that Kennedy do something because "this land of ours is headed for an extreme state of moral degradation with this record, the biggest hit movies and the sex and violence exploited on TV."[20]

Hoover ordered the Indianapolis field office to interview the letter writer in an attempt to obtain evidence that the "Louie, Louie" lyrics were, in fact, obscene. He also ordered FBI agents in Florida to "expedite" their investigation to determine whether enough evidence existed to open an ITOM investigation.[21] The Indianapolis SAC submitted the record to the FBI laboratory, but in the end, laboratory technicians were still unable to ascertain the precise lyrics (as they had likewise failed with the copy submitted from Florida and another from San Diego), given the garbled way they were sung.[22] By May 1964, the U.S. attorney in Indiana, Lester Irvin, decided not to prosecute because the FBI could not determine whether the song's lyrics were obscene.[23]

Almost one year later, the FBI's Detroit field office submitted the record to headquarters again, asking the laboratory to ascertain the song's lyrics. The Detroit SAC also forwarded a copy of his report to the New York City field office, because that is where the song had been recorded. Yet again, the FBI laboratory was unable to determine the song's lyrics. Amazingly, it was not until October 1965 that somebody interviewed a member of the Kingsmen, who commented on the popular but false notion that the song was obscene. Finally, someone in the FBI checked with the copyright office, which had a registered copy of the "Louie, Louie" lyrics that proved, conclusively, that the song was not obscene and therefore not subject to prosecution.[24]

A side note to the FBI's interest in "Louie, Louie" reveals further details about the FBI director's views on obscenity and pornography. On 18 June 1965 a mother who was a teacher in Michigan as well as a member of the General Federation of Women's Clubs wrote to Hoover to express her concern about the song and her failed attempts to have authorities do something about it. She also commented on the general increase in pornography across the country and asked Hoover what her group could do to stop it. She was especially concerned that pornography was contributing to "the alarming rise in venereal disease [rates], perversion, promiscuity and illegitimate births in the teen groups." Hoover responded that although he could not comment on any efforts against the song, he "share[d] the concern you feel in the alarming increase in pornography. I strongly believe that the easy accessability of such material cannot help but divert the minds of young people into unhealthy channels and negate the wholesome training they have already been afforded by their parents." Instead of advice, Hoover sent the woman two FBI publications titled "Poison for Our Youth" and "Combating Merchants of Filth: The Role of the FBI." Yet again, Hoover sought to educate the public about the dangers of obscenity.[25]

Interestingly, "Combating Merchants of Filth" was one of the bureau's attempts to educate the public on the issue and stemmed from the bureau's 1959 subfile of research material on pornography. In the article, which appeared in the *University of Pittsburgh Law Review* in March 1964, Hoover offered various examples of "filth and indecency" while noting that "the pornography racket encompasses a wide range of obscene objects—some so scurrilously vulgar that they defy description." He noted that smut peddlers knew the law and how to get around it, and he outlined federal law dealing with obscenity and pornography. Hoover also took note of the Supreme Court's recent ruling that community standards "dictate what is, and what is not, obscene." Therefore, Hoover warned Americans, "it is essential that high standards of decency be zealously maintained in every phase of community life."[26]

One subject that appears to have interested the FBI when it came to obscenity and, for that matter, homosexuality was Andy Warhol. In November 1968 two FBI agents were dispatched to the San Francisco International Film Festival to witness the midnight screening of a film titled

Lonesome Cowboys, an Andy Warhol production. Quite possibly, though FBI documents do not make it clear, FBI officials were interested in this film because of Warhol's stature as an avant-garde artist and filmmaker—as an artist, he regularly touched on sexuality and obscenity—and the potential publicity value of a case against him. At the very least, FBI officials sought to prosecute Warhol for violating federal anti-obscenity law.

In their report, the two FBI agents described the film's characters, including a woman, a male nurse, a sheriff, and five cowboys. According to the agents, "all of the males in the cast displayed homosexual tendencies and conducted themselves toward one another in an effeminate manner." What's more, and in keeping with contemporary thinking that obscenity and drug use were linked, they noted that "many of the cast portrayed their parts as if in a stupor from marijuana, drugs or alcohol." The agents reported:

> As the movie progressed, one of the actors ran down a hill. The next scene showed a man wearing only an unbuttoned silk cowboy shirt getting up from the ground. His privates were exposed and another cowboy was lying on the ground in a position with his head facing the genitals of the cowboy who had just stood up. A jealous argument ensued between the cowboy who was observed running down the hill and the one wearing the silk shirt. The man in the silk shirt was then seen urinating; however, his privates were not exposed due to the camera angle.[27]

The agents then described a sexual assault against the woman, noting that "the position of the male and female suggested an act of cunnilingus." They also took special note, again in line with contemporary concerns about obscenity and youth, that "at the end of this scene the woman sat up and said. 'Now look—you have embarrassed those children.' [But] There were no children in the movie." The film also depicted homosexuality, such as "a cowboy fondling the nipples of another cowboy" and "suggestive dances" between men that, though they were fully clothed, "suggested love-making between two males." Finally, the FBI agents described the film in general as chock full of "obscene words, phrases and gestures." FBI officials submitted this information to U.S. attorneys in New York, Atlanta, and Phoenix for prosecution, presumably because Warhol had made his movie in Arizona and then crossed state lines to screen it; however, they all declined the case.[28]

From 1957 onward the U.S. Supreme Court repeatedly clarified its legal definition of obscenity. It did so again in April 1969 in a case that would lead FBI Director Hoover to further refine the bureau's policies in pursuing obscenity and using the Obscene File. The case involved Robert Stanley, a known bookie who had been convicted of bookmaking in the past. Federal and state law enforcement officers secured a federal warrant to search Stanley's home for evidence of bookmaking. Although they found no evidence of gambling, they found three pornographic 8mm films in a desk in an upstairs bedroom. The police charged Stanley with possession of obscene matter, for which he was convicted; the Georgia Supreme Court affirmed the conviction.[29]

Stanley appealed to the U.S. Supreme Court, where his lawyer argued that under the provisions of the First Amendment and the Fourteenth Amendment (equal protection under law), the possession of obscene items could not be considered a crime. The Court, noting that the *Roth* decision explicitly held that obscenity was not protected by the First Amendment, nevertheless agreed with Stanley. In all previous obscenity cases, the issue had been the regulation of obscene matter or its dissemination through the mail; the issue of the mere possession of obscene items had never been considered. Therefore, the Court ruled that the *Roth* decision could not be used in a case involving the simple, private possession of obscene items. This resulted in the Court affirming the right of American citizens to keep, for private purposes, obscene items.[30]

In the wake of yet another Supreme Court decision involving obscenity, Hoover was forced to issue new orders to his SACs regarding the seizure of obscene items. He informed the SACs that they were not to seize, "no matter how obscene," anything that clearly fell within the provisions of the *Stanley* opinion. But Hoover also informed them that, in his opinion, "multiple copies [of obscene materials] indicate commercial use." Since the *Stanley* opinion involved only the private possession of obscenity, Hoover decided that the FBI's way of differentiating privately held items from those intended to be sold would be based on the amount of obscenity in an individual's possession. FBI agents were instructed that if they discovered multiple copies of obscene material, they should obtain a warrant and seize it all.[31]

Soon thereafter, the FBI director's anti-obscenity efforts rose from the level of law enforcement and FBI policy to that of presidential and national politics and another sociocultural shift. Just one week after the Supreme Court handed down its *Stanley* opinion, and just twelve weeks after his inauguration, President Richard Nixon launched his ten-point domestic program. Between Nixon's failed bid for the presidency in 1960 and his election in 1968, the United States underwent tremendous upheaval. The turmoil of the Vietnam War and the threat of being drafted sparked intense student protests nationwide. The mass anti-war demonstrations on campuses, in conjunction with the rise of the counterculture movement and the prominence of drug use, suggested that America's youth had somehow lost its way and rejected traditional American values. What's more, some in the civil rights movement began to embrace black nationalism, or Black Power, rejecting both the ideals of assimilation and the nonviolence espoused by Dr. Martin Luther King Jr. Although the advocates of Black Power were only a minority in the civil rights movement, they received focused press attention. Other minorities, inspired by African Americans, also began to seek equality during the 1960s, including women, gays, Latinos, and Native Americans. Their quests for equal rights, and the resultant protests and harassment, seemed to contribute to the sense that traditional American values were under attack. During the campaign in 1968, Nixon capitalized on all this.

As a politician, Nixon had a history of using national events to his advantage. His political career began during the 1940s, when he was a fervent anti-communist member of the House Un-American Activities Committee (HUAC). He sought, at that time, to protect American values from the influence of "subversives." He then served as Eisenhower's vice president, lost the 1960 presidential election, and became a critic of the Kennedy and Johnson administrations' foreign policies. In the process, Nixon revived his political prominence, so when he campaigned for the presidency a second time in 1968, he defined himself, yet again, as a protector of traditional American values. This time, however, he framed himself as the law-and-order candidate, a strategy that proved successful amid the social turmoil of the decade.

Nixon aired political spots on TV showing riots in American cities and mass student protests. He also explicitly blamed President Johnson's attorney general, Ramsey Clark, for the increase in crime, citing the "permissiveness" of America's chief law enforcement officer. He also condemned the various Supreme Court decisions that had altered, for example, American legal standards of obscenity, as well as other decisions handed down by the so-called activist Warren Court. Nixon's strategy was to appeal to middle-class fears about crime, seemingly out-of-control youth, and white resentment toward the black civil rights movement, all of which were negatively affected by the apparent decline in American values. Nixon appealed to what he would later dub the great "silent majority" of Americans—those who wanted to see the Vietnam War end "in a way that we could win the peace"; who wanted to see a decrease in crime; who respected decency, quietly paid their taxes, and did not seek to disrupt American culture. His strategy worked, and Nixon managed to beat Democrat Hubert Humphrey by just 500,000 votes to win the presidency.

It was the American reaction to the social turmoil of the 1960s, and Nixon's ability to capitalize on it, that led to the next great sociocultural shift that caused the issue of obscenity, and the FBI's interest in it, to change yet again. This shift was noticed in 1970 by political analysts Richard Scammon and Ben Wattenberg. They recognized that American voters tended to focus on domestic issues, and in the tumult of the 1960s, a new voting issue emerged that the Republican Party would dominate. Scammon and Wattenberg termed it the "social issue," which encompassed a complex set of variables including crime, race, youth, and obscenity. Scammon and Wattenberg identified the growing public concern with obscenity as one of "values." They wrote in *The Real Majority*: "Pornography blossomed with legal sanction; sexual codes became more permissive; priests were getting married; sex education was taught in schools."[32] As Scammon and Wattenberg rightly noted, these elements all worked in harmony to lead American voters—Nixon's silent majority—to voice their concerns and demand that politicians and the government respond. This social issue, they wrote, "may be defined as a set of public attitudes concerning the more personally frightening aspects of disruptive social change." And in this mix, "pornography, nudity, promiscuity are perceived to tear away the underpinnings of a moral code, and this, too, is frightening."[33] With such issues at the forefront, the authors pointed out, Americans cast their votes largely along these lines.

The Real Majority was widely read at the time, influencing electoral politics and promulgating the obscenity issue. But as Robert Mason points out, Nixon had already made the decision to focus on the issues of patriotism and permissiveness. Nevertheless, Nixon's political strategy and the influence of *The Real Majority* complemented each other at the time.[34] The book was also influential among some important administration officials who would soon be in charge of the obscenity issue. Patrick Buchanan, for instance, wrote an analysis of the book, arguing that the Nixon administration should seek to win over "law and order Democrats" and "conservatives on the 'Social Issue.'" Buchanan advised that these groups' votes could be secured if the administration portrayed "RN as a hard-liner on crime, drugs and pornography, whose legislation is blocked by 'ultra liberals' in the Senate." Nixon was convinced by Buchanan's views and ordered that his analysis of *The Real Majority* be circulated throughout the administration.[35]

In early February 1969, before the appearance of *The Real Majority* and shortly after Nixon's inauguration, the president directed his postmaster general, Winton Blount, and his attorney general, John Mitchell, to meet to evaluate the obscenity problem and propose legislation to deal with it.[36] When the two reported back to the president that they were drafting legislation and seeking to inhibit the mailing of obscenity through administrative means, Nixon was displeased. He found these efforts to be "very minimal," so he asked presidential assistant John Ehrlichman for any "ideas as to how we might best get some good publicity on this matter."[37] Nixon also expressed to his chief of staff, H. R. Haldeman, that he "wanted to take stronger action on obscenity" and implement a "strong program, fast." According to Haldeman, and reflecting the president's interest in the politics and publicity of it, Nixon even suggested that he, Nixon, attend an obscene play in New York and walk out in the middle of it to demonstrate his disgust.[38]

Nixon's demands led presidential assistant and speechwriter Pat Buchanan—one of Nixon's more socially conservative advisers—to write a special report titled "The Pornography Explosion" in which Buchanan characterized "filthy movies" as "pouring out of Hollywood" and from foreign lands "like a plague of locusts." Buchanan pointed out that only a few years ago, these films "would have merited a jail sentence for the producer." Buchanan noted that, given how well Nixon's nomination acceptance speech had been received—in which he promised to "open a new front against the filth peddlers"—"it is clear that pornography and filth are gut issues with millions of decent people." He then suggested that the president "comment quietly and briefly, but strongly" on the issue of obscenity. More specifically, he advised the president that there was "no need to threaten laws or jail sentences or outrage—just presidential disgust, the exercise of the moral leadership of the office." Buchanan concluded his report by stating that he "would be happy to research and draft remarks, which should be made briefly and off the cuff—as something 'on the President's mind.'"[39]

After reading Buchanan's report, Nixon penned on the top of it: "I agree completely." He also wrote instructions for his speechwriter: "find a method." Nixon then handed the report off to Alexander Butterfield, deputy assistant to the president, who advised Buchanan of Nixon's views and, moving beyond the realm of mere publicity, added that he should "continue to give thought to ways and means of remedying this serious national problem and of rebuilding and reinforcing the legal barriers to what can be shown on a public motion picture screen."[40] Thus Buchanan assumed the lead role in handling a political issue that would be of great interest to the Nixon White House over the next two years.

The following month, communications director Herbert Klein wrote to Kenneth Cole, the White House staff secretary who coordinated all presidential communications, to suggest that, because of the publicity it would engender, the president should not make the initial announcement of the administration's anti-obscenity effort; instead, it should be made jointly by the postmaster general and the attorney general. Klein believed "the benefit is bound to be great," given the high degree of public interest in the obscenity issue, but he recognized there was some risk related to issues of censorship and who exactly would set obscenity standards. Nevertheless, he believed it was "highly desirable that the Administration move strongly in the area." Klein further advised that if Nixon were not directly involved, he could "receive benefits from it" but "will not be subject to blame."[41]

A major problem for Nixon in pushing for anti-obscenity legislation was the fact that his Republican Party remained a minority in both the House of Representatives and the Senate. Moreover, Nixon had won the 1968 election by only a slim margin, so he was without an electoral mandate. Given these realities, Nixon sought to publicize the obscenity issue to energize his base and, hopefully, improve Republican prospects in future elections by drawing in more supporters who were interested in his anti-obscenity efforts. Knowing that he was unlikely to achieve new anti-obscenity legislation, and hoping to go beyond merely politicizing the issue, Nixon ultimately sought other avenues to implement his puritanical anti-obscenity agenda by focusing on the courts.

Nixon did not accept Klein's advice regarding his personal involvement with the obscenity issue. In April the president outlined his domestic program in a written message to Congress. This program consisted of ten goals, and close to the top, at number two, were issues dealing with "permissiveness" in American society: the apparent increase in crime, drug use, and obscenity.[42] Nixon proposed three laws designed to beef up existing anti-obscenity statutes and protect Americans from "being bombarded with the largest volume of sex-oriented mail in history." Several weeks later, on 2 May 1969, the president outlined his proposal in more detail in another message to Congress. Nixon noted that dating from 1964, more and more Americans had lodged complaints with the post office about the "unsolicited, unwanted, and deeply offensive" mail they were receiving; in just the past nine months, the White House had received more than 140,000 letters from concerned parents. The president wanted to protect children from being exposed to this mail by making it a crime to send it to anyone under the age of eighteen. He also proposed to ban "advertising designed to appeal to a prurient interest in sex" and to prohibit "smut advertising" from being sent to Americans who did not want it.[43] Nixon claimed that his administration had carefully studied the problem and "discovered some untried and hopeful approaches" to scale back the permissiveness inherent in recent Supreme Court rulings on obscenity and to stamp out "a primary source of this social evil." Classically, Nixon claimed that his proposals were an effort "toward protecting our youth from smut coming through the mails."[44]

Interestingly, not all of Nixon's advisers were advocates of his anti-obscenity stance. Perhaps not surprisingly, Democratic presidential aide Daniel Patrick Moynihan revealed his dissenting views in a letter to Eleanor Boyd, the wife of an old acquaintance from his days as a student at Tufts University. Mrs. Boyd had written to Moynihan to express her concern over the obscenity issue and to ask Moynihan to join the national library board of Morality in Media, an interfaith organization created in 1962 and devoted to extinguishing obscenity in American culture. But Moynihan was not interested. He responded that "in all honesty" he was "not terribly upset by the current flood of pornography and the like." He confessed his belief that the increase in pornography probably reflected "more severe social breakdowns," but Moynihan did not believe that going after pornography would stop those breakdowns, nor did he believe that pornography caused "all that much harm." But Moynihan's views were in the minority among Nixon's advisers, and those views were all but ignored, if sought at all. Nixon would not find an ally in the New York Democrat, but ironically, he would find one in J. Edgar Hoover.[45]

Given the history behind the Nixon-Hoover relationship, it is interesting that the two found common ground here. Nixon's relationship with Hoover began in the 1940s, when the newly minted congressman from California took on communism to make a name for himself. In 1941 *Time* magazine editor Whitaker Chambers, who had joined the Communist Party in the 1920s, decided to turn against the party and cooperate with the U.S. government. Chambers provided the names of people who were allegedly involved in a Communist Party cell and who sought to influence government policy. One of these individuals was Alger Hiss, an official in the State Department. But with no proof other than Chambers's claim that Hiss was a member of the cell, nothing could be done.

Further developments in 1945 pushed the Hiss case forward, giving rise to Nixon's relationship with the FBI director. During that year, Soviet consular official Igor Gouzenko defected to Canada and claimed to have knowledge of Soviet spies in both Canada and the United States. According to Gouzenko, one of the alleged spies was an assistant to the U.S. secretary of state. Given its close intelligence relationship with the United States, Canada shared this information with its neighbor to the south. Based on this new information, combined with what the FBI had already been told, Hoover concluded that this assistant to the secretary of state was none other than Alger Hiss. Thus began the FBI's intensive investigation of Hiss, using both legal and illegal investigative methods such as wiretaps, physical surveillance, and the opening of mail.

The State Department could have initiated loyalty proceedings against Hiss (President Truman had created a loyalty program amid charges that his administration was soft on communism), but it did not do so, probably due to a lack of evidence. Instead, Secretary of State James Byrnes confronted Hiss, who denied the charge. He also denied the charge to FBI agents, after which Hoover sought to build a Hatch Act case again him. The Hatch Act outlawed the government employment of individuals who advocated the violent overthrow of the U.S. government, such as communists. Furthermore, Chambers could not help FBI agents build a case against Hiss because, at the time, Chambers himself was still denying that he was a Soviet espionage agent.

This changed in 1948 when the communist-subversion issue became a dominant topic in American politics. That year, Chambers was subpoenaed to testify before the HUAC, where he publicly stated that Hiss had been a communist during the 1930s. Hiss denied the charge and demanded to do so before the HUAC, of which Nixon was a member. Since Nixon could not prove that Hiss was a communist, he sought to link him to Chambers, which would be enough to satisfy the young California congressman's political interests. In this effort Nixon was successful, but only because he had the help and cooperation of Hoover's FBI. Hoover, ever the coy and careful bureaucrat, did not assist Nixon directly, however. He passed information to Nixon through the anti-communist priest Father John Cronin. Between August and December 1948, if FBI officials developed any information about Hiss they would relay it to Cronin, who would then telephone Nixon and pass it along. Hoover, it should be noted, also maintained helpful relationships with the HUAC, the Senate Internal Security Subcommittee, and Joseph McCarthy.[46]

By the time Nixon became president, his relationship with Hoover had changed. Hoover had turned seventy, the mandatory retirement age at the time, during 1965. He retained his job only because the previous year President Lyndon Johnson had issued an executive order exempting Hoover from mandatory retirement.[47] However, with Johnson out of office and Nixon in, Hoover's tenure as FBI director was in jeopardy because Nixon could reverse Johnson's executive order at any time. Given his tenuous position, and with public protest and skepticism about government (and about Hoover's directorship) at a high, Hoover decided it was too risky to continue the FBI's wide use of illegal investigative techniques, for fear of public exposure and a negative reaction. Yet, as he had done with previous administrations, Hoover continued to provide Nixon with information to satisfy the president's political and policy interests and, no doubt, to protect his own position at the bureau. However, a politically paranoid Nixon was displeased with the FBI's inability to confirm his critics' and staff's disloyalty. This led Nixon to initiate his own internal White House leak-stopping operation—the same "plumbing" operation that would ultimately undo his presidency. Because of Hoover's reluctance to use the FBI to spy for him, and upon the advice of aides such as Buchanan, the president ultimately decided to replace Hoover by persuading him to resign. But in the end, Nixon could not get Hoover to budge.[48]

When it came to social issues such as obscenity, Hoover and Nixon saw eye to eye. By December 1968, after a decade of Supreme Court justices altering the "legal criteria for obscenity," FBI officials, but especially Hoover, had become frustrated with "present standards of obscenity [which] are more liberal than standards used to determine whether evidence was or was not obscene when past decisions were made to add samples of evidence to the Obscene File." This fact, one FBI official observed, had resulted in a mass of material in the Obscene File that "by contemporary standards is not obscene" and therefore "should be removed to make room for the ever growing number of obscene exhibits necessary for reference purposes." An additional concern with removing and then destroying these obscene items was the lack of storage space in FBI headquarters to hold the massive physical portion of the Obscene File.[49]

Among the obscene materials deemed to be of no current value were "nude art type movie films," which were no longer "considered suitable vehicles for prosecution" under current law. Also deemed of little use by late 1968 were nudist magazines, art pamphlets, and still photographs from motion pictures that were used for comparison with more current films. Last, FBI officials no longer considered the Obscene File's index of photograph "order numbers" useful because, to proceed with an obscenity prosecution, agents needed to apply the more exacting legal criteria established over the previous eleven years. As a result, FBI officials ordered the destruction of all these portions of the Obscene File.[50]

Given the changing nature of ITOM prosecutions and the concomitant proliferation of pornography nationwide, just one month after Nixon announced his proposal to eliminate smut from the U.S. mails, Hoover initiated a parallel effort that would effectively buttress Nixon's anti-obscenity plan. Hoover ordered the collection of information for an FBI educational campaign to expose the apparent laxity in obscenity cases. It should be remembered that to score political points with his base, Nixon had lambasted the Johnson administration for its "permissive" attitude toward obscenity. In June 1969 Hoover ordered ten FBI field offices—Baltimore, Chicago, Cleveland, Denver, Detroit, Los Angeles, Miami, New York, Philadelphia, and San Francisco—to submit to headquarters "timely examples of severe [obscenity] cases" involving parole and probation, sex offenders, and pornographic literature. Hoover advised the SACs that he wanted to document "articles, statements, speeches, etc. [from Hoover] showing growing abuses in the handling of such matters and the unwarranted leniency so often noted in their disposition." More specifically, Hoover ordered the SACs to focus on information about "corrupt or inept courts, prosecutors, law enforcement agencies, parole and probation authorities," and anything else that might shed light on "these acute problems." Hoover was careful to order his men not to use standard procedures for submitting data to FBI headquarters; instead, they should direct it specifically to the Crime Records Section, which maintained the special pornography research subfile (as well as the Sex Deviates File) for easy dissemination to trusted recipients.[51]

Since Nixon and Hoover shared the same puritanical values, in 1970 the FBI director sought to help the president create a more conservative Supreme Court and reverse previous Court rulings on obscenity—Nixon's alternative to winning new anti-obscenity legislation from a Democratic Congress. During a 5 June telephone conversation between the two, Nixon expressed interest in any information Hoover might have to back up charges made by Congressman Gerald Ford that Justice William O. Douglas was unfit and should be impeached. Nixon was interested in altering the political makeup of the Supreme Court, and he hoped to help Ford eliminate one justice. The conversation then shifted to the Court's obscenity rulings, and Hoover suggested that the administration press obscenity prosecutions, but especially those involving the seizure of obscene material originating from outside the United States, in an effort to challenge the Court's liberal rulings in obscenity cases. Hoover also suggested a publicity campaign—the director had already initiated one the previous year within the FBI—in the hope that the Court would recognize "raw obscenity" rather than its more lax standard of total content. Hoover advised that such a dual effort would "get some publicity out that the country is sick of this crap they see in the newsstands."[52]

The Nixon administration seemingly accepted Hoover's advice to push for obscenity prosecutions in the courts and to publicize obscenity as a political issue. Since 1970 was a congressional election year, Nixon worked hard to ensure Republican wins by emphasizing, in part, his fight against permissiveness. Hoover's advice also neatly dovetailed with the many letters the White House received demanding that the president do something about pornography. One letter writer, Mrs. S. Murphy, even mentioned Hoover's public claim that pornography "is a major cause of sex crimes and perversion" in the country.[53]

The Nixon administration's publicity effort began in the summer of 1970, prior to the long-awaited release of the final report from the President's Commission on Obscenity and Pornography. Congress had authorized the commission's establishment in October 1967, and in early 1968 President Johnson had appointed its members, who were experts on the issue. After a year and a half of hearings and deliberations, the commission's report was due to come out in the fall of 1970. This report was widely expected to conclude, contrary to Nixon's campaign rhetoric, that pornography was not responsible for the increase in social problems. Nixon decided to utilize the release of the commission's report to publicize his administration's anti-obscenity effort, in part because of congressional Republicans' inability to move anti-obscenity legislation out of committee.[54] Nixon could use the presidential bully pulpit to gain more publicity than his counterparts in Congress prior to the report's release. Interestingly, Haldeman was worried that the commission would "clean up" its report due to negative publicity. He commented, "Obviously we don't want to let them do this." Instead, Haldeman wanted "to develop the issue" of the report and "move hard" on it.[55] Or, as Haldeman confided to his diary, President Nixon "wants the issue of their bad report."[56]

Contrary to previous advice, Nixon himself would spearhead the administration's publicity effort on 11 June 1970. But before he did this, White House staffers had to decide how best to handle the release of the commission's "pro-smut" report. Bud Krogh—who, along with Buchanan, John Dean, and Henry Cashen, made up the White House's "action group" on the report—outlined the administration's two options.[57] First, the White House could replace the commission's "offensive members" with more sympathetic ones. This was the option favored by Buchanan and by Nixon's lone replacement appointee to the commission, Charles Keating, a Cincinnati lawyer and anti-obscenity advocate who led a group called Citizens for Decent Literature and who was described in the press as "a dissident member" of the commission. (Incidentally, Keating, similar to letter writer Mrs. Murphy, noted in private correspondence with Nixon that the FBI director had declared pornography to be "wreaking havoc in our society.") Father Morton Hill, president of Morality in Media and a member of the minority on the commission, secretly provided the White House not only with the names of the so-called offensive members but also with advance copies of the commission's final conclusions. The second option was to encourage the writing of a commission minority report, which, according to Buchanan, needed to be "a vigorous rebuttal" lest the White House have on its hands "a hell of a problem."[58]

Krogh researched the legality of replacing commission members and found that the president had the authority to do so. However, he advised that taking this step "would be bad politics," and he cited several reasons. First, if the offensive members were replaced, that would raise the question of how the White House knew the commission's views before its report was released. The commission had very strict confidentiality rules. Krogh noted that "Hill and Keating would obviously be exposed" as the administration's inside sources. Second, Krogh advised that "if we subvert" the commission at the last moment, the White House's ability to influence future commissions would be jeopardized because "the appearance of impartiality" would be destroyed. Finally, he stated that removing commission members would only lead to more publicity where the administration did not want it focused.[59]

Krogh's suggestion was to bury the commission's report (as other reports had been buried), while keeping the White House at a distance from it. Even if the "left press" intensively covered the report, he argued, the administration could "hammer home in strong moral terms by denouncing any proliferation of smut and exhorting Congress to enact our anti-pornography legislation already there." He also suggested that encouraging the writing of a minority report would "be the best way to siphon off the energy of Keating and Hill," who would be angry if the administration failed to act against the commission. Krogh commented that those two men, "from the moment we came into office," had repeatedly encouraged the White House to condemn the commission and had violated its confidentiality rules in their efforts. In fact, commission chairman William Lockhart, dean of the University of Minnesota Law School, had made complaints to that effect to the White House. Krogh wanted to "deflect the anger of Hill and Keating" because it would not help the administration's publicity efforts. The administration decided to accept, for the most part, Krogh's recommendations.[60]

One significant problem with encouraging a minority report was the fact that the commission's chairman and majority members refused to expend funds to write it, reflecting the tension between them and Hill and Keating. Buchanan, Hill's contact in the White House, suggested to the priest that the White House "might be able to help him with a first-rate writer."[61] Buchanan suggested to Krogh that either the White House should pressure the commission to advance funds for the minority report or the White House should "raise the money ourselves."[62] In the end, the White House found private funds to finance the report and offered any other help that Keating and Hill needed; meanwhile, the White House developed "a plan to combat the effects of the majority report."[63] Buchanan and Dean recommended "a very soft, low key approach" to convince Lockhart to permit the writing of a minority report and to give Keating the necessary time to compose it.[64] Buchanan and Keating fervently believed that the simultaneous release of the minority report was vital to prevent the majority report from being used "to tear down every anti-obscenity law in the country." To put pressure on Lockhart, Buchanan and Dean suggested that Ehrlichman call him.[65]

Buchanan, according to Charles Colson, was put "in charge of attacking the Pornography Commission's findings." Colson was Nixon's special counsel and hatchet man, and his job was to maintain links with outside groups. Colson agreed to telephone religious leaders around the country to encourage them to denounce the majority report, distribute Keating's minority report, and "activate all of the anti-obscenity groups."[66] The administration's "game plan" was that the vice president would make a public statement after the majority report was released, since the president was scheduled to be out of the country; this would be followed by a press conference with the minority members of the commission and their "appear[ance] on appropriate T.V. shows." Dean believed that this plan, which was hammered out by Buchanan, the Justice Department, and the commission's minority members, was the best way "to make the maximum out of the commission's report."[67]

On 11 June 1970—just days after his conversation with Hoover—Nixon began the administration's publicity effort and warned members of Congress that the public would seek retribution at the ballot box if they failed to act promptly to pass his proposals. The president used the occasion of the annual meeting of U.S. attorneys in Washington to begin his anti-obscenity campaign, but he couched it as part of his anti-crime efforts. He warned that "for the Congress to fail to act and go back to the people will be something that the people will remember."[68]

Former Supreme Court justice Arthur Goldberg, who at the time was campaigning to win the Democratic nomination for New York governor, castigated the president's anti-crime ideas as "unconstitutional" and "totalitarian." One overarching concern of Goldberg's was Nixon's proposal that would allow arrested individuals, which presumably included those arrested on obscenity charges, to be detained for up to sixty days without bail. He called this dangerous.[69]

Four days later, Supreme Court Justice Warren Burger (appointed to the Court by Nixon in 1969), whether in league with the White House or not, continued the publicity effort and issued a strong denunciation of the Court's reversal of an obscenity case. In a five-to-two ruling, the Court overturned the conviction of an Ohio newsstand owner who had been found guilty of selling "hard core pornography" in the form of two books and two magazines. Burger said he could "find no justification, constitutional or otherwise, for this Court's assuming the role of a supreme and unreviewable board of censorship for the 50 states, subjectively judging each piece of material brought before it without regard to the findings of conclusions of other courts, state or Federal."[70]

Then, on 22 August 1970, Attorney General John Mitchell gave a speech before the annual meeting of the National District Attorneys' Association in Portland, Oregon, where he reportedly promised to continue the government's crackdown on pornography. Dismissing the expected conclusions of the commission's report, Mitchell said the government should "encourage the best and discourage the worst" in society, and he declared, definitively and contrary to the expected report, that pornography is, in fact, harmful to society. Mitchell also explicitly distanced the Nixon administration from the commission by pointing out that it had been formed during the Johnson administration and that Nixon had appointed only one of the eighteen committee members.[71]

Following suit, on 8 September 1970 Keating, Nixon's lone appointee to the commission, announced that he would seek a judicial injunction to prevent the release of the committee's controversial report. According to the *New York Times,* Keating claimed that his actions were known and supported by the White House. Keating also stated that his motive for seeking the injunction was to give him time to write a thorough dissenting report to rebut the conclusions of the majority. Apparently, the White House's behind-the-scenes efforts to persuade the commission to give

Keating more time had failed. On 9 September a federal district court temporarily halted the release of the report so that Keating could study it and write a dissenting report.[72]

The White House was pleased with these developments. Buchanan was somewhat upset that the *New York Times* had erred, in his view, in reporting that the administration supported Keating's move, since officially, the White House had taken no stand. But, seeing a potential opportunity, Buchanan suggested that "it might not be a bad idea to identify with the effort of Keating to have the report halted"; nevertheless, at this point he told press secretary Ron Ziegler "to say that Keating initiated it on his own." Buchanan also told Haldeman that although he would be on the road, he would have his "porno file" with him so that he could write the president's statement with little or no notice.[73]

On 28 September, as reported in the *New York Times,* Postmaster General Winton Blount "reenforced today the Nixon administration's stand against removing legal restraints on pornography." In addition, Blount criticized the court system for permitting pornography to spread so widely throughout the country. *Times* reporter Richard Halloran, who had been following the story of Nixon's clampdown on smut, picked up on the administration's efforts to publicize the anti-obscenity campaign. He noted that Blount's statement was "another step by the administration to disassociate itself from the pornography commission." What Halloran did not know, of course, was that Blount's statement was part of a larger administration (and FBI) effort to alter recent Supreme Court decisions about obscenity.[74]

The commission finally released its majority report on the afternoon of 30 September 1970. By that time, the Nixon White House had made headway in its efforts to discredit the report. It had, for example, "leaked the substance of Keating's [minority] report" to the *Washington Star, New York Daily News, Boston Herald-Traveler,* and Catholic News Service. The White House had also brought Keating to Washington to participate in the news conference and arranged for him to appear on the *Today Show* the day after the report's release.[75] Furthermore, Dean reiterated in a memo to Larry Higby that the report "provides an excellent opportunity for the Administration to be very vocally placed on the right side of this issue." Additionally, Dean pointed out that "the fact that the nation will be saturated with 'Oh Calcutta' [an obscene play due to be broadcast nationwide on closed-circuit TV] on September 28 will also be useful in our dealing with the subject." This play would become a focus for Nixon advocates and U.S. attorneys.[76]

The White House then followed its plan for responding to the report's release. On 30 September 1970, in a speech at a Republican fund-raising event in Salt Lake City, Utah, Vice President Spiro Agnew referred to the commission's report as a "lame duck" report—referring to the Johnson administration—that was not in line with the current administration's views on obscenity and pornography. He then declared that "as long as Richard Nixon is president, Main Street is not going to turn into Smut Alley." The vice president then laid blame for the proliferation of obscenity over recent years, saying that it "has been abetted by a political hedonism that permeates the philosophy of the radical liberals." Agnew continued: "They may not openly condone indecency, but they help create the climate in which it flourishes by their inability to say no and their unwillingness to condemn." Agnew then linked the Democratic senator from Utah, Frank Moss, with "radical liberals" and asked the people of that state not to return Moss to the Senate in the forthcoming election.[77]

Then, also according to plan, Keating and others held a press conference. Lockhart defended the commission's majority report, but Keating, in a dismissive statement, referred to Lockhart and other commission members as "highly slanted and biased" people who came from either higher education or had links to the sex industry.[78]

After the White House's initial response plan had unfolded, Nixon finally chimed in with a stern denunciation. While stomping the campaign trail in Maryland for Republican candidates during the off-year election cycle, Nixon announced that he rejected "categorically" the "morally bankrupt conclusions and major recommendations" of the commission's report. These included the argument that pornography did no serious harm to society, the statement that open discussion of sex was a normal and natural part of society, and the recommendation that all laws banning sexual material should be lifted. The president strongly disagreed. Nixon retorted that if it were true that pornography did not affect society in a negative fashion, we must also agree that our culture's "great books, great paintings, and great plays also have no ennobling effect on a man's conduct." The president then added: "Pornography can corrupt a society and a civilization. The people's elected representatives have the right and obligation to prevent that corruption." Moreover, and totally contrary to the commission's report, Nixon called for the outlawing of smut everywhere in the United States and encouraged every state to do so quickly and "in unison." He added: "So long as I am in the White House, there will be no relaxation of the national effort to control and eliminate smut from our national life."[79]

In his denunciation, Nixon made special note of the Supreme Court, but he did not castigate it for its recent ruling altering the legal definition of obscenity. Instead, he noted accurately that the Court had historically rejected the view that obscenity was protected by the First Amendment. What Nixon left out, however, was that the Court had differentiated sex from obscenity and had further refined the criteria for the two in a variety of legal opinions. But Nixon did warn, somewhat obliquely, that those "who attempt to break down the barriers against obscenity and pornography deal a severe blow to the very freedom of expression they profess to espouse." The president then applied the domino theory, relating to the spread of communism, to obscenity; he warned that if "permissiveness" was tolerated, then all other aspects of the American "social order" and "our moral principles" would likewise crumble. "American morality," Nixon proclaimed, "is not to be trifled with."[80]

In response, Chairman Lockhart claimed that Nixon's reaction was merely political. He noted that the commission's work was based on science and sought to examine popular notions about obscenity. And Lockhart was right. Nixon's response was, in fact, political. It was, in part, a now classic attempt to energize the Republican base. It was also part of a concerted effort, proposed by Hoover, to influence the Supreme Court to alter its "liberal" standards of obscenity.[81]

In addition to launching a publicity campaign against obscenity and pornography, the Nixon administration and its allies pressed the issue in the courts, as per the FBI director's advice. On 21 September 1970, Charles Keating pursued legal action against another target he regarded as obscene. This time, Keating sued the Shubert Theater in Cincinnati in an effort to prevent it from showing the controversial play Oh! Calcutta. The play, written by British dramatist Kenneth Tynan, included scenes of full nudity by both male and female actors. It was slated to be shown in twenty-six cities nationwide over closed-circuit television, including in the Ohio theater. Keating declared the play a "public nuisance" and claimed it violated Ohio anti-obscenity law because "the dominant theme of the play, as a whole, appeals to a prurient interest in sex."[82]

For a second time Keating was successful in court. The Cincinnati court ruled *Oh! Calcutta* to be obscene under the law and barred the play's producers and AT&T from transmitting it over closed-circuit television. Subsequently, the distributor of the play, Colormedia Inc., filed a lawsuit against Keating, claiming that he had deprived it from freely exercising its First Amendment rights. Shortly thereafter, on 6 October 1970, Dean asked an assistant to draft a letter from the president to Keating to thank him for all his efforts. In Dean's view, Keating "really went beyond the call of duty in his efforts in the court case and the printing and personal expense of copies of his own minority report which we have disseminated here in the White House." What's more, Dean told this aide, Keating "deserves a real pat on the back from the president."[83]

Oh! Calcutta continued to experience trouble. On 19 May 1971 the U.S. attorney in Corpus Christi, Texas, won a federal indictment against the play's distributor and producers (of the videotaped version) for violating the 1873 Comstock Act when Colormedia transmitted the play to fourteen American cities on 28 September 1970. With this indictment, the Nixon administration had a federal obscenity case it could press and a first-ever case involving closed-circuit television. The case was widely expected to raise the question of whether obscene films and plays were protected by the First Amendment, and it was expected to make its way to the Supreme Court. However, the outcome of this case remains unknown. To date, the Justice Department, despite having the case listed in its central index of records, "has been unable to locate this file."[84]

The Nixon administration pursued other obscenity cases, one of which was related to the Commission on Obscenity and Pornography. In December 1970 a pornographically illustrated version of the commission's report was released on the West Coast by a prominent publisher of erotica. It is difficult to determine all the details, but in early 1971 Larry Higby, Haldeman's assistant, asked Dean "about doing something to deal with the illustrated version of the Commission on Obscenity and Pornography."[85] Dean responded with a Justice Department report on the subject.

After the illustrated report was published, a coordinated investigation began in the Los Angeles area and included postal inspectors, FBI agents, and a federal grand jury. They discovered that 80,000 copies of the illustrated report had been printed and then shipped through the U.S. mail and by common carrier, which violated federal anti-obscenity law. Federal prosecutors decided to focus the prosecution in San Diego and Dallas (where the publication had been shipped). But when reporting to Dean about these details, Assistant Attorney General Will Wilson pointed out that "these indictments will be construed by many, including the press, as an outright reprisal directed toward the Presidential Commission" because of its findings. Wilson recommended, and Dean concurred, that the Justice Department's Public Information Office should be prepared to dismiss such allegations and point out that the indictment was the result of an independent prosecution.[86]

By March 1971 three corporations and four individuals had been indicted in San Diego and Dallas for publishing and mailing the illustrated report and the advertising for it. This included forty-nine-year-old William Hamling, a publisher of erotica that the federal government had failed to convict on similar charges in 1965. At trial, defense attorneys called to the stand two members of the Commission on Obscenity and Pornography, who testified that the illustrations actually "clarified and enhanced" the original government-published report. The jury was not wholly convinced, however, and convicted the four individual defendants only for mailing the advertisements for the book. The jury was unable to determine whether the illustrated report itself was obscene, leading the judge to declare a mistrial for those counts.[87]

Hamling was not satisfied with the trial's result and appealed his conviction—ultimately to the U.S. Supreme Court. His lawyers argued that the lower courts had not properly issued procedure and evidentiary rulings and that the proper obscenity test had not been applied in the case. Hamling's attorneys also contended that the prosecution had been a "political move" by the Nixon administration. The Court, in a five-to-four decision, did not agree.[88] Nixon finally had his Supreme Court case, and although it was a victory for the government, it did not lead to any substantive change in obscenity law. And since Nixon would resign in disgrace in less than two months, the publicity value of the case was nil.

Focusing public attention on the prosecution of the illustrated pornography report was not the Nixon administration's only effort to discredit the commission's report. On 23 March 1971 Democratic congressman James Haley of Florida forwarded to the White House a newspaper article sent by one of his constituents claiming that the Commission on Obscenity and Pornography had funneled money to a Methodist minister in San Francisco who, through his National Sex and Drug Forum, sponsored "integrated homosexual [dance] balls." Nixon's staff assistant Jack Caulfield suggested to Dean that the White House ask the FBI and the Internal Revenue Service to investigate the group and consult with Keating to determine whether this story was true.[89] Dean inquired, and Keating's secretary responded that Keating had no knowledge of the commission providing money to any group in San Francisco. However, Keating informed Dean that the minister's organization was in fact listed in the commission's report, and Keating suspected (he gave no reason why) that the commission had issued a contract to the group (possibly for its research). Keating suggested that the White House consult the commission's records in the National Archives. Apparently, Dean only reported these details to Congressman Haley.[90]

Although the Nixon administration mounted an aggressive anti-obscenity publicity campaign, it was never able to build a significant obscenity case that might lead the Supreme Court to change its liberal rulings. In several cases, such as the important *Miller* case (discussed later), the Court did not drastically alter anti-obscenity law but, as historian Paul Boyer has noted, "the net effect was to slow if not reverse a forty-year judicial liberalizing trend on obscenity cases."[91] The reason for this change was the makeup of the Court. In 1969 Nixon appointed the conservative, strict constructionist Warren Burger to the position of chief justice, after President Johnson's choice to replace the outgoing Earl Warren had been blocked by a filibuster in 1968. Then, in 1970 and 1971, Nixon had opportunities to appoint three other conservative justices: Harry Blackmun, Lewis Powell, and William Rehnquist. Thereafter, the Court tended to lean toward the Right, and although it did not significantly alter anti-obscenity law, it tolerated efforts at censorship in close five-to-four rulings (Kennedy appointee Byron White sided with the Nixon justices).

By the late 1960s, the changing legal criteria for obscenity led FBI officials to destroy specific portions of the Obscene File that, under the law, were no longer considered obscene. The stated purpose for this destruction was to make room for materials that did fall under contemporary definitions of obscenity.[92] FBI personnel incinerated obscene books, "art type movies, nudist type magazines, art type pamphlets, still photographs from movie films and index cards bearing [photographic order] numbers." An FBI official who surveyed the Obscene File for 1968–1969 (because the Obscene File was created in late summer, fiscal-year periods were used) noted that FBI personnel made 7,634 searches of the file and identified 4,027 obscene specimens—that is, 52.8 percent of searches were successful, down from the previous year's success rate of 55.9 percent.[93]

When the Obscene File was surveyed a year later in July 1970, the success rate of identifications had plummeted to just 29 percent. This steep drop prompted FBI supervisor Griffith to offer his superiors an explanation for this dramatic failure. His rationale centered, first, on the sheer volume of obscene materials that had flooded the country over the previous two years, given the relaxation in the legal criteria for obscenity. Second, he noted, recent court decisions in obscenity cases "have encouraged the production of more pornographic material that borders on so called hard-core pornography and more material that is readily classified as hard-core pornography." In short, a flood of obscene material in general and the advent of hard-core pornography stymied FBI efforts to achieve successful identifications. Given these developments, Griffith reported that an FBI laboratory technician was now forced to spend his entire time searching the file, whereas in the past these searches required only a fraction of his time.[94]

During the same month that Griffith offered his analysis, the bureau's Baltimore field office forwarded to the FBI director information about the laxity of obscene prosecutions. This was information Hoover had requested previously to supplement his educational campaign. The Baltimore SAC proffered three news clippings. The first detailed a district court decision preventing police raids of bookstores due to improperly worded search warrants; this ruling had reportedly discouraged the pursuit of other pornography cases. Another clipping, from a periodical published by the Knights of Columbus, criticized the argument that abolishing obscenity laws would be a step toward reducing "sex crimes" and the "distribution of pornography." The article cited Denmark's recent relaxation of pornography laws and the subsequent explosion of pornographic literature, including magazines that depicted "all forms of homosexuality, sadism, masochism," and bestiality. The third clipping, from the *Bible Baptist Tribune,* called the growth of unchecked pornography "an evil worse than . . . black slavery" that would infect young minds. Additional "research" submissions were offered by other field offices between July 1970 and March 1972, when they ended (just before Hoover's death in May). Many of these reports are heavily redacted, making it impossible to fully understand the scope of the information being sent to FBI headquarters. Some of them, however, focused on what the bureau called "sex offenders" but were, in reality, homosexuals. In one report, a copy of which was filed in the Sex Deviates File, the Los Angeles field office took note of one bar "featuring male bottomless dancers." Despite Hoover's collection of this material for use in an educational campaign, it appears that this effort never really got off the ground; I found no references to it in FBI press releases or news stories. At the time, the FBI was being roundly criticized in the press, and the FBI director focused much of his attention on defending his embattled bureau. Hoover's sudden death in 1972, just two years after the start of the educational campaign, would also explain why it never materialized.[95]

Hoover's personal interest in the issue of obscenity was, in many ways, the driving force behind the FBI's obscenity cases. Indeed, former assistant director Sullivan notes that "Hoover had always been fascinated by pornography."[96] With Hoover's death, and given the increasingly liberal legal standards of what constituted obscenity, SACs submitted fewer and fewer obscene items to headquarters for identification. By December 1976 field office submissions of obscene materials had decreased markedly, from 8,160 in 1971–1972 (the last year of Hoover's directorship) to only 1,855—a 77 percent decrease. This trend troubled the new FBI director Clarence Kelley, who issued an airtel—an FBI message of the highest priority—to SACs ordering them to step up their submissions of obscene materials. Kelley also sought to reorganize the bureau in an effort to restore its image in the wake of the Watergate scandal and congressional investigations of FBI abuses by the Church and Pike Committees. Kelley was an FBI insider, having been an FBI agent and then a senior official before retiring in 1961 to become the chief of police in Kansas City. Back at the FBI, Kelley attempted to change the Hoover-era culture by stressing a quality-over-quantity approach to investigating, and he laid out specific objectives that he expected his subordinates to meet in a business-like way.

One exception to this quality-over-quantity approach was obscene investigations. Kelley informed his SACs that a vital function of the FBI laboratory was maintaining the Obscene File "as a central intelligence coordinating point in assembling and disseminating information obtained through field investigations concerning the production sources and distributors of pornographic material." Because of this, Kelley wrote, the success of the Obscene File was "totally dependant upon" field submissions of obscene materials; therefore, his own broader focus on "quality versus quantity as related to the FBI's investigative responsibilities" should not preclude SACs from submitting increasing amounts of obscene items, including "film, magazine and other printed matter, limited to obviously explicit 'hard-core' materials and excluding so-called 'rubber goods' and novelty items." Kelley's reason for ignoring his own general orders was his contention that a direct correlation existed between positive obscene identifications and the number of obscene specimens submitted for examination. Kelley also attempted to stimulate obscene submissions by focusing SACs' attention on organized crime, which, he argued, was increasingly involved in the financing, distribution, and selling of pornography. By the 1970s, now able to legally wiretap suspects and armed with the Racketeer Influenced and Corrupt Organizations Act (RICO), FBI officials focused their attention on the Mafia, which intersected with their long interest in obscenity.[97]

On the face of it, the data gathered by FBI agents from 1971 to 1976 suggested a correlation between obscene submissions and identifications, but a critical examination of the broader history of the Obscene File does not bear this out. During the FBI's 1971–1972 fiscal year, SACs submitted 8,160 obscene items, 4,502 of which were identified using the Obscene File, for an identification rate of 55.2 percent.[98] During the next fiscal year (1972–1973), SACs submitted a total of 5,543 obscene items, of which 44.6 percent were identified. Despite this drop, the author of the report concluded that the recent Supreme Court case *Miller v. California* (21 June 1973) would lead to increasing amounts of obscene evidence because the Court had shifted responsibility for defining what was obscene to local authorities and local standards rather than national ones, as had been the case under *Roth*. This meant that federal prosecutors could more easily secure indictments in more conservative local jurisdictions. The Court also relaxed the legal criteria for prosecution—whereas an obscene item previously had to be "utterly without redeeming social value," it now had to meet the less limiting and more easily prosecuted standard of "not hav[ing] serious literary, artistic, politic or scientific value."[99] As it turned out, the amount of obscene evidence and the number of obscene identifications did not increase with the *Miller* case. In fact, during the FBI's 1973–1974 fiscal year, SACs submitted only 3,415 items to the laboratory, and a mere 29 percent of them were identified.[100] During the following fiscal year (1974–1975), obscene submissions dropped to only 1,404 items with 553 identifications; however, this represented an increase in the rate of identification to 39 percent. This flew in the face of Kelley's notion that more submissions would result in more identifications. Again, the author of the Obscene File survey noted that he expected an increase in obscene submissions because of rulings from the Supreme Court.[101] In the next fiscal year the FBI laboratory did see an increase in obscene submissions, but just a slight one for a total of 1,855 items and only 36 percent identified—again contrary to Kelley's claims about the relation between submissions and identifications.[102] During the next fiscal year (1976–1977), the year Kelley ordered an increase in obscene submissions, SACs sent only 1,513 items to the laboratory, and 46 percent of them were identified—fewer submissions but a greater percentage of identifications.[103] Finally, during Kelley's last year as head of the FBI (he resigned in February 1978 amid allegations he had used FBI employees to help furnish his home), SACs submitted a total of 2,604 obscene specimens, of which 40 percent were identified—more submissions resulting in a lower percentage of identifications.[104] In 1979, FBI laboratory technicians received 2,011 obscene submissions and identified only 29 percent of them.[105] In short, Kelley's strategy for increasing obscenity identifications and prosecutions was, by his own criteria and logic, a failure.

Kelley did not limit his reforms of the Obscene File to appeals for more submissions, however. In the wake of Watergate, revelations of Hoover-era abuses, and diminishing bureau resources, Kelley changed other FBI procedures, such as ending "June mail" and reorganizing management of the Obscene File. Kelley attempted to consolidate the work of the FBI's Document Section to keep "reference files and similar kinds of examinations" together. He therefore transferred the administration of the Obscene File from the crime laboratory's "Unit Chief of the Printing and Photocopier Unit."[106] This was a significant change from the Hoover years. Under Hoover's stewardship, the Obscene File had been maintained in the laboratory, but the pornography subunit had been maintained by Crime Records because that unit liaised with Congress and the media and was best situated to leak information to trusted recipients and thus advance the bureau's (i.e., Hoover's) agenda. Under Kelley, the FBI's Obscene File would be kept by professionals who would use it for reference purposes: to identify sources of obscenity. Kelley also officially renamed the Obscene File to better reflect changes in federal law. In 1977 Kelley ordered the file to be maintained as it was, but he renamed it the Pornographic Material File (or the Pornographic Material Reference File).[107] Whereas the term *obscene* was unclear and subject to various judicial interpretations, the term *pornographic* more accurately reflected "sexually oriented material."[108]

With the departure of Kelley in February 1978, President Jimmy Carter appointed William Webster, a lawyer and Nixon-appointed federal judge, as his replacement. Webster, still sensitive about Hoover-era abuses, sought to further reform and diversify the FBI. Part of this effort involved the devising of new obscene submission, collection, and filing guidelines to replace the previous ones, which, in the view of FBI officials, had become "vague and unclear" given the ever-changing legal criteria for obscenity. Webster directed the Criminal Investigative Division, ITOM supervisors, and FBI laboratory personnel to rewrite the FBI manual (i.e., the Manual of Investigative Operations and Guidelines) on obscenity cases. The most significant change effected by these individuals was a new and increasing focus on child pornography cases. And, when it came to prosecuting regular obscenity and pornography cases, the post-Hoover FBI would now take on the Mafia, and it would do so through extensive undercover operations.[109]

CHAPTER 5

The FBI's Anti-Obscenity Undercover Operations

The 1970s and 1980s

William Webster served as director of the FBI from 1978 to 1987 and therefore left his mark on the bureau during the Carter and Reagan years. Like his predecessor, Clarence Kelley, Webster sought to restore the FBI's good image in the public eye after the revelations of abuses during the Hoover years. He did not make domestic security the FBI's priority (although counterespionage cases made headlines during his tenure), as had been the tradition dating from Hoover. Webster began to focus on an area that Hoover had all but ignored: organized crime, white-collar crime, and political corruption. This may have been a reflection of Webster's background in the law—in fact, he preferred to be called "judge" rather than "director." In pursuing these objectives, the Webster-era FBI employed numerous undercover operations. Although undercover operations began under Kelley's directorship, they reached new heights with Webster. This too represented a divergence from the Hoover years, when FBI agents were required to conform to a strict code of conduct and maintain a specific public image: agents wore black suits, white shirts, and ties and were not permitted to drink alcohol. This made it next to impossible for them to engage in true undercover operations. In congressional testimony, Webster quipped about this: "I hope we won't go back to the days, Mr. Chairman, when our agents walked into bars and ordered glasses of milk."[1]

Among the well-known undercover operations of the Webster years was ABSCAM (for Arab scam), an effort to expose political corruption. The undercover operation originated in 1978 when an individual who had been convicted of fraud offered the government information about corrupt public officials in return for a reduced prison sentence. During the sting operation, FBI agents posed as representatives of a fictional Arab sheik named Kambir Abdul, or they posed as another fictional sheik named Yasser Habib. They conducted the operation in a variety of locations from New York to New Jersey and, famously, on a yacht anchored off the Florida coast. In the end, FBI agents arrested seven members of Congress and five New Jersey cops, who were convicted of accepting bribes.[2]

Another well-known undercover FBI operation, dubbed UNIRAC, focused on union racketeering activities. According to Webster, the operation began as a small investigation in mid-1975, but by 1978 it had turned into a major undercover operation in which FBI agents, with the help of at least one union informer, posed as shipping and stevedore management officials who made payoffs to representatives of the longshoremen's union in New York, Miami, Savannah, and Mobile. Meanwhile, FBI agents with accounting backgrounds probed the books of every local union hall in these cities for any questionable transfers of funds. Other FBI agents, including future director Louis Freeh, tailed union members and mobsters and established wiretaps on some of their telephones. By the summer of 1978, federal prosecutors had indicted twenty-two individuals, including Anthony Scotto, a prominent union leader in Brooklyn and reputed captain of the Gambino crime family. Scotto was eventually convicted, along with seventeen other union leaders, and all were given lengthy prison sentences. A Justice Department official commented on the sting operation: "The goal isn't just to get a couple of convictions. The goal is to clean up the union and to change the way business is done on the docks."[3]

A third noted undercover operation targeted corruption in the Chicago judicial system. In operation GREYLORD, FBI agents obtained the cooperation of Cook County prosecutor Terrence Hake. Starting in 1980, Hake pretended first to be a corrupt prosecutor and later a corrupt defense lawyer. FBI agents played similar undercover roles as lawyers, prosecutors, and defendants who offered bribes to judges. What's more, FBI agents employed microphone surveillance in one judge's chambers and concocted nearly a hundred fake cases—controversial tactics that federal judge George Nordberg dismissed as "the only way to root out this corruption." GREYLORD continued for years (until 1991), targeting bribery rings involving judges, lawyers, court officials, and city police officers. In the end, some ninety individuals were convicted, including 6 percent of the circuit court judges in Cook County.[4]

In addition to these three famous FBI undercover operations, four other, previously unknown (except for MIPORN) operations targeted pornography and made extensive use of the Obscene File. The four operations were code-named MIPORN, FAST PLAY, PORNEX, and CLEAN STREETS. By the 1970s and 1980s, FBI officials began to focus their obscenity and pornography investigations in two areas: La Cosa Nostra (LCN)—the umbrella term for the various Italian organized crime families popularly known as the Mafia—and the national distribution of child pornography.

Organized crime had entered the business of distributing pornography nationwide and, according to Webster, was making "huge profits," which mob bosses then used to buttress their other criminal enterprises. With operations PORNEX, MIPORN, and CLEAN STREETS FBI agents were "highly successful" in identifying the links between organized crime and the pornography industry and the means of distribution.[5] With regard to child pornography, FBI officials had uncovered the existence of "a secret culture" in which pedophiles both recruited and transported children while corresponding with one another and trading pornographic photos. Webster noted that although child pornography originated among pedophiles for "self-gratification" and not "for any commercial purposes," it was something that "eventually filters into the pornography industry." Although it was a target of FBI investigations, child pornography never made significant use of the Obscene File and is not examined in depth here except for operation FAST PLAY, which targeted child pornography for the first time.[6]

Webster sought to facilitate the bureau's targeting of pornography and organized crime by directing his SACs in Atlanta, Baltimore, Los Angeles, Miami, San Francisco, and Washington, D.C., to review specific cases (which have been redacted in FBI documents) and enter "appropriate data" into the bureau's Organized Crime Information System (OCIS)—a computer database developed in 1980 by the Detroit field office to help agents better identify and prosecute Mafia figures. At the time, only Los Angeles and Miami were online with OCIS, but Webster expected the remaining field offices listed in his directive to be up and running by the summer of 1983. Webster argued that OCIS would provide FBI agents with "a basic core of information" that should "aid immeasurably in future pornography investigations."[7]

By 1982, one FBI official recognized that the Obscene File was being "used on a daily basis" to identify the sources of pornography and determine where it was being sold and distributed. With the various undercover operations well under way during the 1980–1981 fiscal year, FBI agents had submitted a gargantuan number of obscene specimens to the laboratory: 13,098. However, only 2.6 percent of them had been identified, which was a dramatic failure. To explain this paltry rate of identification, an FBI official noted that of the 13,098 items, nearly half of them—some 6,000 items—were photographs submitted by the Washington field office as part of its FAST PLAY operation. If, he argued, one ignored these photographs, the identification success rate for 1980–1981 would jump to 14.7 percent. However, he also noted that more than 900 specimens originating from the bureau's MIPORN operation had not been included in the total because they were "currently under examination." In any event, the bureau's statistical success and its perceptions of investigative success were clearly muddled at this juncture.[8]

The MIPORN (short for Miami pornography) operation was the bureau's largest and most well-known anti-obscenity effort. It spent some $440,000 to crack down on pornography and, more specifically, organized crime's link to the interstate transportation of obscene materials. Indeed, as Special Agent Gordon McNeil regarded it: "The real emphasis of MIPORN was getting to organized crime—pornography was just the vehicle we used to do it." MIPORN began in 1977 with a seminar at the FBI Academy in Quantico, Virginia, where officials selected their targets. By the summer of 1977, two FBI agents—Patrick Livingston and Bruce Ellavsky—had set up a bogus pornography distribution business in a Miami warehouse. To gather evidence that could be used in court, the warehouse was festooned with electronic listening devices—in FBI parlance, "bugs"—and fitted with video cameras. The FBI agents had a contact in the pornography industry in Los Angeles who served as their entrée into the business. As Ellavsky put it: "You don't walk into the porn industry off the street, okay? We needed somebody to vouch for us." From there they infiltrated the national pornography industry and made arrangements to have distributors across the country ship their merchandise to the Miami warehouse. The agents bought hundreds of pornographic films and videos—everything from standard porn to gay porn to child porn to bestiality. Among the films collected were two famous ones: *Deep Throat*, starring Linda Lovelace, and *Debbie Does Dallas*, the renowned sex comedy film. After a two-and-a-half-year effort, federal prosecutors in Miami indicted fifty-five individuals in ten states for conspiracy and ITOM; many of the targets were of Italian descent and had alleged ties to organized crime.[9]

By January 1981 the first MIPORN trial was in the hands of the jury. Federal prosecutors had charged two men, Bill Jackmore and Phillip Bernsterne of Fort Lauderdale and Los Angeles, respectively, with conspiracy and ITOM. As such, the prosecution had to prove two things: that the films *Deep Throat* and *Debbie Does Dallas* were obscene, and that the defendants had transported the films across state lines. The case hit a roadblock over whether the two films were obscene, a perennial problem for prosecutors dating from the Supreme Court's 1957 *Roth* decision. Experts for both the prosecution and the defense testified on the obscenity issue, but in the end, the jury remained deadlocked over the central issue of what constituted obscenity. The judge in the case scheduled a new trial.[10]

This was not the first or the last time federal authorities were interested in *Deep Throat*. In February 1973 (the film had debuted in New York the previous year) FBI agents from the Milwaukee field office visited that city's Parkway Theatre to conduct a "preliminary survey" of the film to determine whether it was obscene. The two agents watched the entire film, which lasted sixty-one minutes, and reported that it "exhibited a plot dealing with a woman's inability to achieve sexual satisfaction through sexual intercourse, [and] manifested scenes in which explicit acts of cunnilingus, fellatio, analingus, and anal sodomy were depicted." A few days later the agents met with the local U.S. attorney, who concluded that *Deep Throat* met "the criteria for successful prosecution under the ITOM Statute as the film depicted hard-core obscenity" and the agents had established that it had been shipped from New York City to Milwaukee. The U.S. attorney told the agents he intended to prosecute.[11]

FBI agents then obtained a search warrant but failed to win a temporary restraining order to prevent the theater from showing the film. At a subsequent hearing, the agents displayed photographs they had taken of the film from inside the theater to illustrate its obscenity; the judge determined the film to be obscene and ordered it to be seized. The defendants in the case were the theater owners and the producer-director of *Deep Throat*, Gerard Damiano, who had shipped the film to Milwaukee.[12]

When FBI agents arrived to search the Parkway Theatre during the afternoon of 6 March and seize the film, they could not locate it. Inside the projection room the agents found empty film canisters, and just outside the projection room they found sixteen film clippings in a trash can. The agents determined that the clippings were from *Deep Throat,* but they never found the entire film intact.[13]

The theater owners petitioned the judge for the return of the sixteen film clippings, attempting to suppress the primary evidence against the theater. The judge, however, took sixteen months to rule on this motion, which effectively hamstrung the prosecution. In late September 1974 the judge finally ruled against the defendants, and the U.S. attorney considered his next step.[14] In April 1975 the U.S. attorney decided not to pursue the case because the Parkway Theatre had stopped showing "hard core pornographic films" some two years before, after the initial search by the FBI. So FBI agents closed their case in Milwaukee and forwarded the obscene materials they had collected to the FBI laboratory.[15]

FBI officials continued their efforts to make a federal case against those involved with *Deep Throat,* especially its producer-director, in other parts of the country. Buttressing this new national effort was a development stemming from a Supreme Court decision in June 1973. The case involved Marvin Miller of California, who ran a mail-order business that dealt in obscene and pornographic material that Miller euphemistically described as "adult." He was convicted under California law for distributing obscene material, and his appeal to the state's appellate court failed to reverse the lower court's decision. Miller then appealed to the U.S. Supreme Court, which decided to use the case to refine the legal standards for obscenity cases; it also vacated the appellate court's decision and sent *Miller* back to that court. The Supreme Court refined anti-obscenity law by requiring prosecutions to conform to contemporary, local community standards based on whether an average person would regard an allegedly obscene item, on the whole, as obscene.[16]

The decision was a boon to renewed efforts to crack down on obscenity by the Nixon administration. According to an investigation by the *New York Times,* just six weeks after the *Miller* decision, federal authorities began "a major effort to roll back pornography." Assisting their efforts was the new reliance on local community standards in obscenity cases, which meant that it would be easier to prosecute obscenity cases in specific locations where anti-obscenity views were likely tougher, rather than relying on one national standard that might be more liberal. The *Times* found federal prosecutors chasing obscenity of all sorts (including *Deep Throat*) in all regions of the country and from coast to coast.[17]

Although this Supreme Court case was not part of the Nixon-Hoover effort to alter anti-obscenity law (it could not have been, since Miller was prosecuted before Hoover suggested the tactic to Nixon), it made obscenity prosecutions easier for federal authorities, given the new local community standard. What's more, as historian Andrea Friedman points out, the *Miller* decision can be regarded as a move away from the conclusions of the Commission on Obscenity and Pornography. The majority report advocated abandoning the federal regulation of adult pornography, whereas the minority report (partly the result of behind-the-scenes machinations by the Nixon administration) advocated the use of local obscenity standards in court. Friedman also points out that the *Miller* decision "paved the way" for the Reagan administration's own report on obscenity and pornography (discussed later).[18]

Despite the long delay and apparent failure of the Milwaukee case, FBI officials had continued to develop evidence against *Deep Throat*. For example, FBI agents tracked down the motel where the film was shot and established that those involved did stay there. They interviewed multiple individuals connected to the film, including producer-director Gerard Damiano, who freely answered questions about his background, about actress Linda Lovelace, and about making the film.[19] They also obtained information from a detailed *New York Times* article on the film titled "Porno Chic," and they collected reports from FBI field offices and developed additional information in Los Angeles, New York, Miami, and Jacksonville.[20]

An airtel from the SAC of the New York City office reveals the extent of the FBI's national effort to prosecute those involved with *Deep Throat*. The SAC's communication advised, "for the information of all offices conducting investigation regarding 'Deep Throat,'" actress Linda Lovelace had already testified before a federal grand jury in the Eastern District of New York on 8 August 1973, and anyone who wanted a copy of her grand jury testimony was directed to contact the district's strike force on pornography. The field offices involved in the *Deep Throat* investigation included Albany, Boston, Chicago, Denver, Detroit, Houston, Kansas City, Jacksonville, Las Vegas, Los Angeles, Louisville, Miami, Milwaukee, Newark, Norfolk, Phoenix, Tampa, and New York.[21]

By November 1973, FBI agents described Damiano as "a cooperative government witness" who had been subpoenaed "to testify for the government at numerous contemplated trials in various Federal district courts throughout the country." FBI officials were worried, however, that Damiano's testimony would not touch on the interstate transportation of the film, and they and the U.S. attorneys were concerned that this might "jeopardize the successful organized crime prosecution aspect of this investigation." They also wanted to ensure that Damiano's testimony was "not being used for publicity purposes."[22]

The federal case against *Deep Throat* had failed in Milwaukee, and it appears that the federal case against *Deep Throat* in New York never materialized. The likely reason is because the City of New York prosecuted *Deep Throat* between December 1972 and March 1973. On trial in that case were not individuals but the corporation Mature Enterprises Inc., which was responsible for the film's presence in the city since June 1972. The film and the corporation were specifically targeted by Mayor John Lindsay as a test case in his crackdown on obscenity in Times Square. What's more, because the defendant in the misdemeanor case was a corporation, there was no jury trial (in December 1972 a jury in Binghamton, New York, had found that the film was not obscene). In March 1973 the judge declared the film to be obscene and described it as "a Sodom and Gomorrah gone wild before the fire." The following month, he imposed a $100,000 fine against Mature Enterprises. Because the film had been found obscene, it could no longer be shown in the city, effectively negating any federal case.[23]

Far more successful was federal prosecutors' 1976 case against the film in Memphis, Tennessee. There, federal authorities were successful in bringing a federal conspiracy charge, but not an interstate transportation charge, against Herbert Streicher (whose stage name was Harry Reems), the lead male actor in *Deep Throat*. Several weeks after his conviction, Streicher (the first pornography actor prosecuted and convicted on the federal level) hired prominent lawyer and Harvard law professor Alan Dershowitz. In the end, Dershowitz won a new trial for Streicher because the court had used the 1973 *Miller* test for obscenity, even though Streicher's alleged criminal activity had transpired in 1972, prior to adoption of the more stringent *Miller* standards.[24] Streicher was not convicted at his second trial; however, his fellow defendants, who were not retried

because their involvement in the conspiracy to transport the film between states had occurred after the *Miller* case, were sentenced to jail
terms spanning three months to one year with fines of up to $10,000.[25]

In the meantime, federal prosecutors won their first MIPORN conviction.
On 25 February 1981 Walter Bagnell was found guilty on two counts of
interstate transportation of obscene material.[26] Despite this auspicious
beginning, MIPORN soon faced prosecutorial disaster. On 13 May 1982 FBI
Special Agent Patrick Livingston, one of the two undercover operatives
involved in MIPORN, was fired by the bureau six months after being arrested
in Kentucky for shoplifting. When taken into custody, Livingston had
identified himself not by his real name but by his undercover persona. As
it turned out, Livingston was suffering from an undefined mental illness
that ultimately led to his dismissal from the FBI (the shoplifting charges
were also dismissed). But this revelation called into question the agent's
testimony in all MIPORN prosecutions. If he suffered from a mental illness
that caused him to offer false information to the police, defense attorneys
questioned whether his testimony in court might also be tainted.[27]

The court decided yes. In December 1982 a federal judge dismissed
twelve MIPORN indictments that had not yet gone to trial but did nothing
with those cases that had already been tried. When prosecutors appealed
the decision, which was denied, the court also dismissed the convictions
of two New Yorkers—Robert DiBernardo, a reputed Gambino crime family soldier, and Theodore Rothstein—who were in the process of appealing their convictions. Unfortunately for DiBernardo and Rothstein, in November 1985 the Eleventh Circuit Court of Appeals overturned the lower
court's ruling, reinstated their indictments, and ordered the lower court
to either offer them a new trial or reinstate their convictions. Eventually,
the U.S. Supreme Court refused to hear the men's appeal, and their convictions stood.[28]

As for the other FBI undercover operations involving obscenity and
pornography, they, like MIPORN, targeted links with organized crime. CLEAN
STREETS focused on Baltimore, Maryland, and Washington, D.C., and the
operation's file grew to a massive 25,000 pages. PORNEX was centered in
Los Angeles and focused on "the entire LCN [La Cosa Nostra] hierarchy of
the Los Angeles family."[29] The Obscene File was used in these operations
to identify the sources of pornographic materials and the distribution
of those materials by comparing submitted specimens with those main-

tained in the physical file. But these operations also reflected a new era in the history of the FBI, one in which the bureau returned to a focus on criminal matters after the death of Hoover.

At the heart of the CLEAN STREETS investigation was a company called Bon-Jay Sales Inc. It was one of the largest distributors of pornography on the East Coast and one of the top five distributors in the nation. Bon-Jay controlled thirty-six companies in Maryland, Washington, D.C., New York, and North Carolina. Moreover, Bon-Jay was reputed to have close ties to the mob-controlled Star Distributors of New York City. Therefore, Bon-Jay piqued the post-Hoover FBI's interest in targeting organized crime and its links to the pornography industry. FBI agents working the case were told, "under no circumstances is the concept of this operation to be discussed outside [of] the bureau, as the confidential nature of this project and the safety of the personnel involved are paramount."[30]

The investigation first began in August 1976 after a joint raid on Bon-Jay was conducted by the Maryland State Police, the Baltimore police, and the U.S. Customs Service, which then shared the records they seized with the FBI's Baltimore field office. The raid was predicated on information developed by the Customs Service that Bon-Jay was engaged in a smuggling operation from Europe. The FBI cooperated with customs agents in both the surveillance of targets and the analysis of evidence, using the FBI laboratory and the Obscene File to trace seized obscene items.[31] After examining the records seized during this raid, FBI officials realized the size and extent of this distribution operation and decided, "prompted by a long-standing desire to counteract the growth of pornography in WDC and Baltimore," to target Bon-Jay and its associates through a joint undercover operation run out of the FBI's Washington and Baltimore field offices. FBI officials dubbed the operation focusing on Washington, D.C., RINGER, described by the SAC in Baltimore as a "spin-off case"; however, all related documents fell under the CLEAN STREETS program file number, which was the main effort.[32]

By November 1977 FBI agents developed a source "who last did business with BJ [Bon-Jay] approximately two years ago" and agreed to cooperate with the FBI's investigation. This source introduced an undercover FBI agent to someone who worked at Bon-Jay's headquarters in Baltimore, who confirmed that Bon-Jay distributed pornography in Washington, Maryland, and Virginia and had overseas business links. This individual even agreed to "do business" with the two men.[33] So later that month the FBI's source and the undercover agent met again with this Bon-Jay employee, and arrangements were made to sell the undercover agent fifty pornographic films and fifty magazines. In addition, the FBI agent learned that Bon-Jay was involved in selling pornographic videotapes (a new innovation at the time) and pirated Hollywood movies such as *Star Wars*. By December, the undercover agent took possession of the films and magazines.[34]

At this juncture, FBI officials met with a U.S. attorney and a Justice Department official to discuss the undercover operation and the strategy required to see it succeed. The official from Justice, John Dowd, believed "a patient, methodical, multi-level penetration of BJ by Undercover Agents and informants would yield multiple violations prosecutable under RICO, particularly in the fraud area, and would very likely lead to prosecution of organized crime figures." Dowd, in fact, "enthusiastically supported" the effort, which would include cooperation with the FBI's MIPORN investigation in Florida and its undercover operation on the West Coast (PORNEX). It was believed that these three undercover operations would "complement each other nicely," including the coordination of some efforts to help them succeed.[35]

Meanwhile, the FBI had a second undercover agent take a job as a cashier with Bon-Jay. He would serve as a replacement for vacationing employees in six bookstores throughout suburban Maryland. FBI officials believed this would enable him to document the relationship between these stores and Bon-Jay and facilitate future seizures of evidence. His position would also allow him to develop evidence for RICO prosecutions.[36]

In a January 1977 airtel, the SAC of the Washington field office outlined for FBI Director Kelley the operation's four objectives: prosecuting Bon-Jay officials and employees under RICO, seizing the assets of the company and its branches under RICO, identifying the links between Bon-Jay and organized crime, and recovering any pirated Hollywood films. To accomplish this, two undercover FBI agents were directed to infiltrate Bon-Jay as business associates to document illegalities and links to organized crime. In late 1977 FBI and Justice Department officials authorized the use of "transmitting and recording devices" (microphones and video cameras) hidden on the agents themselves and in the vehicles they used. The undercover agents were backed up by two non-undercover FBI agents who would conduct surveillance and two additional agents as information was developed. The estimated cost of the operation for the first year was just over $56,000.[37]

By the end of 1978 it was clear that the FBI's investigation would be a long-term one involving a coordinated effort among the Washington, Baltimore, and Miami field offices. It was at this point that the operation was given the code name CLEAN STREETS. FBI officials were most interested in developing both anti-obscenity prosecutions and "solid RICO violations against Bon Jay." As an example of the former, in March 1979 the Washington field office requested that the FBI laboratory—using the Obscene File—provide information about a pornographic film titled *Lula* or *Lulu* that depicted interracial rape and murder scenes, but the laboratory could offer no useful information. Aiding the FBI's RICO interests was the recent addition of interstate cigarette smuggling to the statute, something the FBI learned Bon-Jay was involved in.[38]

In targeting Bon-Jay, FBI agents created a fake pornographic film distribution company, called Odyssey Productions, in the nation's capital on Eastern Avenue. Out of this office, an undercover agent using the name Joseph Sciandra bought thousands of dollars' worth of obscene videotapes, books, and magazines. Some of this collected evidence was examined in the FBI laboratory, and some of the films were kept "for permanent retention in the Obscene Matter file."[39]

CLEAN STREETS also involved an effort to target Bon-Jay's reputed links to prostitution. A female undercover FBI agent—a post-Hoover innovation—posed as a person interested in developing a prostitution business for Odyssey Productions. Another female undercover agent obtained a secretarial job with Alpha Sentura Business Service, a Bon-Jay subsidiary, during May and June 1980. She "collected evidence showing a nexus between Bon-Jay Sales, Inc., the parent corporation, and its various subsidiaries." The FBI also relied on wiretaps of Bon-Jay's telephones to develop evidence for this particular aspect of the case.[40]

By July 1979 CLEAN STREETS had entered "into a sensitive and significant phase," and officials were nearly ready to prosecute the targets. The FBI's Baltimore and Washington field offices were working closely with two federal prosecutors, who decided the FBI should use pen registers—an electronic device that records all numbers dialed from a specific telephone. The prosecutors noted that the U.S. Supreme Court had recently ruled in *Smith v. Maryland* that a warrant was not necessary for the use of pen registers because people voluntarily offered phone numbers to the telephone company when they made calls. FBI officials and prosecutors regarded the use of pen registers as "crucial to a complete and successful penetration of [the] target company as well as being integral to a comprehensive prosecution and potential linking of various elements of organized crime throughout the United States involved in the production and distribution of pornography." They believed that RICO offered the best hope for successful prosecution because Bon-Jay and its owner, Jacob "Jack" Gresser, maintained links with the mob-controlled Star Distributors and because Gresser was the only distributor of *Deep Throat* in the Baltimore area—and, according to FBI agents, the film was "LCN owned." Moreover, FBI surveillance had established that Bon-Jay employees had traveled between states and made contact with Star Distributors. They hoped to charge Bon-Jay and its associated companies with interstate transportation of stolen property, interstate transportation in aid of racketeering (ITAR), interstate transportation of obscene material, copyright violations, wire fraud violations, ITAR involving extortion, extortionate credit transactions, police corruption, cigarette smuggling, white slave trafficking, and bribery with links to organized crime.[41]

By November 1979 the FBI completed its wiretap surveillance (called "tesur," or technical surveillance, by FBI agents) and microphone surveillance ("misur") and began an "extensive analysis" of the collected evidence. Based on the results of this analysis, as well as information developed from informants and undercover FBI agents, a federal judge issued search warrants for four businesses controlled by Bon-Jay. FBI agents seized "voluminous records," including business checks, and began to analyze them. But FBI officials and prosecutors were not yet prepared for indictments, and they kept CLEAN STREETS "in the covert stage utilizing UCAs [undercover agents], informants, cooperating witnesses and consensual monitoring techniques." The SAC in Baltimore anticipated that indictments, arrests, and prosecutions would begin by the end of July 1980. The covert phase of CLEAN STREETS was scheduled to terminate with the issuance of indictments.[42]

Meanwhile, on 15 May 1980, defense attorneys working for Bon-jay attempted to have the affidavit on which the FBI search warrants had been based unsealed, but Judge Edward Northrop in Baltimore denied their motion. By the end of May, the U.S. attorney's office in Baltimore advised the FBI field office there that it had completed "an initial rough draft indictment," thirty pages long, of Bon-Jay and its associates. The indictment contained, at that juncture, twenty-two counts of RICO violations. But because this was only a draft indictment, the FBI continued its undercover phase of CLEAN STREETS, leading the SAC in Baltimore to comment to FBI Director Webster that the primary undercover agent in the case "continues to enjoy a good rapport with subjects associated with this criminal enterprise."[43]

On 3 June 1980 a special federal grand jury was impaneled in Baltimore to hear testimony from witnesses involved in CLEAN STREETS. FBI agents also prepared extensive lists of people who would be either interviewed or subpoenaed to appear before the grand jury, and according to the Baltimore SAC, several of these individuals agreed to cooperate with the investigation. Another individual, whose name is redacted in FBI files but who is described as "a major subject in the Clean Streets investigation," concluded a plea agreement with prosecutors and provided a wealth of information to FBI agents, including "numerous consensually monitored telephone calls" and "approved recordings of in-person meetings between himself" and various investigative targets in CLEAN STREETS.[44]

By the end of May 1981, federal prosecutors went forward with their indictments, and the FBI ended its undercover phase of the operation. Eight individuals in Maryland and one in Florida were indicted and then arrested simultaneously on 27 May, including the owner of Bon-Jay, Jack Gresser. They all posted bonds of between $10,000 and $100,000 and were released. The final indictment described Bon-Jay as operating "a major East Coast pornography ring" that was involved in the distribution of pornographic books and films and pirated Hollywood films, as well as operating prostitution rings in Baltimore and Washington, D.C. It also alleged that those who had not paid their bills to Bon-Jay were subject to death threats and that Bon-Jay had conspired to bomb a competing pornographer. The final indictment contained fifty-two counts, but interestingly, none of them involved violations of federal anti-obscenity law. Instead, federal prosecutors chose to focus exclusively on RICO violations, wire and mail fraud charges, copyright infringement, and various interstate transportation violations, including prostitution. Prosecutors chose this route because of the difficulty of winning obscenity cases under the *Roth* community standards test for obscenity. Commenting on this, Thomas Baker from the Washington field office said, "We're not trying to say something is obscene or is not obscene. We're attacking it from the financial end."[45]

By July 1981 two of the indicted individuals in Maryland took plea agreements and pled guilty (it is impossible to determine their identities due to redactions in the FBI files).[46] Shortly thereafter, a tenth man, George Louis Sharkey, was indicted and arrested in Rockville, Maryland, and charged with illegally distributing videocassettes. He also accepted a plea agreement and pled guilty.[47] In December 1981 the indictment against one of the targets (again, it is impossible to determine who) was dismissed. Apparently, this had something to do with this person being indicted twice by the same federal grand jury, but the details are not clear.[48] The trial for the remaining individuals was scheduled for 7 July 1982.[49]

Prosecutors then ran into further difficulties when, in April 1982, a Maryland state court found that the search warrants issued against Bon-Jay in August 1976 and November 1978 and executed by the Baltimore police were "defective." This raised the issue of whether the evidence FBI agents had received from the Baltimore police was tainted.[50] The evidentiary hearings about this matter became, in the words of the Baltimore SAC, "more involved than both government and defense counsel [had] anticipated."[51] By May 1982, four of the nine defendants had pled guilty, and five remained to face trial. Also in that month, federal prosecutors "conceded that the BPD searches [of Bon-Jay in 1976 and 1978] were illegal." The defense would have to prove which aspects of the prosecution were tainted, and the prosecution would have to find a way, if possible, to prove its case without the tainted Baltimore evidence.[52] Meanwhile, prosecutors worked to secure "plea agreement[s] with [the] remaining defendants."[53] They were successful, and by 29 July the "remaining defendants . . . pled guilty" and were sentenced on 9 September 1982; all received supervised probation in addition to a $400,000 forfeiture by (apparently) Gresser.[54]

Despite obvious difficulties, FBI officials were successful in their undercover efforts to root out pornography and its links to organized crime on the East Coast and Florida. They also gained experience in conducting complicated undercover operations and developing strategies to target obscenity and pornography, which new federal legal standards had made more difficult. FBI officials next focused their efforts on the West Coast.

The FBI's undercover anti-obscenity operation dubbed PORNEX was centered in Los Angeles. Like the bureau's other efforts against pornography in the 1970s and into the 1980s (namely, MIPORN and CLEAN STREETS),

PORNEX's primary focus was on links to organized crime. It had first been proposed to FBI Director Kelley by the Los Angeles field office's assistant director in charge (ADIC)[55] in October 1975. The ADIC suggested targeting Michael Zaffarano and Anthony Peraino of the Galante and Colombo crime families, respectively, since each was heavily involved in the pornography industry.[56]

Zaffarano was a made member of the Galante crime family based in New York City, but he also maintained a residence in Los Angeles. FBI agents in California learned that, since 1970, Zaffarano had maintained a "controlling interest in pornographic operations" through a company called Miracle Films. They believed Zaffarano's role was that of a loan shark, providing money to others so that they could purchase obscene films and establish theaters nationwide in which to show them. Zaffarano managed his criminal enterprise with a heavy hand and "jealously guarded" his turf. If anyone outside his circle publicly screened the films he distributed, Zaffarano's men would reportedly threaten these people, steal their copies of the film, and vandalize or even incinerate their theaters.[57]

Peraino, also a made man from New York City but affiliated with the Colombo crime family, was, according to FBI information, "one of the prime movers" in the interstate transportation of both obscene and legitimate films. Peraino, for example, was infamous for his involvement in the distribution of *Deep Throat*. Similar to Zaffarano, Peraino would threaten anyone who dared to screen his films, going so far as to intimidate theater owners into not reporting him to the police.[58]

But prosecuting these individuals under the anti-obscenity laws would not be easy. As the Los Angeles ADIC told Kelley, prosecutions of individuals under the ITOM statutes "have been unsuccessful due to the moral interpretations of the law by jurors hearing these cases." What's more, since Zaffarano was careful to conceal his involvement in his pornographic interests, the ADIC recognized that "unless his confederates testified against him, it is inconceivable that his prosecution could be realized." Clearly, FBI officials recognized that, given the problems associated with ITOM cases and the way Zaffarano and Peraino conducted themselves and their operations, making a case would be very difficult.[59]

Given these realities, the Los Angeles ADIC proposed the following "plan of action" for Zaffarano and Peraino, hoping that experienced undercover agents could help refine it. He proposed that his office "attack" the two men through an undercover operation in which FBI agents would establish a bogus film distribution company, called Bedco, housed in a leased Los Angeles movie theater. He suggested that four "mature" and "glib" FBI agents from outside Los Angeles be brought in because they would be unknown to the local police and criminal elements. Two teams would target theaters around the country and offer them the same films they received from Zaffarano and Peraino, but under terms that gave the theater owners greater personal profits. It was hoped that, because of their fear of the Mafia, these theater owners would report Bedco to Zaffarano or Peraino, who would then have their "groups [check] out our operation." When that happened, FBI agents would be in place "to act as authentic pornographers with the ability to simulate possession of almost any type of pornographic film for distribution." In the end, the ADIC believed, Zaffarano and Peraino, or their representatives, would "approach" the agents and try to either extort them or establish business relationships with them. This "would enable this Bureau to collect evidence to be used against them in future proceedings."[60]

The Los Angeles ADIC consulted with the chief of the Los Angeles strike force about the legalities of the operation. In their opinion, the undercover operation did not run the risk of entrapment issues, and if an attempt at extortion took place, Zaffarano and Peraino could be prosecuted under either RICO or ITAR statutes. What's more, the undercover agents themselves would not be violating ITOM law—a real concern for the FBI—because the films, slides, and brochures they would carry over state lines as part of the operation would not be distributed or sold commercially.[61]

Kelley did not authorize the undercover operation at this time. He saw problems in the plan and requested "a more in depth analysis," including more detailed and specific information about the extortionist activities of the targets in relation to theater owners to show a pattern of RICO violations. He asked whether the Los Angeles office had "any specific information" about Zaffarano and Peraino personally threatening anyone, since they seemed to be isolating themselves from any direct links to crime. Kelley was also concerned that some of the theater owners might actually accept the better deal offered by undercover agents. What would the FBI do then? Would the agents have to go through with the deal and supply the films, thus violating ITOM law themselves? Finally, Kelley advised the Los Angeles office that the FBI laboratory had 35mm copies of the films *Deep Throat* and *The Devil and Miss Jones,* which could be offered to theaters as part of the undercover operation. But where would the Los Angeles office get the other films not contained in the Obscene File? He also advised that FBI headquarters would confirm with federal authorities whether the operation was free of entrapment issues.[62]

The Los Angeles office immediately responded to Kelley's questions. First, the ADIC reported various examples of extortionist tactics used by members of both the Zaffarano and the Peraino groups, developed through "investigative efforts by numerous Field Divisions." Second, although the FBI could show that Peraino himself had engaged in extortion, it could not prove that Zaffarano had done so. However, the ADIC hoped to develop further evidence via undercover agents and various FBI listening devices. Third, as to whether the FBI was prepared to offer contracts to theater owners who accepted its offer, the ADIC reiterated his belief that this would not happen, but if it did, FBI agents would "stall the sending of any film" and would "never . . . distribute a film or enter a contract with anyone desiring one." Last, if copies of illicit films were not available from the Obscene File, in at least one instance an informant could "obtain one surreptitiously but . . . the cost of a 35 millimeter film is in excess of $1,000 per copy." Even with this information, Kelley still did not authorize the undercover operation.[63]

An opportunity to develop further information about the Mafia and its links to pornography on the West Coast arose in January 1976. The Los Angeles ADIC learned through one of his informants—"who is a dealer in sex films in the LA area"—that a pornography convention was being held in the city that month. The ADIC asked Kelley for permission to send an undercover agent to this convention to develop contacts in the industry, which would assist in the FBI's establishment of "the undercover pornographic business [previously] suggested." Attending this convention, the ADIC advised, would allow the agent "to gain knowledge and exposure to this business."[64] Kelley authorized the Los Angeles office to send an undercover agent to the pornography convention, where he would "gain firsthand information of distribution, pending production, and future plans of the pornographic industry, including LCN members." Because of "stringent budget limitations," Kelley could not authorize the all-encompassing undercover operation outlined by the Los Angeles field office. But, Kelley asserted, "if at a later date Los Angeles feels that the operation still has merit, you should resubmit the facts for consideration."[65]

Two months later the ADIC in Los Angeles did just that. He based his second request for authorization of an undercover operation "on tremendous ongoing intelligence data from reliable hoodlum informants that the Los Angeles family, supported by the Chicago LCN family, is planning to extort pornographers in the Southern California area in the near future." Members of the Los Angeles Mafia or their underlings planned "to move in on pornographers" in an attempt to extort "monthly payments from them," and they were "totally prepared at this time to make examples of individuals who refuse to pay . . . through physical beatings." The Mafia did not intend to operate these pornographic businesses but to extort pornographers who were violating the law. Because these Mafia targets were "not law enforcement oriented"—that is, because they were engaged in criminal activity—the mafiosos considered them unlikely to be undercover operatives. In addition, these targets were "already conditioned to extortionate attempts," particularly because they earned "above average income which is easily skimmed and profits not declared on clear business ledgers," making them tempting Mafia targets.[66]

The ADIC also advised the FBI director that the use of listening devices would not be "an effective tool because once the threat is made and agreed to, the only other contact would be to receive payments." Or, as he put it, "there would be a rediscussion of a threat earlier made and the payments could always be explained away." In any event, the ADIC wrote, both the Mafia figures and the pornographers, given their criminal enterprises, were already wary of listening devices, so their use would probably not reap any benefits. He also believed that because "pornographers could not openly testify against organized crime figures," owing to their own illegal operations, an alternative plan was needed. He recommended that "the best manner to attack this situation" was to undertake an undercover operation, including setting up a false business "dealing in the foreign distribution of pornographic films." This, he continued, "would place us in the role of a potential extortion victim." To establish the bona fides of this business, the ADIC proposed "accelerating contact with informants and planting with them the fact that the FBI investigation had determined such activity [i.e., foreign distribution]." By posing as a distributor of foreign films, the ADIC pointed out, a "retail outlet" would not be needed, and in any event, the FBI's bogus business would be viewed by mafiosos as "an enticing victim of extortion." "It would be our intent," he continued, "to go along with these illegal payments with the hope of not only involving those who originally contacted us, but of establishing a conspiracy upward in order to compile evidence to convict all involved for RICO."[67]

The Los Angeles ADIC further refined the details of the proposed undercover operation. Instead of leasing a movie theater, which was a budget-busting idea, FBI agents would simply rent office space, an apartment with a view of the business front, and a car for the undercover agents. The Los Angeles office would also liaise with the San Diego office by establishing a "sister" company there "at little additional cost." The sister company would be used to prove to the mafiosos that the company indeed "engaged in foreign distribution of pornographic film to South America," as well as to target organized crime in San Diego.[68]

By April 1976, after careful consideration, FBI officials authorized the Los Angeles and San Diego field offices' proposal for an undercover operation, and they named it PORNEX (pornography extortion). One interesting sidelight was the advice of the FBI's legal counsel. He suggested that if PORNEX were a success, the FBI director could be embarrassed if the pornographers publicly thanked him for removing their Mafia overseers. To avoid this, he suggested extending the operation to include legitimate businesses being extorted by the Mafia, so that the FBI "would be subject to more beneficial publicity than is likely to be the case in the present proposal." Robert McCarthy, section chief of the FBI's Special Investigative Division, ordered that this advice be "considered," but he pointed out that the focus should be the Mafia, and either way, "the public will benefit."[69]

With approval secured, the Los Angeles office set up its fake film distribution company—named Forex—in an office suite in Van Nuys, California. Even though FBI officials did not think technical surveillance would lead to any evidence, they requested and received Justice Department approval to install a microphone in the office suite "to provide security for our Agents and also to secure evidence should threats be made against them." FBI officials also authorized the use of closed-circuit television. PORNEX was expected to begin after installation of the technical equipment on 6 May 1976.[70]

During the first two weeks of the operation, undercover FBI agents reached out to informants to confirm that pornographers in Los Angeles were aware of Forex and, significantly, that they did not suspect it was a front. Undercover FBI agents were even admitted into "four pornography labs" where films were developed and processed, and they engaged in "detailed discussions regarding price structures with the key operators of each lab." This indicated to FBI officials that the undercover agents had been accepted by the pornography industry.[71]

The first Mafia contact established through the PORNEX operation occurred on 7 June. That morning a man appeared at the Forex office, told the two undercover FBI agents that he had experience selling films, and asked if Forex would hire him. The agents asked him where he had heard of Forex, but he did not answer. The agents informed him that Forex was not hiring at the present time but likely would in the future. They also informed him that they would have to check the background of anyone they hired because they "were concerned with heat." The job seeker stated that he would have someone stop by and "vouch for him." He then left, got into the passenger side of a brown Lincoln Continental with license plate 538 NBX, and departed. The FBI agents traced this license plate and discovered the car was registered to "Michael Anthony Rizzi, one of the targets of this investigation" and the "right-hand man" of Jimmy Fratianno, the underboss of the Los Angeles Mafia. The FBI later learned that Rizzi "has been given the assignment by the Los Angeles LCN 'family' to extort the operators of FOREX Corporation." They also learned that on 11 June, mafioso Jack LoCicero and another Mafia figure "surveilled the FOREX office for a lengthy period of time."[72]

By July 1976, the San Diego SAC reported to FBI headquarters that "any LCN approach to the Forex office in San Diego is remote." Kelley therefore decided to end San Diego's involvement in PORNEX, noting, "there does not appear to be sufficient justification to continue this operation in San Diego at the present time."[73] Meanwhile, there were no further developments in Los Angeles through August, but FBI agents learned from informants and from the Los Angeles and New York City police departments that the Mafia intended to move on Forex in the near future. In the meantime, Rizzi was in New York City, apparently consulting with fellow mafiosos there. For that reason, FBI officials decided to continue the undercover operation.[74]

Finally, on 19 August 1976, mafiosos Jack Lo Cicero and Thomas Ricciardi made contact with one of the undercover agents at Forex. The two men informed the agent that nobody in Los Angeles worked in the pornography business without their permission, and then Lo Cicero said, "I get a piece of your business, you know, like I come over, we [get] a piece and that's all's I doing. You know, of course, if you don't do so you might as well a close up tonight, pack in all everything and move out. I telling you this now."[75] Following the FBI's plan, the agent informed Lo Cicero and Ricciardi that Forex was already making (extortion) payments to another individual. The next day Lo Cicero and Ricciardi met two FBI agents—one the Forex agent and the other posing as the extortionist to whom Forex was making payments—at a restaurant in the San Fernando Valley. Lo Cicero asked the FBI agent posing as the extortionist: "Who do you think you are, taking money from this man? Where do you come from? Who told you you could talk to this man?" After a brief conversation, he said, "You don't take no more money from nobody in this town 'cause it ain't healthy for you if you do, understand?" Lo Cicero then told the undercover agent, "I don't want to see your face no more. Do you understand me? It ain't healthy for you in this town, you get out." The agent then left with the understanding that he was to repay Lo Cicero the $2,500 he had supposedly extorted from Forex. Shortly thereafter the second undercover agent from Forex joined them, as did Michael Rizzi, whereupon the undercover agents were told that if they did not cooperate they would be put out of business no matter where they lived, because the mafiosos "had people in all parts of the United States." The agents were then told they needed to pay a certain amount of money (the amount is redacted in the FBI files) up front and then pay an additional amount each week. If they failed to do this, they would be put out of business.[76]

FBI agents in Los Angeles developed information indicating that other pornographers were also being extorted and determined, after consulting with the Los Angeles strike force, that these various examples constituted a RICO violation. The Los Angeles FBI office therefore recommended that PORNEX continue and that the undercover agents go ahead and make the extortion payments. Their rationale was that this would enable the agents to develop further information about exactly who in the Mafia was involved in these crimes. In their undercover roles, it would also enable them to contact fellow pornographers who were being extorted to develop "insight into their payments with the goal of using these individuals as witnesses against LCN at a later date."[77]

Kelley authorized the Los Angeles office to make extortion payments to the Mafia for at least four weeks.[78] On 27 August the undercover agents met with Lo Cicero and Ricciardi at the restaurant again to deliver their payment. Lo Cicero insisted that they sign a promissory note. They then discussed buying and selling pornographic films, and during the conversation Ricciardi told them a story about a pornographer who had refused to make his weekly payments. This man, Ricciardi said, was taken "to the top of a tall building," where they had a conversation next to a window; afterward, the man never missed a payment. The agents also attempted to gain access to "higher ups" in organized crime. They wanted to target Jimmy Fratianno, who, they knew, refused to hold meetings in Los Angeles. So they called their Mafia contacts later that day and told them that the Los Angeles police had questioned them about their previous meeting. They asked to have the next one in Las Vegas—where they hoped to goad Fratianno into attending. The goal, wrote the Los Angeles ADIC, was to enable the undercover agents to "move into the higher echelon of LCN."[79]

The following month, with authorization from headquarters, FBI agents tried to determine the extent of the Los Angeles Mafia's involvement in pornography and extortion nationwide. After being told by their Mafia contacts that mobsters "could help us [the fake Forex company] in other parts of the country," FBI agents in Los Angeles decided to test this assertion. The plan was to dispatch an undercover FBI agent from the Los Angeles office to Cleveland, Ohio, where he would stay at the Holiday Inn, Lakeside. Another undercover agent would then inform the Los Angeles Mafia that this man in Cleveland owed Forex money, to see what the Mafia would do. FBI agents would install a microphone in the hotel room to record any conversations, and the hotel would be covered by "photographic surveillance" while the undercover agent was there.[80]

A member of the Los Angeles Mafia confirmed that, "for a fee," he could collect the money owed to Forex from this man in Cleveland. Undercover agents arranged for the meeting to take place between 8 and 10 September 1976,[81] but it never occurred. Moreover, on 9 September Ricciardi terminated his relationship with Forex, saying "each could go their separate ways." To determine why these events transpired, FBI agents questioned their informants and learned that "a series of events . . . possibly explain this current posture taken by the Los Angeles LCN family."[82] The Los Angeles ADIC offered Kelley four possible explanations for the Mafia's reaction, but three of the four were redacted in the FBI files. The one explanation not blacked out was that Rizzi had been arrested and charged with insurance fraud. In any event, the Los Angeles office concluded that "the Los Angeles LCN family is becoming super cautious in their pornography extortions." This development was somewhat disappointing for FBI agents, who had made only one extortion payment before the relationship was ended. Nevertheless, the Los Angeles office proposed to continue the undercover operation for one more month to see whether contact could be reestablished with their targets, but especially with Rizzi, Lo Cicero, Ricciardi, and Fratianno.[83]

By October, no further developments had transpired in the PORNEX operation. The Los Angeles field office then became aware of information (redacted in FBI files) that led to the issuance of subpoenas for various individuals (names redacted) to appear before a federal grand jury. This development led the Los Angeles office to close its false business, Forex. By November the Los Angeles office believed it had developed enough evidence to warrant the indictments, based on RICO violations, of Rizzi, Ricciardi, Lo Cicero, and other individuals (names redacted). The undercover phase of PORNEX had come to an end, and the prosecutorial phase had begun.[84]

With their evidence marshaled, U.S. attorneys sought the indictments of Michael Rizzitello (Mike Rizzi), Tommy Ricciardi, Jack Lo Cicero, and others (names redacted),[85] and the indictments were handed down on 22 November.[86] In the meantime, the FBI director gave the Los Angeles and San Diego field offices two weeks "to prepare a blind memorandum . . . setting forth procedures, techniques, and guidelines you consider important in the establishment and operation of a long-term undercover operation." The FBI director wanted other field offices to use this information to develop their own "long-term undercover operations" and so that FBI headquarters could thoroughly analyze the operation. Given the expected success of PORNEX, Kelley believed that its "investigative techniques, efforts, and ideas" would inform "future undercover seminars" and would greatly "assist other field offices."[87]

As FBI agents summarized PORNEX for headquarters, other agents sought to arrest the operation's targets.[88] Ricciardi and one of the others (name redacted) disappeared and became fugitives.[89] They did not remain fugitives for long, however; by the end of November 1977 both men had surrendered to FBI agents at the Los Angeles field office. They were arraigned, photographed and fingerprinted, and placed in the custody of the U.S. Marshal Service, where they stayed until they posted bonds. The other three defendants—Rizzitello, Fratianno, and Lo Cicero—were arrested by FBI agents on 22 November. The trial was set for Valentine's Day, 14 February 1978.[90]

By February 1978 the government's prosecution against organized crime expanded beyond PORNEX when prosecutors decided to indict "the entire leadership structure of the Los Angeles LCN 'family.'" This decision was made partly because of PORNEX, but also because of the FBI's GANGMURS case. The GANGMURS case began in January 1978 when various organized crime factions in Youngstown, Ohio, descended into internecine war—or what is popularly dubbed a gangland war. At the insistence of the Los Angeles organized crime task force, prosecutors agreed to include charges of conspiracy and murder, related to the killing of San Diego consigliere Frank Bompensiero, the highest-ranking Mafia informant in FBI history to date. The Mafia had murdered Bompensiero because of his cooperation with FBI agents in the PORNEX case, and the FBI had investigated his murder as part of the GANGMURS case. By increasing the scope of the government's organized crime prosecution, Justice Department officials expected "widespread publicity" and "much public interest." They also viewed the expanded case as "a substantial accomplishment against organized crime in this country."[91]

By 10 March 1978, six individuals had been indicted for various RICO violations: Michael Rizzitello, a capo; Jack Lo Cicero, a consigliere; Dominick Brooklier, West Coast mob boss; Louis Dragna, former acting boss; Samuel Orlando Sciortino, Mafia underboss; and Thomas Louis Ricciardi. Aladena "Jimmy the Weasel" Fratianno pled guilty and testified against his compatriots to avoid a death sentence. He had been involved in Bompensiero's murder, but because of his relationship with FBI agents in San Francisco, he volunteered to provide information. Noting that Fratianno "presents a unique opportunity to illuminate the LCN structure on a national level," prosecutors accepted his offer of cooperation. This was significant because, for the first time, "a 'made' member has testified about the structure of his own family of the LCN."[92]

But within two months, the prosecution faced disaster. The defense raised a motion to dismiss the indictment because there had been leaks to the press—Time magazine as well as various newspapers—while the federal grand jury was deliberating.[93] One month later Judge Harry Pregerson ruled in favor of the motion and dismissed the indictments of all the defendants. He explained that the grand jury's "manifestation of fairness" had been compromised because jurors were not warned to avoid publicity about the case, only fourteen jurors heard all the presented testimony, and the jurors read and discussed the *Time* and newspaper articles and even brought them into the grand jury room.[94]

Prosecutors did not give up. They prepared a new indictment targeting all the previous defendants, and they still had Fratianno's cooperation. In mid-February 1979 Ricciardi suffered a heart attack in Folsom Prison and died during bypass surgery, but this did not significantly affect the government's indictment of the other five defendants. On 21 February they were reindicted, and the trial was set for June. By that time, however, Lo Cicero had been dropped from the trial due to his own recovery from major heart surgery. Another complication was the alleged bribe offered to Judge Pregerson by one of the defendants—Sam Sciortino. Pregerson was forced to recuse himself, and a new judge was assigned to the trial. Then, as a result of further delays and defense motions, the trial was pushed back to November 1979 and then again to March 1980 as a result of a conflict with other federal prosecutions.[95]

With a new judge in place, defense attorneys argued again for dismissal of the indictments. They claimed that because only ten of the sixteen grand jurors had heard "all the live testimony presented in this case," this raised the issue of "informed grand jurors." The new judge, Terry Hatter, agreed, noting that having transcripts of the missed testimony was not sufficient. The Los Angeles organized crime task force believed the government would win an appeal of this decision, but because this was expected to take a full year's time, the prosecutors decided "that a reindictment will be undertaken within a few weeks."[96]

On 15 May 1980, for a third time, indictments were issued for Brooklier, Lo Cicero, Sciortino, Dragna, and Rizzitello. All the defendants pled not guilty, and the trial was set for September 1980 but did not actually begin until October of that year.[97] Within about one month's time, the jury had its verdicts. All the defendants were found guilty of both substantive and conspiracy-related (except Sciortino) RICO violations, and Rizzitello and Lo Cicero were found guilty of extorting the FBI's dummy business Forex; all five defendants were found not guilty in the murder of FBI informer Frank Bompensiero. Prosecutor James Henderson commented that this result "destroys the myth that the Mafia cannot be prosecuted."[98]

On 21 January 1981 the defendants were sentenced to terms "far below" those recommended by both the Los Angeles strike force and the

U.S. Probation Department. Lo Cicero was sentenced to two years in prison, Rizzitello received five years in prison, Brooklier received four years, Sciortino was sentenced to four years in prison and a $25,000 fine, and Dragna received two years in prison and a $50,000 fine.[99] Afterward, FBI officials planned "to remain alert" for new mafiosos to replace the defendants, and they believed the testimony offered about the structure of the Mafia could "be applied to any LCN family in the country." They further believed that this "prosecution may lead the way for other witnesses to cooperate in future trials."[100] As for Fratianno, the Mafia issued a $100,000 contract on his life. He went on, however, to write books about his experiences in organized crime.[101]

Different from the bureau's other undercover operations that focused on adult pornography, FAST PLAY targeted child pornography. Moreover, owing to the sensitive nature of this effort, we know only the broad outlines of the operation; because of federal privacy laws, all the names of and details about FBI targets and their victims have been redacted in FBI files. FAST PLAY's origins, however, date to 1978, when a police detective from Prince George's County, Maryland, provided an FBI agent with information about an individual who "was involved in the production [and distribution] of child pornography." Because this was a new area of concern for federal law enforcement, FBI agents could develop information about child pornography but "often lacked the necessary credibility needed for federal prosecution." By early 1981 FBI officials decided to remedy this problem and assigned several undercover agents to investigate child pornography. First they reviewed the mass of literature about child pornography and then developed an informant who provided information about "a large number of pederasts throughout the United States," including "a massive volume of names, addresses, and other data . . . [that was acquired] on a daily basis."[102]

Originally dubbed FOWL PLAY, the operation involved agents buying examples of "hard-core child pornography" while seeking to identify the pornographers, dealers, and victims and the various connections among them all. FBI officials took a step-by-step approach to (1) "identify the major producers and distributors of child pornography," (2) "infiltrate their secretive sub-world," and (3) arrange for the sale of child pornography to undercover agents to create cases for prosecution.[103] FBI officials learned that 500,000 children in the United States were victims of the child pornography industry, which was able to produce its merchandise at minimal cost. This led FBI officials to believe that the child pornography industry "may be growing at an alarming rate."[104] Additionally, because of popular notions that organized crime might be involved in the production and distribution of child pornography—as reflected in contemporary media reporting—FBI officials hoped to either "confirm or discount claims" of the Mafia's alleged involvement.[105]

The operation was extensive and resulted in the collection of a large volume of documentation. As a result, by September 1981 FBI officials had created "sixteen substantive subfiles" and had identified twenty-seven subjects for whom FBI officials created specific subfiles.[106] Additionally, FBI agents collected a huge volume of child pornography specimens, including "thousands of photographs, slides, and negatives, many depicting several FAST PLAY subjects and victims" in Alexandria, Virginia (as previously noted, these photographs were examined using the bureau's Obscene File). These samples were duplicated by the Photographic Operations Unit at FBI headquarters and then returned to Alexandria for prosecutorial purposes.[107]

The undercover phase of FAST PLAY concluded in early 1982, "after approximately 12 months of 'deep cover'" that was mostly focused on Richmond, Virginia, and New York City.[108] FBI officials found no links between organized crime and the child pornography industry. In fact, they ascertained that child pornography was best described as a "cottage industry" that "does not involve a complex network as is popularly referred to by law enforcement officials and news media." Instead, it was composed of "a loosely knit group of pederasts located throughout the United States" who "corresponded and held meetings in furtherance of their pederast activities." Because of this reality, FBI agents were unable to locate the "major producers and distributors of child pornography." They were, however, able to prosecute several individuals for the transportation of minors and the distribution of child pornography, and additional prosecutions of other individuals were planned in the future. These potential prosecutions involved sharing information with local and state prosecutors to secure convictions of these criminals.[109]

The FBI's targeting of organized crime in the 1970s and 1980s reflects two primary developments in its history. First, it illustrates the bureau's shift away from the noncriminal intelligence collection and anti-subversive and anti-American priorities of J. Edgar Hoover and a return to criminal investigations. These investigations also reflect a change in the strict image Hoover demanded of his agents at all times, such as wearing suits and not indulging in alcohol. Part of this image included an all-male contingent of FBI agents, but in the post-Hoover era, female and other minority agents became part of the bureau. Second, it reflects an evolutionary change in how FBI officials targeted obscenity. Because obscenity prosecutions became more difficult after the 1957 *Roth* decision, FBI officials focused less on anti-obscenity statutes and more on RICO. In this way, they could kill two birds with one stone: reduce the effectiveness of the Mafia, and curtail the pornography business. Yet during the 1980s and 1990s, obscenity prosecutions, and hence the FBI's Obscene File, would evolve even more, given the political priorities of new administrations.

CHAPTER 6

The End of the Obscene File and the Temporary Revival of the FBI's Role in Adult Obscenity

FBI supervisors who were responsible for overseeing the administration of the Obscene File continued Webster's reforms during the early 1980s. The FBI began to computerize some of its information, especially that related to organized crime and obscene materials, using the OCIS database. FBI officials also began to impose a management system on the Obscene File, first implemented under Kelley, to increase the efficient use of FBI resources. The system was called management by objective (MBO), and its purpose was to set specific "goals and milestones" that Webster expected his personnel to meet in obscene investigations. By February 1981, FBI officials had set three goals for the Obscene File: (1) to review the "reference section" to determine whether it met current obscenity standards and should therefore be maintained, (2) to train another ITOM examiner, and (3) to review backlogged cases and create a ninety-day tickler filing system—a now-archaic system that used numbered folders to organize data coherently. Yet FBI officials were unable to meet any of these goals in a timely manner owing to a personnel shortage and the priority given to other FBI cases. Starting in January 1982 the FBI began to assume a role in drug enforcement—a priority of the Reagan administration. Reagan's War on Drugs, one of his major political initiatives, now took precedence over obscenity cases.[1]

During 1982 the bureau's MBO write-up, as FBI officials called their review of the Obscene File, reflected new goals that would continue until 1984. These goals included maintaining the Obscene File as a "reference file of pornographic materials being sold and distributed throughout the

United States" and providing agents with "all available information regarding the source of pornographic materials to assist in their investigations." The most important investigations FBI officials had in mind were
the various undercover operations they expected to continue.[2]

By the summer of 1984, mainly as a result of personnel shortages,
the administration of the Obscene File shifted yet again. Since 1977 the
Obscene File had been supervised by the bureau's Document Section in
an effort to consolidate FBI reference files. But given the bureau's new
priorities—such as Reagan's War on Drugs and Webster's desire to work
more closely with the Drug Enforcement Administration—examiners in
the already understaffed Document Section were reassigned. One, for
example, was reassigned to examine drug records, and another was reassigned to help administer polygraphs. These personnel transfers caused
one official to state that "manpower shortages . . . are critical," and they
left no one to work with the Obscene File. FBI officials found a solution
to this problem in the bureau's Special Photographic Unit of the Special
Projects Section of the Laboratory Division. That unit's chief had some
experience working with the Obscene File, and "since many of the examinations are photographic in nature," it was "logical" for this unit to take
over the Obscene File.[3]

FBI officials continued to experience difficulty with the Obscene File
for the next two years, however, leading them to alter their policy for
the submission of obscene materials. By this time, the Obscene File was
composed primarily of "adult pornographic publications, films, and videotapes which are home or commercially produced." Yet in recent years
the Justice Department had seen fewer and fewer ITOM prosecutions—
between 1978 and 1986 only 100 people were charged with ITOM violations, and only 71 were convicted—while the FBI laboratory continued
to receive large amounts of obscene specimens from the various field offices. This continued flow of obscene items into FBI headquarters, along
with a recent court ruling that prohibited the FBI from destroying pornographic evidence, led to storage problems, so FBI officials decided to
streamline the Obscene File.[4]

In July 1986, however, the Attorney General's Commission on Pornography released a report that called for a renewed national effort to
clamp down on smut. In May 1984, responding to pressure from conservative groups, President Reagan had directed his attorney general, William French Smith, to form the commission "to study the scope and na-

ture of pornography in the United States."[5] Edwin Meese replaced Smith as attorney general the following year, and he later commented about the extent of pornography in the 1980s: "even I was not prepared for the present depth of depravity, nor was President Reagan."[6] After fourteen months of hearings, the commission concluded—contrary in many ways to the findings of President Johnson's commission—that there was a relationship between pornography and sexual violence, as well as a relationship between pornography and organized crime. It called for stronger enforcement of existing anti-obscenity laws rather than new laws to define obscenity. The commission's report also recommended a more intense focus on child pornography and the creation of a national computerized filing system for pornography cases. By 1987, when Reagan introduced his child protection and obscenity enforcement bill to Congress, the president claimed that in recent years purveyors of smut and child pornography had begun to use new technologies, such as computers, and had expanded their reach. He declared that "neither our Constitution, our courts, our people, nor our respect for common decency and human suffering should allow the trafficking in obscene material—which exploits women, children, and men alike—to continue."[7] The bill would pass in 1988, but in 1986 Meese's Justice Department had already created an Obscenity Enforcement Unit within its Criminal Division, and the FBI had begun to focus on the sexual exploitation of children. The FBI also sought to make searches of the Obscene File easier, hoping to make the file "an active resource for investigators [and] not a historical library of pornography." Indeed, with the conservative Reagan in office, FBI officials began to devote greater efforts to anti-obscenity investigations.[8]

The FBI's new policy included several changes. First, it mandated that FBI agents solicit legal opinions as to whether evidence was obscene only from their "local prosecuting jurisdiction," not from the FBI's Investigative Division or laboratory. Previously, officials at FBI headquarters or the Justice Department had made this determination. Second, because of the new focus on child pornography, FBI agents were directed to submit to headquarters only commercially produced examples of child pornography and "commercial adult pornography dealing with sadomasochism, bestiality, and coprophilia." FBI agents were further directed not to submit any noncommercial items unless there were unique circumstances.[9]

Another innovation for the Obscene File was the creation of "a section in the single fingerprint file devoted exclusively to the fingerprints of manufacturers and major distributors of obscene material." This section, called the Obscene Matter Dealers Section, was supposed to be devoted to developing obscene materials as evidence, and FBI agents were instructed to follow evidentiary rules when requesting fingerprint identifications.[10]

In addition to FBI officials' concern about properly developing evidence for prosecution purposes, they stated that the FBI "is vitally interested in ascertaining the original source of obscene material." This stemmed from the belief that most obscene material "emanates from a common source" and is distributed by a handful of "commercial purveyors." FBI officials thus informed agents that it was "extremely desirable" that field offices submit all commercially produced obscene items, irrespective of the source and regardless of whether there was a violation of federal law. They were specifically directed to gather this type of material from local police forces "to increase the effectiveness of the obscene matter file."[11]

One aspect of FBI policy—dating from the Hoover years—did not change. FBI officials still recognized that some obscenity investigations had "potential publicity value." Webster directed all SACs to closely monitor their respective obscene investigations to identify those with publicity value. Before taking action on such cases, SACs were ordered to obtain prior approval from headquarters.[12]

Last, FBI officials outlined the means by which obscene materials could be obtained. The usual method involved interviewing investigative subjects. During such interviews a subject might voluntarily hand over the items or FBI agents might, in some unspecified manner, conduct a search of the subject's person or dwelling. The other two methods for obtaining obscene materials were a search of the subject's premises with his permission and a search conducted after the issuance of a warrant. Regarding warrants, FBI officials were careful to direct FBI agents that before obtaining obscene films they must *first* have a warrant. This stemmed from a 1973 Supreme Court case, *Roaden v. Kentucky,* in which the Court ruled that a film could not be seized until it had officially and legally been declared obscene. The only exception to this rule occurred when it was determined that, without the film, "evidence will be unavailable." These procedures reflected the ongoing difficulty and complexity of obscenity investigations and prosecutions, and they may explain why there were so few successful ones.[13]

For the remainder of 1986 FBI officials worked assiduously to convert the Obscene File into a searchable computerized database, as called for by the Meese report (the attorney general also ordered the formation of a special team of prosecutors to pursue obscenity cases). FBI programmers created a data entry program, and by September they had spent "150 manhours" testing it. These tests convinced FBI officials that they could have a complete, working program that would allow them to upload "bulk" data by December. As that date approached, however, they realized that, given the gargantuan amount of data to be entered into the computer system—some 26,880 records—it would take more than three years, or about 6,272 working hours, to do so.[14]

What is interesting about this computerization effort is the FBI's internal rationalization for it. Not surprisingly, one rationale was the new national interest in pornography promoted by the conservative Reagan administration during the 1980s. But the more compelling rationale for computerizing the Obscene File was the simple fact that the single FBI technician who had maintained and searched the file since 1969 had announced his plan to retire by June 1987. FBI officials regarded the bureau's successful searches over the years to be "directly attributable to his personal knowledge of the file and its contents." One FBI official stated bluntly that "the computerization effort is an attempt to convert the years of expertise acquired by this technician and his record keeping system into an efficient, consistent, and readily retrievable data base." The primary stumbling block for this effort was time: it was "highly unlikely" that the FBI could complete the computerization project and find a successor to the retiring technician before he left. Perhaps this particular situation foreshadowed the ultimate destiny of the FBI's Obscene File: within seven years it would be terminated.[15]

The final evolutionary stage in the life of the Obscene File, ironically enough, returned to an issue that had occupied the FBI some forty-four years earlier and had never been successfully resolved. During 1944–1945, FBI officials attempted to effect an information-sharing liaison with the U.S. Customs Bureau, which also collected large amounts of obscene items in its effort to thwart the importation of foreign sources of obscenity. This effort failed because of the belief by the head of the Customs Bureau that his agency was compelled by the 1930 Tariff Act to destroy all obscene items it collected. In mid-November 1988 the FBI's assistant director in charge of the Laboratory Division, Roger Castonguay, again raised the possibility of a liaison between the FBI and the U.S. Customs Service's Pornography Task Force "relative to the exchange of information and materials." His reasoning was based on the fact that both the FBI and the Customs Service operated obscene reference files to aid in the enforcement of anti-obscenity statutes.[16]

Before this idea reached the assistant director level, however, the respective supervisors of the two agencies' files met and agreed that each was "collecting and retaining materials that are mutually beneficial." Moreover, each agent agreed that his agency was disposing of obscene materials that might "be of significant value to the other agency." They believed that "significant benefits and enhancements" would be possible through a collaborative effort, such as "substantial additions" to each file, as well as the ability to reference a second, largely different obscene collection. Agreeing with this assessment were the FBI's supervisory special agent who handled ITOM investigations in the Criminal Division and FBI laboratory personnel. As in the past, FBI personnel believed that supplementing the Obscene File would somehow lead to more success in anti-obscenity prosecutions. It would not.[17]

Before effecting the liaison, Assistant Director Castonguay authored a memorandum of understanding that would form the basis of the relationship between the FBI and the Customs Service, and he submitted this and a background memorandum to the bureau's Legal Council Division for an opinion as to its legal efficacy. A staff member from the Legal Council Division then interviewed the Obscene File's supervisory agent, who added that the type of obscene materials that would be shared between the FBI and the Customs Service were "those that no longer had evidentiary value." Given that the information would be used only for comparison and identification purposes and not as evidence in court, the Legal Council Division gave its seal of approval to the liaison arrangement, which, in its view, was consistent with contemporary federal laws and regulations covering the sharing of information between law enforcement agencies.[18]

The FBI and Customs Service shared their respective collections of obscene items between June 1989 and May 1990. The Customs Service, for example, forwarded to the FBI hundreds of obscene magazines, books, videotapes, and films covering all manner of pornographic subjects. Presumably, although the Obscene File contains no record of it (the administrative file has frequent gaps), FBI officials forwarded similar items to the Customs Service.[19]

One curious collection of materials the Customs Service turned over to the FBI was an assortment of eighty-five homosexual magazines. As detailed in earlier chapters, FBI officials began to collect information on homosexuals in 1937, and by 1951 it had created a Sex Deviates File to use to ensure that gay and lesbian government employees were terminated. In 1977 the Sex Deviates File—totaling over 330,000 pages—was incinerated. By the late 1980s FBI officials had decided to focus their anti-obscenity efforts on child pornography. This raises the question: why did the FBI take custody of eighty-five homosexual magazines? Extant FBI records do not offer any conclusive answers. One possibility relates to the common and inaccurate perception that homosexuals were akin to pedophiles. Another possibility relates to the FBI's own history. During the 1950s FBI officials attempted to use anti-obscenity statutes to silence gay civil rights organizations. Although it is unlikely that the FBI planned to use the same tactic in the 1980s (which would not succeed in light of previous Supreme Court rulings), we do know that the FBI monitored the radical gay activist group ACT-UP (AIDS Coalition to Unleash Power) at the time, given the explosion of HIV cases and the Reagan administration's failure to respond to these developments.[20] So even though we do not have FBI documents explaining the collection of these homosexual magazines, the fact that they were collected should, at the very least, be regarded with skepticism and scrutiny.

Within just three years of instituting its liaison with the Customs Service, the FBI decided to discontinue the Obscene File. By the 1990s, federal prosecutors had all but stopped prosecuting ITOM cases. Judicial interpretations of what was obscene and therefore illegal had been relaxed, and Presidents George H. W. Bush and Bill Clinton lacked Nixon's and Reagan's interest in anti-obscenity efforts. As Clinton's FBI director, Louis Freeh, put it: "ITOM matters are now all but nonexistent except for child pornography cases." And since child pornography cases did not require evidence to be compared with the Obscene File, Freeh saw no reason to continue devoting already stretched bureau resources to maintaining it.[21]

Given the termination of the FBI's Obscene File, the logical next step in the process would be destruction of the physical file—that is, the file containing the actual obscene films, magazines, and whatnot (as noted earlier, there was also an administrative file containing primarily memoranda about the Obscene File). The final extant document in the administrative file ordered the discontinuance of the Obscene File. In it, Freeh reminded the SACs of the various field offices that FBI regulations concerning the "disposing of pornographic materials are long-standing and well-established." He then directed, "in the remote event that the file contains a submission that should be returned and not destroyed, each field office" should notify FBI headquarters "with either a negative or positive answer *NO LATER THAN APRIL 30, 1993*." Although Freeh did not explicitly state that the Obscene File would be destroyed, the context of his order suggests that it was going to be incinerated.[22]

The FBI's use of the Obscene File and its active pursuit of ITOM cases (except those involving child pornography) thus ended during the administration of Democrat Bill Clinton. Despite the Clinton administration's unsurprising effort to focus almost exclusively on child pornography, Deputy Attorney General Eric Holder paid lip service to adult obscenity in June 1998 when he sent a memorandum to U.S. attorneys to "remind" them of the Justice Department's "policies and priorities" with respect to "large-scale distributors" of obscenity with links to organized crime.[23]

The end of the Obscene File was not a surprising development. Legally, ITOM cases had become more difficult to prosecute, given the legal definition of obscenity and the more relaxed cultural perceptions of sexuality. Additionally, it was more common for conservative Republican administrations—such as Nixon's and Reagan's—to push obscenity cases as a means of shoring up their political bases and to satisfy and pander to the social mores of socially conservative American voters. But the FBI's role in pursuing general obscenity still had one last gasp of life.

After the controversial election of 2000, George W. Bush, a reborn fundamentalist Christian who closely cultivated his right-wing evangelical political base of support rather than appealing to the moderate middle, began to feel pressure to do something about adult obscenity. Bush declared a "Protection from Pornography Week" in October 2003, but it did little to satisfy his base. For example, Focus on the Family, a right-wing evangelical group, began to criticize Attorney General John Ashcroft in December 2003 for failing to make any serious efforts to target adult obscenity. (The puritanical Ashcroft did, however, order a bare-chested female statue called the "Spirit of Justice," displayed in the Justice Department's Great Hall, covered with a blue drape.) Given these political pressures, Ashcroft quietly directed the FBI to renew its work in general obscenity cases in early 2004. Through its Child Exploitation Section, the Justice Department created "an initiative to combat purveyors of illegal adult obscene material." As part of this effort to resume traditional obscenity investigations, FBI officials also created a special anti-obscenity squad—called Squad CR-18—consisting of six FBI agents who were stationed at the Tysons Corner Resident Agency in Fairfax County, Virginia, which was part of the Washington field office.[24]

The anti-obscenity squad focused on only the "largest purveyors/producers of obscene material that depicts graphic violence, bondage, bestiality and defecation." The squad was also instructed to investigate violations of the ITOM statutes and "other illegal practices prevalent within the industry." These prevalent practices included "unwanted solicitation, unsolicited bombardment of obscenity, 'mouse trapping,' money laundering, tax evasion, trademark fraud, narcotics trafficking, [and] involuntary servitude," among other unspecified items. FBI agents were specifically reminded of the Supreme Court's *Miller* test for obscenity and were advised that the Justice Department intended to use the federal grand jury in Virginia's Eastern District "during the initial stage of any investigation to issue grand jury subpoenas." Presumably, this district's more conservative perspective on obscenity would ensure relatively easy indictments (a technique first used by Anthony Comstock in the late nineteenth century). Afterward, cases would be assigned to the appropriate jurisdictions.[25]

Because no FBI agents had conducted general (or adult) obscenity investigations since the 1980s, the Justice Department's Child Exploitation Section sought to train the bureau's six-man squad during February 2004. The previous autumn, that section had instructed assistant U.S. attorneys, FBI agents, and others about obscenity investigations and cases. FBI officials made arrangements for the Los Angeles Police Department's vice squad, which had significant experience in the field, to provide additional instruction to the FBI's new squad and to "assist in the development of an obscenity specific intelligence base for the FBI." In other words, when seeking to create an "intelligence base," FBI officials apparently sought to re-create something akin to the old Obscene File. The physical portion of the Obscene File had been, in essence, an intelligence base of specimens used for comparison and identification purposes to locate and identify the sources of smut and its purveyors.[26]

A year later, having won reelection with what the president described as "political capital," the Bush administration publicly announced its effort to step up the government's prosecution of the interstate transportation of not just child pornography but also, as FBI officials called it, "adult obscenity." In July 2005 Bush's new attorney general, Alberto Gonzales, announced the formation of the Obscenity Prosecution Task Force and made what came to be known as the Adult Obscenity Initiative "one of the top priorities" of the Justice Department; this meant it would also become a top priority of both U.S. attorneys and the FBI via its Criminal Investigative Division (CID). Congress funded the initiative as part of its 2005 fiscal year budget—1 October 2004 to 30 September 2005. As a result, after well over a decade of not pursuing general obscenity cases, the FBI leadership officially and publicly renewed the bureau's efforts in this area. In explaining this move, Assistant Attorney General Christopher Wray predictably cited "advances in technology and mass marketing, particularly over the past decade, [that] have enabled the traffic in obscenity to take on a more national and even global reach." Bush administration officials decided to focus the effort within the Washington field office and earmarked special funds to assign ten agents—nine FBI agents plus one supervisory agent—to what was now called Squad CR-8. FBI officials permitted other field offices to conduct obscenity investigations, but only if resources permitted them to do so without affecting higher-priority cases, such as those involving public corruption.[27]

In early November 2005 the Justice Department issued a press release on its new anti-obscenity effort. Although the specific case mentioned in the statement apparently did not involve the FBI (probably because it was centered in Colorado), the statement reveals the Bush administration's attitude about obscenity and the means of pursuing it. Assistant Attorney General Alice Fisher, of the department's Criminal Division, said:

> The Department of Justice, with other law enforcement agencies, will pursue those, like Edward Wedelstedt, who transport adult obscene material in violation of our criminal laws with all available tools. This will include jail time, tax penalties, and forfeiture of business interests where those businesses engage in the distribution of obscene material. This guilty plea [of Wedelstedt's] is a warning to others who are pandering such hard-core pornography that the

Department of Justice will bring to justice those who violate our Nation's obscenity laws.[28]

The revival of the FBI's role in pursuing adult obscenity cases was not popular with some FBI agents. One anonymous agent who was interviewed by the *Washington Post* stated, in a dismissive tone, "I guess this means we've won the war on terror." He elaborated by commenting on the FBI's already stretched funding: "We must not need any more resources for espionage." The FBI agent explained that, for some agents, the effort was nothing but "a running joke" and noted, "honestly, most of the guys would have to recuse themselves."[29]

In January 2006 investigative journalist Paul Krassner (he refers to himself as an investigative satirist) interviewed an anonymous FBI agent involved with the new anti-obscenity squad. Reiterating the views expressed by the agent interviewed for the *Washington Post* article, he told Krassner, "To tell you the truth, the guys I had worked with, they all thought it was just a big joke." He explained that the Washington field office, where the new anti-obscenity effort was located, was heavily involved in important national security matters, and FBI agents thought the focus on obscenity would detract from what should be, in their view, the FBI's priority post 9/11. However, the agent also told Krassner he had applied to work for the new anti-obscenity squad because he "was feeling burnt out" and "needed something less stressful."[30]

Krassner asked this agent why he thought the Bush administration had made adult obscenity a priority. In the agent's view, the Bush administration "figure[d] that pornography is an easy target." He believed the effort was political and that the Bush administration was "sucking up to the religious right." He also cited the fact that Congress had authorized the anti-obscenity effort and observed that, as a political matter, "nobody wants to come out *for* porn." Additionally, the FBI agent called Bush administration policy makers "control freaks" who had an interest in shifting attention away from "their own insidiousness and incompetence."[31]

FBI officials were concerned that agents conducting this new anti-obscenity program would encounter "many legal issues including first amendment claims." SACs of the various field offices were therefore directed "to focus on clearly obscene conduct." The Washington field office, working in tandem with the CID's Violent Crimes Section, the Justice Department's Child Exploitation and Obscenity Section, and the

U.S. attorney's office for the Eastern District of Virginia, would "identify and predict the most significant targets and initiate appropriate investigations." Members of the CID reviewed the bureau's history of successful obscenity cases and, given the evolution of obscenity law, directed field offices to focus only on the creators and distributors of "the most egregious obscene material." Included in this category was material "depicting rape, 'snuff' films, scat, bestiality, bondage, urination, defecation, [and] sadistic and masochistic conduct." Specifically excluded from the FBI's new anti-obscenity initiative was, as one agent wrote, behavior "typically portrayed on 'Girls Gone Wild' videos" and shown on cable TV and DirecTV. Or, as the FBI agent interviewed by Krassner put it, they were directed to focus on "the kind of material that tends to be most effective with local juries, because it's been shown that the best odds of conviction are in pornography cases that involve bestiality, urination, defecation, sadism and masochism." What's more, given the sensitivity of such investigations, FBI field offices were ordered to implement "safeguarding mechanisms . . . to protect WFO [Washington field office] Agents from long-term exposure to AOI [Adult Obscenity Initiative] materials." Moreover, before initiating one of these investigations, FBI agents were "encouraged" to contact the Violent Crimes Unit for direction.[32]

It is not clear whether FBI officials actually revived the physical portion of the old Obscene File, either as it had been used in the past or, as noted in 2004, as an intelligence base for obscenity. But given the focused nature of the new anti-obscenity efforts, a massive physical file for comparing obscene specimens from across the country was probably not necessary. FBI officials apparently did, however, create something similar to the administrative portion of the Obscene File. In a memorandum to the Washington field office, the supervisory special agent in the Violent Crimes Unit advised that "FBIHQ file 319W-HQ-A1487699-CID is reserved for issues relating directly to program guidance." As such, agents were instructed not to use this file number in communications to CID.[33] For decades, beginning with Hoover, FBI officials had used file 80-662, the administrative portion of the Obscene File, to maintain memoranda relative to the massive collection of obscene items.

In testimony before the Senate Committee on Commerce, Science, and Transportation, the FBI's deputy assistant director of the Criminal Division, James Burrus, reported in 2006 that the FBI was "taking an aggressive course of action in the area of obscenity." He outlined the

FBI's creation in the Washington field office of what he called an adult obscenity squad, noting that it worked intimately with the Justice Department's Obscenity Prosecution Task Force. He then described how the bureau conducted obscenity investigations. According to Burrus, agents would first consult with the Justice Department's task force to determine whether allegations met the legal criteria for obscenity; only then would they begin an investigation. This differed from the old standard, when FBI agents sought the advice of the local district attorney because local community standards were the determinants of obscenity. In 2006, stated Burrus, the FBI's primary focus for adult obscenity was the Internet.[34]

Burrus then offered the committee some general, and not altogether clear, statistics on the FBI's most recent anti-obscenity effort. Since the start of the Bush administration, the FBI had opened seventy-nine ITOM cases; of these, fifty-two had been opened since October 2003 (almost as many cases had been pursued from the late 1970s to the late 1980s). Burrus's mention of 2003 was a reference to the launch of the FBI's Innocence Lost national initiative, a program focusing on the sex trafficking of children, which inevitably involved child pornography. Burrus then went on to describe the FBI's child pornography efforts—its anti-obscenity bailiwick since closure of the Obscene File—and he cited several examples of the bureau's work in this area. He said very little about adult obscenity cases (other than the focus on the Internet) and did not mention the number of cases stemming for the FBI's adult obscenity squad. Burrus concluded his remarks by reiterating that the FBI was "committed to curbing the production and distribution of obscene materials and child pornography."[35]

Although precise data are not readily available, it appears that the Bush administration made no significant headway in prosecuting adult obscenity cases, and the Obama administration has expressed little interest in doing so. The only information released by the Justice Department about obscenity enforcement—caseload data for U.S. attorneys—is very general in nature, but it shows that between fiscal years 2001 and 2009 (essentially, during the Bush administration) a total of 151 obscenity cases were filed, 197 cases were pending, and 167 cases were terminated.[36] The Justice Department did not elaborate on what kinds of obscenity cases these data reflect.

In April 2010, Utah senator Orrin Hatch pressured the Obama Justice Department to do more to combat adult obscenity. During a Senate hearing, Hatch reiterated to Attorney General Eric Holder that "there has been a pattern at the Department of Justice to prosecute only the most extreme obscene materials. This particular type of material may virtually guarantee a conviction but it is not the most widely produced and consumed and therefore its prosecution may have very little impact on the obscenity industry." Hatch was frustrated because, in his view, the Bush administration had not done enough about the broader issue, despite its revival of adult obscenity targeting. He called the Justice Department's work with obscenity cases "misguided and narrow."[37] One year later, Hatch and forty-one other senators—mostly but not exclusively socially conservative ones—appealed to Holder "to urge the Department of Justice vigorously to enforce federal obscenity laws against major commercial distributors of hardcore adult pornography." In these senators' view, the federal government must "combat the growing scourge of obscenity in America." Hatch cited so-called experts who claimed— contrary to the scientific report of the Johnson-Nixon era and more in line with the unscientific Meese report of the 1980s—that adult obscenity "contributes to violence against women, addiction, harm to children, and sex trafficking."[38]

Hatch and company were particularly upset because, after several years, it was clear that the Obama administration had little interest in pursuing adult obscenity. When Obama took office, his Justice Department declined to initiate any more adult obscenity indictments and allowed only three adult obscenity cases held over from the Bush administration to proceed.[39] Moreover, the Justice Department's response to Senator Hatch indicated that since October 2008 "the Department has charged violations of the federal obscenity statutes over 150 times" and secured guilty pleas "in several cases," with one pending case in California due to go to trial in the spring of 2011.[40] More significantly, in the spring of 2011 Holder shut down the Justice Department's Obscenity Prosecution Task Force and presumably, with it, the FBI' s adult obscenity squad, both created during the Bush administration. Citing limited resources, the Holder Justice Department decided to prioritize child pornography cases over adult obscenity cases. Indeed, in the department's response to Hatch, it even cited the increase in child pornography crimes since the 1990s as the reason behind its decision. The move elicited the following response from the moralist Hatch: "Rather than initiate a single new case since President Obama took office . . . the only development in this area has been the dismantling of the task force. As the toxic waste of obscenity continues to spread and harm everyone it touches, it appears the Obama administration is giving up without a fight."[41]

In any event, given the history of obscenity targeting, it is not surprising that the Obama administration would back away from adult obscenity cases. It is, however, still too soon for historians to fully understand these developments in any meaningful way until substantive records are released. Nevertheless, the ebb and flow of obscenity targeting continue unabated, and the pattern of conservative administrations reacting to perceived permissiveness in American culture continues its own historical rise and fall, while the post-Hoover FBI responds to the political and policy goals of its superiors.

CONCLUSION

For more than eight decades FBI officials maintained an interest in targeting obscenity and pornography. This interest, however, was influenced and characterized by a complex and multifaceted confluence of forces. First and foremost were overarching sociocultural developments that defined the FBI's focus to a large degree. These sociocultural developments constituted great cultural shifts in which American value systems were challenged, notably during wartime or periods of cultural upheaval. These events put tremendous political pressure on the FBI, which is responsive to both public pressure and the political and policy interests of its superiors. These influences were complemented, for example, by advances in technology. Technological innovations (whether motion pictures, videotapes, or the Internet) helped facilitate the distribution of obscenity and make it more widespread, spurring public interest in the obscenity issue and leading federal law enforcers and politicians to focus on these new developments. The new legal focus was characterized by constantly changing court rulings on obscenity, which altered how FBI officials targeted obscenity and pornography. Finally, affecting the FBI's interest in obscenity were the personal agendas of its various directors. For almost fifty years J. Edgar Hoover took great interest in using the FBI to influence American values, especially through his various educational campaigns. Whether they were campaigns to educate Americans about the threat of communism or the moral perils of obscenity, Hoover pushed his own particular and puritanical value system in an effort to prevent what he saw as undesirable changes in American culture. Those who followed had their own special interests that influenced how the FBI dealt with obscenity, but none had the influence or the political legerdemain of Hoover.

The first great sociocultural shift affecting the FBI was America's rapid industrialization during the Progressive Era. At this time the bureau focused on breaking up prostitution rings via the Mann Act, which had its origins in the popular fear that naïve young women moving into the cities would fall prey to criminals. These investigations led to the increasing collection of obscenity. The FBI's focus on obscenity really advanced, however, with the trauma of the First World War, another great sociocultural shift. Following that conflict, many Americans were concerned about the apparent decline in Victorian morality. This led the FBI—headed by moralist J. Edgar Hoover—to devise a procedure in 1925 for filing in field offices and mailing to headquarters obscene items collected by FBI agents during the course of their investigations. Despite the intense public interest in obscenity, the FBI's interest in the 1920s was still limited because it was part of and responsive to the anti-statist administrations of conservative Republicans Calvin Coolidge and Herbert Hoover. In any event, obscenity efforts were still spearheaded mainly by private organizations and the U.S. Customs Bureau. The FBI's interest had not yet developed into any overarching and significant law enforcement effort.

It was only when the FBI assumed a broader role in federal law enforcement during the New Deal era and established its vaunted crime laboratory that FBI officials realized how much obscene evidence agents had submitted for examination. Even so, it would take another major and traumatic sociocultural event—namely, the Second World War—before FBI officials felt public pressure to target obscenity rings. This development paralleled similar public pressure exerted on the federal government toward the end of the Civil War to protect young and seemingly innocent American soldiers from immoral influences. And in their effort to curtail smut peddlers, FBI officials were largely successful, even if wartime priorities later forced them to nearly abandon obscenity targeting.

The next sociocultural shift came with the end of the Second World War and the advent of the Cold War. The idea of conformity became dominant in American culture in the face of the perceived global threat of communism and the concomitant threat of domestic subversion. Containment was the solution to the threat of communism, but it also seemed to be the solution to domestic threats to American culture and values. FBI officials began to use the Obscene File not only to curb crime but also to regulate social morality, a concomitant goal of Hoover's. They first focused on African American musicians and record distributors, then on gay and lesbian Americans, who were seen as a unique subversive threat. Hoover also used the Obscene File to have FBI agents submit sensitive information that the director found to be of particular personal and bureaucratic interest.

By the late 1950s, as the federal legal definition of obscenity underwent several changes, starting with the Warren Court, FBI officials responded to these developments. Hoover used the Obscene File to quietly keep tabs on state obscenity laws, viewing them as foreshadowers of possible changes to federal anti-obscenity law. He also directed his agents to single out specific obscenity cases that could be used in bureaucratic maneuvering, for publicity, or as part of his various educational campaigns in the fields of anti-communism or morality. The significant sociocultural development in this era took place in presidential politics and originated with the political rebirth of Richard Nixon. Campaigning in 1968, Nixon capitalized on the obscenity issue and related Supreme Court rulings to mobilize his silent majority to win the presidency. He then executed an intensive anti-obscenity campaign that, significantly, paralleled the interests of Hoover, who shared Nixon's puritanical values. Nixon's anti-obscenity efforts, however, had two purposes: to pander to his conservative base and others in an effort to construct a Republican political majority, and to publicize and promote Nixon's (and Hoover's) puritanical conservative values during the social and cultural tumult of the 1960s. Even though Nixon was not successful in getting significant anti-obscenity legislation passed (he lacked the necessary congressional majorities), he promoted the issue and focused his battle in the courts— both pushing obscenity cases (per Hoover's advice) and changing the makeup of the Supreme Court. He was arguably successful, inasmuch as his conservative appointments to the Court slowed the liberal trend in its obscenity rulings. Overall, Nixon was able to promote his and Hoover's values in the face of significant cultural change.

With the political demise of Nixon and the death of Hoover, the FBI's role in obscenity issues changed again in response to sociocultural shifts. The first was the revelation of various FBI abuses. These abuses merely added to the public's distrust of the government resulting from the Vietnam War and Watergate. Directors after Hoover tried to rebuild the bureau's image and refocus its work, at least publicly, on combating crime. This led FBI agents to concentrate on obscenity and its links to organized crime. This period was further characterized by changes in obscenity law that shaped how FBI officials targeted obscenity, the proliferation of pornography, and a new federal focus on the Mafia with the recently enacted RICO statute. FBI officials increasingly used undercover operations, another move away from the image of the clean-cut agent of the Hoover era.

The post-Hoover era was further defined by the priorities of the FBI directors. Clarence Kelley stressed a quality-over-quantity approach, but he did not require this in obscenity cases. He believed that larger amounts of obscene submissions would lead to greater obscene identifications. As it turned out, this was not the case. William Webster continued the undercover operations that began under Kelley and preferred to attack obscenity and the money behind it via RICO. By FBI officials' own assessments, obscenity prosecutions had become more difficult with the changing legal definition of what constituted obscenity, given the different community standards of the various jurisdictions FBI agents worked in.

With the Reagan administration, the FBI's targeting of obscenity changed yet again. With a conservative back in the White House, public pressure grew for the president to do something to curb the perceived growth of immorality. Part of this demand was rooted in technology, as the VCR was becoming more prominent and radically changing the pornography industry. The Reagan administration responded with a special commission headed by the attorney general to study the issue and make recommendations. This commission was, in many ways, the conservative antithesis to the Johnson-Nixon presidential commission on obscenity. The Reagan administration implemented the commission's recommendations, and FBI officials responded to the political priorities of their superiors. Yet federal obscenity cases had become increasingly difficult to prosecute, and fewer and fewer went forward. FBI officials therefore tried to reorganize the Obscene File, computerize it, and expand the scope of obscene specimens—through liaison with the Customs Service—in the hope of overcoming legal obstacles and the larger political priorities of the Reagan administration (the War on Drugs and child pornography).

By the 1990s the American public had become more accepting of obscenity. After twelve years of conservative Republican rule (although the George H. W. Bush administration showed less interest in obscenity than his predecessor), FBI officials terminated the Obscene File during the Clinton administration. The reason given was the paltry level of federal obscenity prosecutions over the years, primarily as a result of changing legal definitions and a new and almost exclusive focus on child pornography.

With the controversial election of George W. Bush, a reborn fundamentalist Christian and cultural conservative, the FBI's interest in obscenity would also be reborn. This development can be understood in a couple of ways. First, there is a clear and discernible pattern during the latter half of the twentieth century of conservative administrations coming to power and focusing on obscenity issues. This political interest in the issue developed during the Nixon era, when the Democratic Party held a political advantage in economic issues and the Republican Party dominated in social issues. Republicans realized the electoral advantage of pushing social issues such as obscenity, and Nixon undoubtedly hoped to advance the values of his core base of support. For Bush this effort was even more crucial; his election strategy rested not on attracting moderate voters but in energizing his conservative base with the hope (like Nixon) of creating a permanent Republican majority. Second, Bush's first attorney general who spearheaded these efforts was moralist John Ashcroft. It is no surprise that, given Ashcroft's fundamentalist Christian background and interests and the political pressures being exerted on the administration from its right-wing evangelical base, the FBI would suddenly be directed to return to adult obscenity investigations.

Despite its eighty-year involvement in the obscenity and pornography issue, the FBI was a latecomer to the federal enforcement of obscenity laws. When they did enter the field, FBI agents and officials were influenced by and reacted to the same traditional influences that had shaped obscenity regulation for centuries. But the FBI's methods of targeting obscenity and pornography were different, inasmuch as FBI agents and officials had to operate within the federal legal system, even though they lent assistance to local and state entities. FBI efforts were also significantly shaped by the fact that FBI officials, especially after Hoover, responded to the political and policy interests of their White House superiors and the new contours of anti-obscenity law, which brought national political interests and legal hurdles into the picture. In the end, we see a long and unique interest in a complicated topic by a complex and highly bureaucratic federal law enforcement body.

NOTES

Introduction

1. See, for example, James Paul and Murray Schwartz, *Federal Censorship: Obscenity in the Mail* (Westport, CT: Greenwood Press, 1961); Paul S. Boyer, *Purity in Print: Book Censorship in America from the Gilded Age to the Computer Age*, 2nd ed. (Madison: University of Wisconsin Press, 2002); Richard F. Hixson, *Pornography and the Justices: The Supreme Court and the Intractable Obscenity Problem* (Carbondale: Southern Illinois University Press, 1996); Maureen Harrison and Steve Gilbert, eds., *Utterly without Redeeming Social Value: Obscenity and Pornography Decisions of the United States Supreme Court* (Carlsbad, CA: Excellent Books, 2000).

2. Robert W. Haney, *Comstockery in America: Patterns of Censorship and Control* (New York: DaCapo Press, 1974); Jay Gertzman, "John Saxton Sumner of the New York Society for the Suppression of Vice: A Chief Smut-Eradicator of the Interwar Period," *Journal of American Culture* 17, 2 (Summer 1994): 41–47.

3. Molly McGarry, "Spectral Sexualities: Nineteenth-Century Spiritualism, Moral Panics, and the Making of U.S. Obscenity Law," *Journal of Women's History* 12, 2 (Summer 2000): 8–29; Helen Lefkowitz Horowitz, "Victoria Woodhull, Anthony Comstock, and Conflict over Sex in the United States in the 1870s," *Journal of American History* 87, 2 (September 2000): 403–434. See also John D'Emilio and Estelle B. Freedman, *Intimate Matters: A History of Sexuality in America*, 2nd ed. (Chicago: University of Chicago Press, 1997).

4. The two best studies that, read together, offer a comprehensive, two-century view are Donna Dennis, *Licentious Gotham: Erotic Publishing and Its Prosecution in Nineteenth-Century New York* (Cambridge, MA: Harvard University Press, 2009), and Andrea Friedman, *Prurient Interests: Gender, Democracy, and Obscenity in New York City, 1909–1945* (New York: Columbia University Press, 2000).

5. Robert Mason, *Richard Nixon and the Quest for a New Majority* (Chapel Hill: University of North Carolina Press, 2004); Rick Perlstein, *Nixonland: The Rise of a President and the Fracturing of America* (New York: Scribner, 2008); Whitney Strub, *Perversion for Profit: The Politics of Pornography and the Rise of the New Right* (New York: Columbia University Press, 2011).

6. Will Brantley, "The Surveillance of Georgia Writer and Civil Rights Activist Lillian Smith: Another Story from the Federal Bureau of Investigation," *Georgia Historical Quarterly* 85, 1 (Spring 2001): 59–82.

7. See Athan Theoharis, *The Boss: J. Edgar Hoover and the Great American Inquisition* (Philadelphia: Temple University Press, 1988), 5, 94–96; Athan Theoharis, *The FBI and American Democracy: A Brief Critical History* (Lawrence: University Press of Kansas, 2004), 35.

8. Paul Boyer notes this phenomenon, building on the work of British sociologist Alan Hunt, who describes "crisis tendencies" at particular historical points that lead to increases in moral regulation and result in political and cultural infighting. See Boyer, *Purity in Print*, 294.

9. Mason, *Richard Nixon*; Perlstein, *Nixonland*; Strub, *Perversion for Profit*.

10. In the 1980s, as a result of Federal District Court Judge Harold H. Greene's ruling concerning the FBI's plans for the disposal of records, National Archives officials examined FBI files and records classifications in detail and made recommendations for records retention. In the process, they also created a useful survey of the types and general scope of FBI records.

11. Gerald K. Haines and David A. Langbart, *Unlocking the Files of the FBI: A Guide to Its Records and Classifications System* (Wilmington, DE: Scholarly Resources, 1993), 33, 141, 70–71, 168, 172.

1. The Evolution of American Obscenity Regulation and the FBI

1. Donna Dennis, "Obscenity Regulation, New York City, and the Creation of American Erotica, 1820–1880" (Ph.D. dissertation, Princeton University, 2005), 11–20.

2. Donna Dennis, *Licentious Gotham: Erotic Publishing and Its Prosecution in Nineteenth-Century New York* (Cambridge, MA: Harvard University Press, 2009), 34, 38–39, 40.

3. Ibid., 43–49; Dennis, "Obscenity Regulation," 20–28.

4. Dennis, *Licentious Gotham*, 57–70; James Paul and Murray Schwartz, *Federal Censorship: Obscenity in the Mail* (Westport, CT: Greenwood Press, 1961), 11.

5. Paul and Schwartz, *Federal Censorship*, 12; the Tariff Act is also reprinted in that volume (347–348). On the Whigs and their politics, see Michael F. Holt, *The Rise and Fall of the American Whig Party: Jacksonian Politics and the Onset of the Civil War* (New York: Oxford University Press, 1999), 32, 131, 148, and Daniel Walker Howe, *What Hath God Wrought: The Transformation of America, 1815–1848* (New York: Oxford University Press, 2007), 593.

6. Paul and Schwartz, *Federal Censorship*, 17; Dennis, *Licentious Gotham*, 182–198, 204.

7. Soldier quoted in Dennis, *Licentious Gotham*, 201.

8. Paul and Schwartz, *Federal Censorship*, 17–18; Section 16, An Act Relating to the Postal Laws, chapter 89, 13 Stat. 507 (1865).

9. Paul and Schwartz, *Federal Censorship*, 18–21.

10. "Comstock Act," 18 USC 1461 (1873), reprinted in ibid.

11. Dennis, *Licentious Gotham*, 268–269, 272–273.

12. On the federal government's law enforcement role during Reconstruction, see Rhodri Jeffreys-Jones, *The FBI: A History* (New Haven, CT: Yale University Press, 2007), 17–38.

13. David J. Langum, *Crossing over the Line: Legislating Morality and the Mann Act* (Chicago: University of Chicago Press, 1994), 3, 17–19, 21–23.

14. Ibid., 9; Stanley Finch, "The White Slave Traffic," in *Self Knowledge and Guide to Sex Instruction*, ed. Thomas W. Shannon (Marietta, OH: S. A. Mullikin, 1913).

15. Stanley W. Finch, "The White-Slave Traffic," in *White Slavery Today*, ed. Ernest A. Bell (Chicago: Lincoln Walter, 1917), 91.

16. For an account of the FBI's targeting of Jack Johnson, see Jeffreys-Jones, *The FBI*, 57–58, 62, 63–65. Memo, [deleted] to Rosen, 25 August 1944, FBI 80-662-[40?] (in some cases the serial number is illegible; the likely number is indicated by brackets and a question mark).

17. Athan Theoharis, *The FBI and American Democracy: A Brief Critical History* (Lawrence: University Press of Kansas, 2004), 24–27; Robert K. Murray, *Red Scare: A Study in National Hysteria, 1919-1920* (Minneapolis: University of Minnesota Press, 1955), 58–68, 193–194; William Preston Jr., *Aliens and Dissenters: Federal Suppression of Radicals, 1903-33,* 2nd ed. (Chicago: University of Illinois Press, 1994), 208–212, 216–217.

18. For Hoover's background, see Richard Gid Powers, *Secrecy and Power: The Life of J. Edgar Hoover* (New York: Free Press, 1987), 5–35.

19. Paul S. Boyer, *Purity in Print: Book Censorship in America from the Gilded Age to the Computer Age,* 2nd ed. (Madison: University of Wisconsin Press, 2002), 55–57. Baker quoted in Fred D. Baldwin, "The Invisible Armor," *American Quarterly* 16 (Autumn 1964): 432.

20. See T. W. Shannon, *Ethics of the Unmarried, or Spooning* (Cincinnati: S. A. Mullikin, 1913).

21. John D'Emilio and Estelle B. Freedman, *Intimate Matters: A History of Sexuality in America,* 2nd ed. (Chicago: University of Chicago Press, 1997), 240–241; Frederick Lewis Allen, *Only Yesterday: An Informal History of the 1920s* (New York: Harper & Row, 1931), 83; Paul and Schwartz, *Federal Censorship,* 40; Boyer, *Purity in Print,* 69–74, 208–209.

22. SAC letter no. 512, Hoover to all SACs, 24 March 1925, FBI 66-04-x92. On the Clean Books crusade, see Boyer, *Purity in Print,* 99–127.

23. On the early 1930s "crime wave," see Bryan Burrough, *Public Enemies: America's Greatest Crime Wave and the Birth of the FBI, 1933-34* (New York: Penguin Press, 2004), 15–18. Letter, John Dillinger to Henry Ford, 6 May 1934, FBI 62-29777-1338.

24. Memo, [deleted] to Rosen, 25 August 1944, FBI 80-662-[40?]; memo, E. P. Coffey to E. A. Tamm, 26 August 1944, FBI 80-662-[39?].

2. The Development of a Centralized Obscene File

1. See Douglas M. Charles, *J. Edgar Hoover and the Anti-interventionists: FBI Political Surveillance and the Rise of the Domestic Security State, 1939-45* (Columbus: Ohio State University Press, 2007).

2. "Sumner Sees Danger of Vice Rise in War," *New York Times,* 23 May 1942; "War Need Is Stressed for Vice Suppression," *New York Times,* 13 June 1943.

3. Memo, [deleted] to Rosen, 25 August 1944, FBI 80–662-[40?] (in some cases the serial number is illegible; when possible, the likely number is indicated by brackets and a question mark).

4. Memo, E. P. Coffey to E. A. Tamm, 26 August 1944, FBI 80-662-[39?].

5. Ibid.; memo, Coffey to Tracey, 30 September 1942, FBI 80-662-1.

6. Memo, Rosen to Hoover, 30 September 1942, FBI 80-662-2; memo, Coffey to Tracey, 23 October 1942, FBI 80-662-3; memo, [deleted] to Coffey, 21 December 1942, FBI 80-662-4.

7. Memo, [deleted] to Coffey, 21 December 1942, FBI 80-662-4; "5 Seized by FBI as Lewd Book Ring," *New York Times,* 24 November 1942; memo, [deleted] to Rosen, 25 August 1944, FBI 80-662-[40?], p. 3.

8. Memo, [deleted] to Coffey, 21 December 1942, FBI 80-662-4; laboratory report, 15 March 1943, FBI 80-662-5.

9. Memo, J. A. Martin to Coffey, 3 August 1944, FBI 80-662-33.

10. Memo, Martin to Coffey, 8 March 1943, FBI 80-662-16. The number 80 is the FBI file classification for Laboratory Research Matters—Headquarters. In other words, it is a bureau policy file.

11. Memo, J. A. Martin to Coffey, 3 August 1944, FBI 80-662-33; bureau bulletin no. 16, 2nd series 1943, 31 March 1943, FBI 66-03-474; memo, Coffey to Hoover, 31 July 1944, FBI 80-662-[31?]; memo, FBI Executive Conference to Hoover, 4 October 1944, FBI 80-662-NR (not recorded).

12. Memo, Coffey to Hoover, 31 July 1944, FBI 80-662-[31?].

13. Ibid.; memo, Clegg to Hoover, 1 August 1944, FBI 80-662-32.

14. Memo, Coffey to Tamm, 26 August 1944, FBI 80-662-[?]; memo, [deleted] to Rosen, 25 August 1944, FBI 80-662-[40?]. On file burning, see also memo, [deleted] to Rosen, 18 August 1944, FBI 80-662-37; memo, Martin to Coffey, 23 August 1944, FBI 80-662-[?].

15. Memo, Coffey to Tamm, 26 August 1944, FBI 80-662-[?].

16. Memo, [deleted] to Rosen, 25 August 1944, FBI 80-662-[40?].

17. Ibid.

18. Ibid.

19. Memo, Coffey to Tamm, 26 August 1944, FBI 80-662-[?].

20. Memo, FBI Executive Conference to Hoover, 4 October 1944, FBI 80-662-NR; memo, Martin to Coffey, 29 September 1944, FBI 80-662-44.

21. Will Brantley, "The Surveillance of Georgia Writer and Civil Rights Activist Lillian Smith: Another Story from the Federal Bureau of Investigation," *Georgia Historical Quarterly* 85 (2001): 70.

22. Ibid., 70–72.

23. Memo, [deleted] to Nichols, 17 November 1942, FBI 94-4-5826-7.

24. Letter, Hoover to Spellman, 18 November 1942, FBI 94-4-5826-NR.

25. Letter, Spellman to Hoover, 25 November 1942, FBI 94-4-5826-5.

26. Letter, Spellman to Hoover, 30 November 1942, FBI 94-4-5826-8; letter, Hoover to Spellman, 10 December 1942, FBI 94-4-5826-8.

27. "Blames Broken Homes for Juvenile Crime," *New York Times,* 17 February 1944, 16; J. Edgar Hoover, "A 'Third Front'—Against Juvenile Crime," *New York Times,* 27 February 1944, SM8; "Wider Aid to Youth Urged by Hoover," *New York Times,* 5 May 1944, 21.

28. Letter, Spellman to Hoover, 10 May 1944, FBI 94-4-5826-NR.

29. Memo, Special Agent [deleted] to SAC Conroy, 8 May 1946, FBI 94-4-5826-16; "Award Goes to Hoover," *New York Times,* 6 January 1946, 41; "FBI Head Assails Communists Here: Awarded 1945 Club of Champions Medal," *New York Times,* 9 January 1946, 16.

30. Memo, SAC Miami to Hoover, 2 June 1944, FBI 80-662-29.

31. Memo, Guy Hottel to Hoover, 16 September 1944, FBI 80-662-[?]; memo, Hoover to Hottel, 29 November 1944, FBI 80-662-[?].

32. Memo, Hottel to Hoover, 18 December 1944, FBI 80-662-54; memo, Hottel to Hoover, 7 February 1945, FBI 80-662-62.

33. Memo, [deleted] to Rosen, 25 August 1944, FBI 80-662-[40?], p. 5.

34. On the bureaucratic wrangling over foreign intelligence, see Douglas M. Charles, "'Before the Colonel Arrived': Hoover, Donovan, Roosevelt, and the Origins of

American Central Intelligence," *Intelligence and National Security* 20 (Summer 2005): 225–237.

35. Athan Theoharis, *J. Edgar Hoover, Sex, and Crime* (Chicago: Ivan R. Dee, 1995), 48–49; Athan Theoharis, *The Quest for Absolute Security: The Failed Intelligence Relations among U.S. Intelligence Agencies* (Chicago: Ivan R. Dee, 2007), 94–95; memo, [deleted] to Rosen, 25 August 1944, FBI 80-662-[40?], p. 5.

36. Theoharis, *Hoover, Sex, and Crime,* 48–49.

37. Memo, Martin to Coffey, 9 November 1944, FBI 80-662-[56?].

38. Examples include letter, SAC Washington Field Office to Hoover, 11 January 1943; letter, SAC Pittsburgh to Hoover, 25 January 1943; letter, SAC New Haven to Hoover, 18 February 1943; letter, SAC San Antonio to Hoover, 6 March 1943 [from Army Air Corps]; letter, SAC Newark to Hoover, 19 March 1943; letter, SAC New Haven to Hoover, 22 March 1943; letter, SAC Pittsburgh to Hoover, 31 March 1943 [from district attorney]; report, SAC Huntington, WV, to FBI HQ, 8 April 1943; letter, SAC New York to Hoover, 3 May 1943 [from citizen]; letter, SAC New Haven to Hoover, 25 May 1943; letter, SAC Philadelphia to Hoover, 6 July 1943 [from district attorney]; letter, SAC New Haven to Hoover, 28 August 1943 [from citizen]; memo, SAC New York to Hoover, 15 August 1944 [anonymous submission of obscene letter found in subway station]; memo, SAC Baltimore to Hoover, 29 September 1944; memo, SAC Chicago to Hoover, 6 October 1944; memo, SAC El Paso to Hoover, 20 March 1945 [from town marshal]; memo, SAC San Francisco to Hoover, 11 October 1945 and 12 August 1946 [from U.S. Navy]; and letter, [deleted, but U.S. Marine Corps office] to FBI, 14 August 1946, all in FBI 80-662.

39. Bureau bulletin no. 56, series 1944, 11 October 1944, FBI 90-662-NR.

40. Memo, FBI Executive Conference to Hoover, 18 June [*sic;* actually July] 1945, FBI 80-662-72.

41. See bureau bulletin no. 37, series 1946, 10 July 1946, FBI 66-03-759.

42. Ibid.

43. Ibid.

44. Ibid.

45. Memo, [deleted] to Rosen, 18 August 1944, FBI 80-662-37.

46. Memo, Sizoo to Harbo, 25 April 1947, FBI 80-662-[?]. For the "paid in full" exhibit, see memo, SAC Los Angeles to Hoover, 18 March 1948, FBI 80-662-[?].

47. Memo, Sizoo to Harbo, 3 May 1948, FBI 80-662-[?]; memo, [deleted] to Rosen, 10 June 1949, FBI 80-662-224; memo, Sizoo to Harbo, 2 June 1949, FBI 80-662-224; memo, [deleted] to [deleted], 12 January 1951, FBI 80-662-[?]; memo, [deleted] to Harbo, 21 August 1952, FBI 80-662-NR; memo, [deleted] to Rosen, 28 August 1952, FBI 80-662-[?].

48. Memo, [deleted] to Louis Nichols, 10 January 1948, FBI 74-[?].

49. Ibid.

50. Ibid.

51. Airtel, SAC Los Angeles, to Hoover, 5 March 1958, FBI 145-1375-1.

3. The Postwar Obscene File and Social Regulation

1. James T. Patterson, *Grand Expectations: The United States, 1945–1974* (New York: Oxford University Press, 1996), 30.

2. See William R. Ferris Jr., "Racial Repertoires among Blues Performers," *Ethnomusicology* 14 (September 1970): 439–449.

3. Memo, SAC Boston to Hoover, 4 March 1948, FBI 80-662-[?] (in some cases the serial number is illegible, as indicated by a bracketed question mark).

4. Memo and list of records, Hoover to SAC Boston, 11 March 1948, FBI 80-662-[?]; memo, SAC Boston to Hoover, 18 March 1948, FBI 80-662-[?]; memo, Hoover to SAC Boston, 29 March 1948, FBI 80-662-[?].

5. Memo, Rosen to Ladd, 16 September 1948, FBI 80-662-[?]; memo, Rosen to Ladd, 15 September 1948, FBI 80-662-[?].

6. Memo, Sizoo to Harbo, 7 January 1949, FBI 80-662-198; memo, [deleted] to Harbo, 1 March 1950, FBI 90-662-[?]; "Obscene Record Ruling; Curb on Literature Is Held Not Applicable to Disks," *New York Times,* 1 June 1949; Lewis Wood, "Supreme Court Rulings," *New York Times,* 7 February 1950; *United States v. Alpers,* 175 F.2d 137 (9th Cir. 1949); *United States v. Alpers,* 338 US 680 (1950); U.S. Senate, Judiciary Committee Report, "Transportation of Obscene Matters (Phonograph Records)," Report No. 1305, 27 February 1950, 81st Cong., 2nd sess.; U.S. House of Representatives, Judiciary Committee Report, "Transportation of Obscene Matters," Report No. 2017, 5 May 1950, 81st Cong., 2nd sess. I attempted to gain access to the Justice Department's files on the Alpers prosecution, which have not yet been deposited in the National Archives. After a flurry of correspondence, I was informed that these records "have either been misfiled or destroyed due to age in accordance with records disposal schedule." Letter, Rena Y. Kim, Chief, Criminal Division FOIA Unit, Justice Department, to Douglas M. Charles, 13 April 2010. Because I cannot prove that Alexander L. Alpers is deceased, I cannot request his file from the FBI and therefore cannot confirm that he was one of the FBI's West Coast targets.

7. On the Lavender Scare, see David K. Johnson, *The Lavender Scare: The Cold War Persecution of Gays and Lesbians in the Federal Government* (Chicago: University of Chicago Press, 2004); Robert Dean, *Imperial Brotherhood: Gender and the Making of Cold War Foreign Policy* (Amherst: University of Massachusetts Press, 2001); and Athan Theoharis, *Chasing Spies: How the FBI Failed in Counterintelligence But Promoted the Politics of McCarthyism in the Cold War Years* (Chicago: Ivan R. Dee, 2002), 170–197.

8. Memo, [deleted] to Rosen, 22 October 1954, FBI 62-93875-NR (not recorded).

9. Memo, Henry Wolfinger, Records Disposition Division, to Directors of NCD and NNF, re: Disposition Job No. N01-65-78-5, 28 December 1977; Request for Records Disposition Authority, James W. Awe, 15 January 1978; letter, Emil Moschella, Chief of FBI FOIA Section, to Seth Rosenfeld, 11 September 1990, all in author's possession; memo, [deleted] to DeLoach, 7 July 1959, FBI 80-662-NR. The 330,000-page Sex Deviates File was destroyed in 1977–1978.

10. Memo, SAC San Antonio to Hoover, 1 September 1947, FBI 80-662-[?].

11. Letter, Lieutenant [deleted] to FBI Crime Lab, 5 March 1964; FBI lab worksheet, 13 March 1964; FBI lab report, Hoover to Oak Park Police, 26 March 1964, all in FBI 80-662-308.

12. Douglas M. Charles, "From Subversion to Obscenity: The FBI's Investigations of the Early Homophile Movement in the United States, 1953–1958," *Journal of the History of Sexuality* 19, 2 (May 2010): 267–268.

13. Ibid., 270.

14. Ibid., 271–272.

15. Ibid., 276–277.

16. Ibid., 280–281.

17. Ibid., 281–282.

18. Ibid., 284.

19. Ibid., 285.

20. Memo, [deleted] to [deleted], 12 January 1951, FBI 80-662-[?].

21. Ibid.

22. Memo, [deleted] to Harbo, 15 January 1951, FBI 80-662-[?]. For a discussion of the FBI's records destruction policies, see Athan Theoharis, "Secrecy and Power: Unanticipated Problems in Researching FBI File," *Political Science Quarterly* 119, 2 (2004): 285–288.

23. Athan Theoharis, *J. Edgar Hoover, Sex, and Crime* (Chicago: Ivan R. Dee, 1995), 49–52.

24. See the FBI's annual reports on the Obscene File: 20 August 1944, 23 January 1945, 1 March 1950, 15 January 1951, 14 January 1952, 14 January 1953, 2 February 1954, 18 January 1955, 13 January 1956, 29 January 1957, 11 February 1958, 30 January 1959, 22 January 1960, 10 January 1961, 12 January 1962, 21 January 1963, 20 January 1964, 29 January 1965, 16 July 1965, 11 July 1966, 14 July 1967, 11 July 1968, 15 July 1969, 14 July 1970, 16 July 1971, 12 July 1972, 9 July 1973, 3 July 1974, 7 July 1975, 14 July 1976, 3 October 1977, 10 October 1978, 17 October 1979, 7 October 1980, 4 January 1982, all in FBI 80-662.

25. Memo, [deleted] to Harbo, 14 January 1952, FBI 80-662-[?]; memo, [deleted, but initials ABE] to Rosen, 30 January 1952, FBI 80-662-[?].

26. Memo, [deleted] to Harbo, 14 January 1953, FBI 80-662-241.

27. Memo, [deleted] to Q. Tamm, 2 February 1954, FBI 80-662-260; memo, [deleted] to D. J. Parsons, 18 January 1955, FBI 80-662-273; memo, [deleted] to Parsons, 13 January 1956, FBI 80-662-[?].

28. Patterson, *Grand Expectations,* 370; "Congress Studies the Problem of Juvenile Delinquency," *Congressional Digest* 33 (December 1954): 289–310; "Smut Held Cause of Delinquency," *New York Times,* 1 June 1955, 35. See also James Gilbert, *A Cycle of Outrage: America's Reaction to the Juvenile Delinquent in the 1950s* (New York: Oxford University Press, 1986).

29. "FBI Head Asks Aid in Crime War," *New York Times,* 4 October 1955, 24; "Lax Parents Assailed," *New York Times,* 4 March 1956, 82; "FBI Head Indicts Adult Community," *New York Times,* 26 May 1957, 67.

30. Memo, FBI Executive Conference to Tolson, 5 August 1955, FBI 80-662-[?]; "Senate Contempt Is Laid to 3 Here," *New York Times,* 13 July 1955, 54.

31. Athan Theoharis and John Stuart Cox, *The Boss: J. Edgar Hoover and the Great American Inquisition* (Philadelphia: Temple University Press, 1988), 96. For the documents relating to this episode marked "OBSCENE," see Dwight Eisenhower Folder, Official & Confidential file of Louis Nichols, Special Collections, Marquette University Library.

32. Memo, [deleted] to Parsons, 29 January 1957, FBI 80-662-[?]; memo, [deleted] to Parsons, 11 February 1958, FBI 80-662-[?]; memo, Griffith to Parsons, 30 January 1959, FBI 80-662-[?]. A card index file (consisting of seven index files) for the Obscene File was created in 1958 to facilitate its use.

33. Memo, SAC Indianapolis to Hoover, 11 June 1957, FBI 62-105761-X; memo, Hoover to SAC Indianapolis, 21 June 1957, FBI 62-105761-X; Jonathan Gathorne-Hardy, *Sex, the Measure of All Things: A Life of Alfred C. Kinsey* (Bloomington: Indiana University Press, 1998), 241.

34. Memo, Sullivan to Belmont, 18 June 1959, FBI 62-105761-X2; memo, SAC Indianapolis to Hoover, 19 July 1957, FBI 62-105761-X1; memo, Sullivan to Belmont, 28 September 1959, FBI 62-105761-[?]; memo, Hoover to Assistant Attorney General Malcolm Wilkey, 13 November 1959, FBI 62-10561-2; memo, Sullivan to Belmont, 13 November 1959, FBI 62-105761-3 (emphasis in original).

35. SAC letter no. 57-52, 16 September 1957, FBI 80-662-NR; Dwight D. Eisenhower, Executive Order 10501, "Safeguarding Official Information in the Interests of the Defense of the United States," 18 *Federal Register* 7049 (5 November 1953); Public Law 83-703, "Atomic Energy Act" (30 August 1954). On the June mail procedure, see Athan Theoharis, *The FBI and American Democracy: A Brief Critical History* (Lawrence: University Press of Kansas, 2004), 111–112.

36. SAC letter no. 57-52, 16 September 1957, FBI 80-662-NR. This document, ironically, was labeled "Obscene Material."

4. Changing Judicial Views on Obscenity, the Nixon Administration, and the FBI

1. On *Hicklin,* see James Paul and Murray Schwartz, *Federal Censorship: Obscenity in the Mail* (Westport, CT: Greenwood Press, 1961), 9–17.

2. *Roth v. United States & Alberts v. California,* 354 US 476 (1957); Paul and Schwartz, *Federal Censorship,* 134–135; Del Dickson, ed., *The Supreme Court in Conference, 1940–1985: The Private Discussions behind Nearly 300 Supreme Court Decisions* (New York: Oxford University Press, 2001), 353.

3. Dickson, *Supreme Court in Conference,* 353–357; *Roth v. United States & Alberts v. California; Kingsley Books, Inc., v. Brown,* 354 US 436 (1957).

4. *Roth v. United States;* John D'Emilio and Estelle B. Freedman, *Intimate Matters: A History of Sexuality in America,* 2nd ed. (Chicago: University of Chicago Press, 1997), 287–288.

5. D'Emilio and Freedman, *Intimate Matters,* 287–288.

6. Memo, [deleted] to DeLoach, 7 July 1959, FBI 80-662-NR (not recorded); Alfred C. Roller, "Merchants of Smut: Pornography Billion-Dollar Business," *Newark Evening News,* 19 June 1959, FBI 80-662-[?] (in some cases the serial number is illegible, as indicated by a bracketed question mark); Marjorie Holmes, "Of Love and Laughter: Parents Are Key in Fight against Pornography Racket," *Evening Star,* 2 June 1959, FBI 80-662-[?].

7. Memo, [deleted] to DeLoach, 7 July 1959, FBI 80-662-NR.

8. Memo, Henry Wolfinger, Records Disposition Division, to Directors of NCD and NNF, re: Disposition Job No. N01-65-78-5, 28 December 1977; Request for Records Disposition Authority, James W. Awe, 15 January 1978; letter, Emil Moschella, Chief of FBI FOIA Section, to Seth Rosenfeld, 11 September 1990, all in author's possession; memo, SAC New York Scheidt to Hoover, 17 April 1952, FBI 94-40980-984, and index card, Adlai Ewing Stevenson, Sex Deviate, both in folder 143, Adlai Stevenson, Hoover Official & Confidential file; memo, [deleted] to DeLoach, 7 July 1959, FBI 80-662-[NR].

9. Memo, SAC Jacksonville to Hoover, 13 July 1959, FBI 80-662-[?]; memo, [deleted] to DeLoach, 27 August 1959, FBI 80-662-[?]; memo, Hoover to SAC Baltimore, 7 August 1959, FBI 80-662-287; memo, SAC Baltimore to Hoover, 18 August 1959, FBI 80-662-288; memo, SAC Jacksonville to Hoover, 14 July 1961, FBI 80-662-[?]; memo, SAC Milwaukee to Hoover, 12 February 1962, FBI 80-662-299; memo, SAC Boston to Hoover, 30

April 1963, FBI 80-662-302; memo, SAC New Orleans to Hoover, 23 August 1966, FBI 80-662-319; memo, SAC Philadelphia to Hoover, 3 April 1967, FBI 80-662-NR; memo, SAC Kansas City, Kansas, to Hoover, 24 March 1967, FBI 80-662-32[?].

10. Ibid.

11. Athan Theoharis, *J. Edgar Hoover, Sex, and Crime* (Chicago: Ivan R. Dee, 1995), 63–65; SAC letter no. 66-19, 29 March 1966, FBI 80-662-NR.

12. Ibid.

13. William C. Sullivan, *The Bureau: My Thirty Years in Hoover's FBI* (New York: W. W. Norton, 1979), 140–141.

14. As quoted in Sanford J. Unger, *FBI* (Boston: Little Brown, 1975), 164.

15. Theoharis, *Hoover, Sex, and Crime*, 64–65.

16. Ibid.

17. Memo, SAC Tampa to Hoover, 17 February 1964, FBI 145-2961-1.

18. Memo, Hoover to SAC Tampa, 28 February 1964, FBI 145-2961-1.

19. Report, FBI laboratory, to SAC Tampa, 4 March 1964, FBI D-443153 AV.

20. Memo, Herbert J. Miller Jr. to Hoover, 13 March 1964; letter, [deleted] to Attorney General Robert Kennedy, 7 February 1964, both in FBI 145-2961-4.

21. Airtel, Hoover to SACs Indianapolis and Tampa, 16 March 1964, FBI 145-2961-4.

22. Memo, SAC Indianapolis to Hoover, 27 March 1964, FBI 145-2961-5; reports, FBI laboratory, to SAC Indianapolis, 17 and 30 April 1964, FBI 145-2961-5.

23. Memo, SAC Indianapolis to Hoover, 20 May 1964, FBI 145-2961-8.

24. Memo, SAC Detroit to Hoover, 22 April 1965, FBI 145-2961-9; memo, SAC New York to Hoover, 23 August 1965, FBI 145-2961-17; report, SAC Detroit, 29 October 1965, FBI 145-2961-18; report, Special Agent [deleted] of Detroit, 6 December 1965, FBI 145-2961-NR.

25. Letter, [deleted] to Hoover, 18 June 1965; letter, Hoover to [deleted], 25 June 1965, FBI 145-2961-13.

26. J. Edgar Hoover, "Combating Merchants of Filth: The Role of the FBI," *University of Pittsburgh Law Review* 25, 3 (March 1964): 469–478.

27. Report, by Special Agents [redacted], 6 November 1968, FBI SF 145-653.

28. Ibid.

29. *Stanley v. Georgia*, 394 US 557(1969).

31. Ibid.; Richard F. Hixson, *Pornography and the Justices: The Supreme Court and the Intractable Obscenity Problem* (Carbondale: Southern Illinois University Press, 1996), 96–97.

31. SAC letter no. 71-44, 13 July 1971, FBI 80-662-NR.

32. Richard M. Scammon and Ben J. Wattenberg, *The Real Majority*, 2nd ed. (New York: Donald I. Fine, 1992), 40–42.

33. Ibid., 43.

34. Robert Mason, *Richard Nixon and the Quest for a New Majority* (Chapel Hill: University of North Carolina Press, 2004), 82.

35. Ibid., 84.

36. Memo, Nixon to Blount, 4 February 1969; memo, Nixon to Mitchell, 4 February 1969, both in Pornographic and Obscene Literature 1969–70 folder, box 27, White House Central Files [WHCF]: Subject Files, PU 2-6, Richard Nixon Presidential Library [RNPL], National Archives and Records Administration, College Park, MD.

37. Memo, Cole to Ehrlichman, 14 March 1969; memo, Butterfield to Blount and Mitchell, 13 March 1969; memo, Butterfield to Ehrlichman, 13 March 1969, all in

Pornographic and Obscene Literature 1969–70 folder, box 27, WHCF: Subject Files, PU 2-6, RNPL.

38. Stephen E. Ambrose, ed., *H. R. Haldeman Diaries: Inside the Nixon White House* (New York: G. P. Putnam's Sons, 1994), 43 (entry for 28 March 1969).

39. "Special Report: The Pornography Explosion," Patrick J. Buchanan to Nixon, 31 March 1969, News Summaries—March 1969 folder, box 30, White House Special Files [WHSF]: Staff Member and Office Files [SMOF], President's Office Files, RNPL; "Transcripts of Acceptance Speeches by Nixon and Agnew to GOP Convention," *New York Times,* 9 August 1968, 20.

40. Personal and confidential memo, Butterfield to Buchanan, 2 April 1969, Pat Buchanan 1969 folder, box 50, WHCF: Subject Files, H. R. Haldeman files, RNPL.

41. Memo, Klein to Cole, 11 April 1969, Pornographic and Obscene Literature 1969–70 folder, box 27, WHCF: Subject Files, PU 2-6, RNPL.

42. Robert Semple, "President Offers Ten-Point Program in Domestic Area," *New York Times,* 15 April 1969; "Text of President's Message to Congress," *New York Times,* 15 April 1969, 28.

43. Walter Rugaber, "Nixon Asks 3 Laws to Stop Increase in Obscene Mail," *New York Times,* 3 May 1969; "Text of Nixon Message on Rise in Obscene Mail," *New York Times,* 3 May 1969, 14.

44. "Text of Nixon Message on Rise in Obscene Mail," 14.

45. Letter, Eleanor Boyd to Moynihan, 4 May 1969; letter, Moynihan to Boyd, 7 May 1969, both in Pornographic and Obscene Literature 1969–70 folder, box 28, WHCF: Subject Files, PU 2-6, RNPL.

46. Athan Theoharis, *Chasing Spies: How the FBI Failed in Counterintelligence But Promoted the Politics of McCarthyism in the Cold War* (Chicago: Ivan R. Dee, 2002), 120. See also John Donovan, *Crusader in the Cold War: A Biography of Fr. John F. Cronin, S.S., 1908–1994* (New York: Peter Lang, 2005).

47. Administratively confidential memo, Dean to Ehrlichman, 16 December 1970; Johnson Executive Order 11154, 8 May 1964, both in Hoover Retirement folder, box 38, WHSF: SMOF, John Dean III files, RNPL.

48. Ambrose, *Haldeman Diaries,* 243, 270 (entries for 4 February and 12 April 1971); memo, Buchanan to Nixon, 12 February 1971, Presidential Memos 1971 folder, box 3, WHSF: SMOF, Pat Buchanan files, RNPL; memo, Buchanan to John Dean, 12 April 1971, and memo, Dean to Buchanan, 16 April 1971, both in Hoover Retirement folder, box 38, WHSF: SMOF, John Dean III files, RNPL.

49. Memo, Griffith to Conrad, 26 December 1968, FBI 80-662-326.

50. Ibid.

51. Memo, Hoover to SACs Baltimore, Chicago, Cleveland, Denver, Detroit, Los Angeles, Miami, New York, Philadelphia, and San Francisco, 17 June 1969, FBI 80-662-NR.

52. As quoted in Theoharis, *Hoover, Sex, and Crime,* 64; Athan Theoharis and John Stuart Cox, *The Boss: J. Edgar Hoover and the Great American Inquisition* (Philadelphia: Temple University Press, 1988), 406–407; Alexander Charns, *Cloak and Gavel: FBI Wiretaps, Bugs, Informers, and the Supreme Court* (Urbana: University of Illinois Press, 1992), 116.

53. Letter, Mrs. S. Murphy to Nixon, 14 April 1970; letter, Donald Santarelli to Murphy, 29 April 1970, both in folder 1 of 4, box 1, WHCF: Subject Files, FG-95, Commission on Obscenity and Pornography, 1969–1970, RNPL.

54. Memo, William Timmons to Nixon, 23 April 1970, Pornographic and Obscene Literature 1969–1970 folder, box 27, WHCF: Subject Files, PU 2–6, RNPL.

55. Memo, Haldeman to Buchanan, 7 September 1970, Staff Memos 1970 B–C folder, box 64, WHSF: SMOF, H. R. Haldeman files, RNPL.

56. Ambrose, *Haldeman Diaries,* 191 (entry for 7 September 1970).

57. Memo, Cole to Ehrlichman, 4 August 1970, 1969–1970 folder, box 1, WHCF: Subject Files, FG-95, Commission on Obscenity and Pornography, 1969–1970, RNPL.

58. Memo, Krogh to Ehrlichman, 10 June 1970; memo, Buchanan to Ehrlichman, 18 May 1970, both in Obscenity and Pornography 1969–1970 folder, box 16, WHSF: SMOF, Egil Krogh files, RNPL; letter, Keating to Nixon, 10 January 1970, folder 2 of 4, box 1, WHCF: Subject Files, FG-95, Commission on Obscenity and Pornography, 1969–1970, RNPL.

59. Memo, Krogh to Ehrlichman, 10 June 1970, Obscenity and Pornography 1969–1970 folder, box 16, WHSF: SMOF, Egil Krogh files, RNPL.

60. Ibid.

61. Memo, Buchanan to Krogh, 22 July 1970, Obscenity and Pornography 1969–1970 folder, box 16, WHSF: SMOF, Egil Krogh files, RNPL.

62. [Second] memo, Buchanan to Krogh, 22 July 1970, Obscenity and Pornography 1969–1970 folder, box 16, WHSF: SMOF, Egil Krogh files, RNPL.

63. Memo, Cole to Ehrlichman, 4 August 1970, 1969–1970 folder, box 1, WHCF: Subject Files, FG-95, Commission on Obscenity and Pornography, 1969–1970, RNPL.

64. Memo, [unknown] to Ehrlichman, 25 August 1970, 1969–70 folder, box 1, WHCF: Subject Files, FG-95, Commission on Obscenity and Pornography, 1969–70, RNPL.

65. Confidential memo, Buchanan to Ehrlichman, 19 August 1970, 1969–1970 folder, box 1, WHCF: Subject Files, FG-95, Commission on Obscenity and Pornography, 1969–70, RNPL.

66. Memo, Charles Colson to John Brown, 14 September 1970, Pornographic and Obscene Literature 1969–1970 folder, box 27, WHCF: Subject Files, PU 2–6, RNPL.

67. Memo, John Dean to Haldeman, 26 September 1970; memo, Dean to Larry Higby, 18 September 1970, both in Obscenity Commission 2 of 2 folder, box 52, WHSF: SMOF, John Dean III files, RNPL.

68. Fred P. Graham, "Nixon Scores Lag in Bills on Crime," *New York Times,* 12 June 1970, 23.

69. Ibid.

70. "Burger Criticizes Obscenity Ruling," *New York Times,* 16 June 1970, 42.

71. "Pornography Curbs Urged by Mitchell," *New York Times,* 23 August 1970, 59; "Concern on Smut Held Unfounded," *New York Times,* 6 August 1970, 22; "Panel's Draft Urges Liberal Pornography Laws," *New York Times,* 9 August 1970, 31.

72. Richard Halloran, "Dissenter Seeks Smut Report Ban," *New York Times,* 9 September 1970, 8; Richard Halloran, "Report on Smut Held up by Court," *New York Times,* 10 September 1970, 23. This is the same Charles Keating who was involved in the 1980s Lincoln Savings and Loan Association scandal.

73. Memo, Buchanan to Haldeman, 9 September 1970, Obscenity Commission 2 of 2 folder, box 52, WHSF: SMOF, John Dean III files, RNPL; Halloran, "Dissenter Seeks Smut Report Ban," 8.

74. Richard Halloran, "Nixon Postal Aide Backs Smut Laws," *New York Times,* 29 September 1970, 11.

75. Confidential eyes only memo, Magruder to Haldeman, 30 September 1970, Obscenity Commission 2 of 2 folder, box 52, WHSF: SMOF, John Dean III files, RNPL.

76. Confidential memo, Dean to Larry Higby, 18 September 1970, Obscenity Commission 2 of 2 folder, box 52, WHSF: SMOF, John Dean III files, RNPL.

77. James M. Naughton, "Epithets Greet Agnew in Salt Lake City," *New York Times*, 1 October 1970, 22.

78. Richard Halloran, "A Federal Panel Asks Relaxation of Curbs on Smut," *New York Times*, 1 October 1970, 1.

79. "Text of Nixon's Statement Rejecting the Report of Obscenity Panel," *New York Times*, 25 October 1970, 71.

80. Ibid.

81. "Smut Panelist Sees Politics in Rebuke," *New York Times*, 26 October 1970, 74.

82. "Nixon Obscenity-Unit Man Sues to Block 'Calcutta!'" *New York Times*, 23 September 1970, 39.

83. Memo, John Dean to David Miller, 6 October 1970, Obscenity Commission 2 of 2 folder, box 52, WHSF: SMOF, John Dean III files, RNPL; "Nixon Obscenity-Unit Man Sues to Block 'Calcutta!'" 39. It is not entirely clear whether Dean was referring to Keating's *Oh! Calcutta* case or the one over the commission's report. The timing, and Dean's previous comment about the play, suggests he may have meant the former. In any event, he sought to praise Keating's efforts.

84. Richard Halloran, "TV 'Oh! Calcutta!' Leads to Charges," *New York Times*, 20 May 1971, 83; letter, Rena Y. Kim, Chief DoJ FOIA Unit, to author, 23 October 2009.

85. Memo, John Dean to Larry Higby, 3 March 1971, Obscenity Report (Illustrated) folder, box 52, WHSF: SMOF, John Dean III files, RNPL.

86. Memo, Assistant Attorney General William Wilson to John Dean, 25 February 1971, Obscenity Report (Illustrated) folder, box 52, WHSF: SMOF, John Dean III files, RNPL.

87. "Illustrated Version of Obscenity Study Brings Indictments," *New York Times*, 6 March 1971, 24; "Smut Trial Goes to Jury on Coast," *New York Times*, 19 December 1971, 71; "4 Are Convicted in Smut Mailing," *New York Times*, 25 December 1971, 22.

88. Everett R. Holles, "Erotica Publisher Tries Today to Win Rehearing in High Court," *New York Times*, 15 October 1974, 23; *Hamling v. United States*, 418 US 87 (1974).

89. Letter, James Haley to William Timmons, 23 March 1971; memo, Jack Caulfield to John Dean, 6 April 1971, 1971–1972 folder, box 1, WHCF: Subject Files, FG-95, Commission on Obscenity and Pornography, 1969–1970, RNPL.

90. Letter, John Dean to Charles Keating, 9 April 1971; letter, Martha A. Lang to Dean, 6 May 1971; letter, Dean to Haley, 25 June 1971, all in 1971–1972 folder, box 1, WHCF: Subject Files, FG-95, Commission on Obscenity and Pornography, 1969–1970, RNPL.

91. Paul S. Boyer, *Purity in Print: Book Censorship in America from the Gilded Age to the Computer Age*, 2nd ed. (Madison: University of Wisconsin Press, 2002), 310.

92. It is interesting to note, however, that FBI officials had a long history of destroying either sensitive or embarrassing documents, and this may have factored into their reasoning. Even today, the FBI destroys files that it has deemed to be of no historical value, without consulting historians.

93. Memo, Griffith to Conrad, 26 December 1968, FBI 80-662-326; memo, Griffith to Conrad, 15 July 1969, FBI 80-662-327; memo, Griffith to Conrad, 11 July 1968, FBI 80-662-325.

94. Memo, Griffith to Conrad, 14 July 1970, FBI 80-662-331.

95. Memo, SAC Baltimore to Hoover, 24 July 1970, FBI 80-662-332; "Ruling Curbs Store Raids," *Baltimore Sun,* 3 June 1970; Elmer Von Feldt, "Comment," *Columbia,* April 1970; "'Pornography Pollution' Theme of Former Judge," *Bible Baptist Tribune,* n.d.; subsequent reports: memo, SAC San Francisco to Hoover, 23 July 1970, FBI 80-662-NR; memo, SAC Philadelphia to Hoover, 22 July 1970, FBI 80-662-NR; memo, SAC Detroit to Hoover, 24 July 1970, FBI 80-662-333; memo, SAC Los Angeles to Hoover, 24 July 1970, FBI 80-662-334; memo, SAC Boston to Hoover, 27 July 1970, FBI 80-662-335; memo, SAC Cleveland to Hoover, 4 August 1970, FBI 80-662-[?]; memo, SAC Cleveland to Hoover, 16 March 1972, FBI 80-662-NR.

96. Sullivan, *The Bureau,* 140.

97. Airtel, Kelley to SACs and assistant directors, 22 December 1976, FBI 80-662-NR.

98. Memo, [deleted] to Conrad, 12 July 1972, FBI 80-662-338.

99. Memo, [deleted] to [deleted], 9 July 1973, FBI 80-662-339; *Miller v. California,* 413 US 15 (1973).

100. Memo, [deleted] to [deleted], 3 July 1974, FBI 80-662-340.

101. Memo, [deleted] to [deleted], 7 July 1975, FBI 80-662-341.

102. Memo, [deleted] to [deleted], 14 July 1976, FBI 80-662-342.

103. Memo, [deleted] to [deleted], 3 October 1977, FBI 80-662-[?].

104. Memo, [deleted] to [deleted], 10 October 1978, FBI 80-662-[?].

105. Memo, [deleted] to [deleted], 17 October 1979, FBI 80-662-[?].

106. Memo, [deleted] to [deleted], 7 April 1977, FBI 80-662-NR.

107. For the sake of continuity and to avoid confusion, I will continue to refer to it as the Obscene File.

108. Memo, [deleted] to [deleted], 3 October 1977, FBI 80-662-[?].

109. Memo, [deleted] to [deleted], 21 October 1980, FBI 80-662-349; memo, [deleted] to [deleted], 7 October 1980, FBI 80-662-350.

5. The FBI's Anti-Obscenity Undercover Operations

1. Athan Theoharis, *J. Edgar Hoover, Sex, and Crime* (Chicago: Ivan R. Dee, 1995), 157; Ronald Kessler, *The Bureau: The Secret History of the FBI* (New York: St. Martin's Press, 2002), 198–199; Webster quoted in Rhodri Jeffreys-Jones, *The FBI: A History* (New Haven, CT: Yale University Press, 2007), 163.

2. Leslie Maitland, "High Officials Are Termed Subjects of a Bribery Investigation by FBI," *New York Times,* 3 February 1980; Athan Theoharis, *The FBI and American Democracy: A Brief Critical History* (Lawrence: University Press of Kansas, 2004), 150.

3. Anthony Marro, "Investigation of Port Corruption Brings Indictment of 22 in Miami," *New York Times,* 9 June 1978, 15; "Virginia Official of Longshoremen's Union Is Indicted," *New York Times,* 9 July 1980, A12; Edward T. Pound, "Informer Tells of Threats and Payoffs of $200,00 in Shipping Industry," *New York Times,* 18 February 1981, A12; Louis J. Freeh, *My FBI* (New York: St. Martin's Press, 2005), 105–112.

4. "Chicago's Court System Is under FBI Inquiry," *New York Times,* 8 August 1983, A12; "Jury Finds Clerk in Chicago Guilty," *New York Times,* 16 March 1984, A13; Athan Theoharis et al., eds., *The FBI: A Comprehensive Reference Guide* (Phoenix: Oryx Press, 1999), 85.

5. Airtel, FBI Director William Webster to SACs Atlanta, Baltimore, Los Angeles, Miami, San Francisco, Washington Field, 18 March 1982, FBI 80–662-[?] (in some cases the serial number is illegible, as indicated by a bracketed question mark).

6. Ibid.

7. Ibid.; memo, [deleted] to [deleted], 24 March 1982, FBI 80-662-353. FBI officials began using computers in December 1978 at the bureau's Washington headquarters.

8. Memo and enclosure, [deleted] to [deleted], 4 January 1982, FBI 80-662-352.

9. Leggs McNeil and Jennifer Osborne, *The Other Hollywood: The Uncensored Oral History of the Porn Film Industry* (New York: HarperCollins, 2005), 199, 200; "Area Porn Distributor Indicted," *Washington Post*, 15 February 1980; "55 Indicted by US as Pornographers and in Film Piracy," *New York Times*, 15 February 1980, A1.

10. Associated Press, "Government's Prosecution Off to a Shaky Start," 24 January 1981.

11. Report of FBI agents [deleted], 16 March 1973, FBI 145-5139-1A.

12. Ibid.

13. Ibid.

14. Memo, SAC Milwaukee to Acting Director FBI, 28 April 1973, FBI 145-5139-2; memo, SAC Milwaukee to FBI director, 31 October 1973, FBI 145-5139-5; memo, SAC Milwaukee to FBI director, 30 September 1974, FBI 145-5139-9.

15. Report, SAC Milwaukee, 21 April 1975, FBI 145-5139-10.

16. *Miller v. California*, 413 US 15 (1973).

17. Judith Kinnard, "Crackdown on Hard-Core Pornography Has Followed Supreme Court Decision," *New York Times*, 7 August 1973, 13.

18. Andrea Friedman, *Prurient Interests: Gender, Democracy, and Obscenity in New York City, 1909–1945* (New York: Columbia University Press, 2000), 198.

19. Results of Interviews with Participants in Making of Motion Picture Film, Entitled, "Deep Throat," n.d., FBI NY 145-3400.

20. Report, SAC Los Angeles, 23 July 1973, FBI 145-5049-12; airtel, SAC New York to FBI director, 26 July 1973, FBI 145-5049-13; airtel, SAC Miami to FBI director, 1 August 1973, FBI 145-5049-14; airtel, SAC Jacksonville to FBI director, FBI 145-5049-16.

21. Airtel, SAC New York to FBI director, 8 August 1973, FBI 145-5049-17.

22. Airtel, SAC New York to FBI director, 15 November 1973, FBI 145-5049-26.

23. Paul Montgomery, "Obscenity Trial of 'Throat' Ends," *New York Times*, 4 January 1973, 34; Paul Montgomery, "'Throat' Obscene, Judge Rules Here," *New York Times*, 2 March 1973, 73; "Exhibitor of 'Deep Throat' Is Fined $100,000," *New York Times*, 13 April 1973, 24.

24. "'Deep Throat' Jury Brings Conviction," *New York Times*, 2 May 1976, 26; Tom Goldstein, "Notables Aid Convicted 'Deep Throat' Star," *New York Times*, 29 June 1976, 26; "Judge Grants New Trial for 'Deep Throat' Star," *New York Times*, 11 April 1977, 12.

25. "8 in 'Deep Throat' Case Receive Prison Sentences," *New York Times*, 1 May 1977, 26.

26. Associated Press, "LA Man Convicted of Trafficking in Obscenity," 25 February 1981.

27. Associated Press, "Dual Life Unravels, Agent Fired by FBI," 15 May 1982.

28. *U.S. v. DiBernardo and Rothstein*, 755 F.2d 1470 (11th Cir. 1985); Associated Press, "Court Won't Hear Appeal in FBI Obscenity Case," 5 May 1986; McNeil and Osborne, *The Other Hollywood*, 205.

29. Memo, Additional Successes against Organized Crime, John Roberts to Kenneth Star, 8 June 1983, Organized Crime Folder, Correspondence Files of Kenneth Star, 1981–1983, box 5, Record Group 60, National Archives and Records Administration (NARA), College Park, MD; telephone conversation between the author and the FBI's Freedom of Information Act (FOIA) office, 19 June 2009.

30. Memo, [deleted] to [deleted], 18 January 1978, FBI 145-5627-37; memo, SAC Miami to FBI director, 19 April 1978, FBI 145-5627-NR (not recorded).

31. Memo, FBI Director Kelley to Assistant Attorney General, Criminal Division, 24 October 1975, FBI 145-5627-5; U.S. Customs Service, Report of Investigation, 18 September 1975, ICE.10.1367.0000018 (FOIA document).

32. Airtel, SAC WFO to FBI director, 9 January 1977, FBI 145-5627-35. For the "spin-off" description, see airtel, SAC Baltimore to FBI director, 5 April 1982, FBI 145-5627-NR.

33. Airtel, SAC WFO to FBI director, 9 January 1977, FBI 145-5627-35.

34. Ibid.

35. Ibid.

36. Ibid.

37. Ibid.; memo, [deleted] to [deleted], 18 January 1978, FBI 145-5627-37.

38. Airtel, SAC Baltimore to FBI director, 15 February 1979, FBI 145-5627-140; airtel, SAC Washington Field Office to FBI director, 13 March 1979, FBI 145-5627-143; airtel, FBI director to SAC Washington Field Office, 19 March 1979, FBI 145-5627-144.

39. Joe Pichirallo, "FBI Arrests 7 in Md. in Pornography Probe," *Washington Post,* 28 May 1981; memo, SAC Baltimore to FBI director, 9 July 1979, FBI 145-5627-NR; airtel, SAC Miami to FBI director, 5 January 1979, FBI 145-5627-125; Airtel, FBI director to SAC Baltimore, 27 February 1979, FBI 145-5627-131.

40. Joe Pichirallo, "FBI Arrests 7 in Md. In Pornography Probe," *Washington Post,* 28 May 1981; airtel, SAC Baltimore to FBI director, 4 November 1980, FBI 145-5627-327.

41. Airtel, SAC Baltimore to FBI director, 12 July 1979, FBI 145-5627-169X; airtel, SAC Baltimore to FBI director, 24 October 1979, FBI 145-5627-202.

42. Airtel, SAC Baltimore to FBI director, 29 April 1980, FBI 145-5627-318.

43. Airtel, SAC Baltimore to FBI director, 4 November 1980, FBI 145-5627-327.

44. Ibid.

45. Pichirallo, "FBI Arrests 7 in Md. Pornography Probe"; Associated Press, "Eight Indicted in Federal Pornography Investigation," 28 May 1981; teletype, SAC Baltimore to FBI director, 28 May 1981, FBI 145-5627-371; teletype, SAC Baltimore to FBI director, 19 May 1981, FBI 145-5627-372.

46. Airtel, SAC Baltimore to FBI director, 22 July 1981, FBI 145-5627-383.

47. Airtel, SAC Baltimore to FBI director, 3 August 1981, FBI 145-5627-386; Pichirallo, "FBI Arrests 7 in Md. Pornography Probe."

48. Airtel, SAC Baltimore to FBI director, 26 January 1982, FBI 145-5627-393X.

49. Teletype, SAC Baltimore to FBI director, 2 March 1982, FBI 145-5627-394X.

50. Teletype, SAC Baltimore to FBI director, 19 April 1982, FBI 145-5627-397X.

51. Teletype, SAC Baltimore to FBI director, 27 April 1982, FBI 145-5627-400.

52. Teletype, SAC Baltimore to FBI director, 8 May 1982, FBI 145-5627-400X.

53. Teletype, SAC Baltimore to FBI director, 23 July 1982, FBI 145-5627-408.

54. Airtel, SAC Baltimore to FBI director, 14 September 1982, FBI 145-5627-413; criminal docket for *USA v. Gresser et al.,* case #1:81-cr-00251-1, U.S. District Court, District of Maryland (Baltimore), 9 September 1982.

55. Normally, a special agent in charge (SAC) commands an FBI field office. But in very large field offices such as those in New York City, Washington, D.C., and Los Angeles, the field office also oversees smaller resident agencies, and the person in charge is an ADIC (which outranks an SAC).

56. Airtel, ADIC Los Angeles to FBI director, 8 October 1975, FBI 183-386-1.

57. Ibid.

58. Ibid.

59. Ibid.

60. Ibid.

61. Ibid.

62. Airtel, FBI director to SAC Los Angeles, 17 October 1975, FBI 183-386-2. The document uses the title SAC.

63. Airtel, ADIC Los Angeles to FBI director, 20 October 1975, FBI 183-386-5.

64. Nitel, Los Angeles to Director, 13 January 1976, FBI 183-701-X3.

65. Nitel, FBI director to SAC Los Angeles, 15 January 1976, FBI 183-701-X3; airtel, FBI director to ADIC Los Angeles, 20 January 1976, FBI 183-701-X4.

66. Airtel, ADIC Los Angeles to FBI director, 23 March 1976, FBI 183-701-X6.

67. Ibid.; teletype, Los Angeles to FBI director, 21 November 1977, FBI 183-701-78.

68. Ibid.; airtel, SAC San Diego to FBI director, 30 March 1976, FBI 183-701-X7.

69. Memo, R. J. McCarthy to Mr. Fehl, 9 April 1976, FBI 183-701-1; nitel, FBI director to SACs Los Angeles and San Diego, 26 April 1976, FBI 183-701-4.

70. Memo, FBI director to Assistant Attorney General, Criminal Division, 28 April 1976, FBI 182-701-5; airtel, FBI director to SAC Los Angeles, 30 April 1976, FBI 182-701-5; teletype, Los Angeles to Director, 23 April 1976, FBI 183-701-7; nitel, Los Angeles to Director, 5 May 1976, FBI 183-701-9; action memo, FBI director to Assistant Attorney General, Criminal Division, 25 May 1976, FBI 183-701-11; action memo, FBI director to Assistant Attorney General, Criminal Division, 26 May 1976, FBI 183-701-12.

71. Teletype, SAC Los Angeles to FBI director, 21 May 1976, FBI 183-701-11.

72. Teletype, SAC Los Angeles to FBI director, 7 June 1976, FBI 183-701-13; unspecific document, Special Investigative Division, 14 June 1976, no file number but in PORNEX file; teletype, ADIC Los Angeles to FBI director and SAC San Diego, 14 June 1976, FBI 183-701-16; airtel, ADIC Los Angeles to FBI director, 16 August 1976, FBI 183-701-35.

73. Airtel, SAC San Diego to FBI director, 14 July 1976, FBI 183-701-29; airtel, FBI director to SAC San Diego, 19 July 1976, FBI 183-701-27.

74. Teletype, ADIC Los Angeles to FBI director, 16 August 1976, FBI 183-701-34; airtel, ADIC Los Angeles to FBI director, 16 August 1976, FBI 183-701-35.

75. Microphone transcription of conversation between undercover FBI agent [deleted] and Jack Lo Cicero and Tommy Ricciardi, 19 August 1976, in report, ADIC Los Angeles, 8 November 1976, FBI 183-701-65.

76. Memo, E. J. Sharp to Mr. Fehl, 25 August 1976, FBI 183-701-38; transcription of recorded conversation between undercover FBI agents [deleted] and Jack Lo Cicero and Tommy Ricciardi, 23 August 1976, in report, ADIC Los Angeles, 8 November 1976, FBI 183-701-65.

77. Ibid.

78. Teletype, FBI director to ADIC Los Angeles, 27 August 1976, FBI 183-701-39.

79. Unspecific document, Special Investigative Division, 30 August 1976, no file number but in PORNEX file; teletype, ADIC Los Angeles to FBI director, 27 August 1976, FBI 183-701-40; report, ADIC Los Angeles, 8 November 1976, FBI 183-701-65.

80. Teletype, ADIC Los Angeles to FBI director, 7 September 1976, FBI 183-701-42; teletype, FBI director to ADIC Los Angeles, 8 September 1976, FBI 183-701-42.

81. Memo, FBI director to Assistant Attorney General, Criminal Division, 10 September 1976, FBI 183-701-48.

82. Teletype, ADIC Los Angeles to FBI director, 14 September 1976, FBI 183-701-52.

83. Ibid.; teletype, ADIC Los Angeles to FBI director, 10 September 1976, FBI 183-701-54.

84. Teletype, ADIC Los Angeles to FBI director, 14 October 1976, FBI 183-701-60; teletype, ADIC Los Angeles to FBI director, 5 November 1976, FBI 183-701-64.

85. Airtel, ADIC Los Angeles to FBI director, 16 March 1977, FBI 183-701-70.

86. Teletype, Los Angeles to FBI director and New York, 22 November 1977, FBI 183-701-79.

87. Airtel, FBI director to ADIC Los Angeles, 10 June 1977, FBI 183-701-NR.

88. Teletype, Los Angeles to FBI director, 21 November 1977, FBI 183-701-78.

89. Memo, SAC Los Angeles to FBI director, 22 November 1977, FBI 183-701-74; memo, SAC Los Angeles to FBI director, 22 November 1977, FBI 183-701-75.

90. Teletype, San Francisco to FBI director, 23 November 1977, FBI 183-701-76; teletype, SAC Los Angeles to Bureau [HQ] and New York, 28 November 1977, FBI 183-701-77; report, SAC Los Angeles, 28 November 1977, FBI 183-701-80.

91. Teletype, Los Angeles to FBI director, 7 February 1978, and DoJ memo on GANG-MURS, 8 February 1978, FBI 183-701-83; teletype, Los Angeles to FBI director, San Francisco, San Diego, Cleveland, 1 March 1978, FBI 183-701- 84; teletype, San Diego to FBI director, 22 May 1978, FBI 183-701-99; DoJ memo on GANGMURS, 1 March 1978, FBI 183-701-84; memo, Additional Successes against Organized Crime, John Roberts to Kenneth Star, 8 June 1983, Organized Crime Folder, Correspondence Files of Kenneth Star, 1981–1983, box 5, Record Group 60, NARA.

92. Teletype, Los Angeles to FBI director, 16 March 1978, FBI 183-701-86; report, SAC Los Angeles, 20 March 1978, FBI 183-701-89; teletype, San Diego to FBI director, 22 May 1978, FBI 183-701-99; teletype, Los Angeles to FBI director, [?] November 1980, FBI 183-701-183.

93. Teletype, Los Angeles to FBI headquarters, San Diego, San Francisco, 26 May 1978, FBI 183-701-95; teletype, Los Angeles to FBI headquarters, 12 May 1978, FBI 183-701-96.

94. Teletype, Los Angeles to FBI director, 16 June 1978, FBI 183-701-101.

95. Teletype, Los Angeles to FBI director, 21 October 1978, FBI 183-701-122X1; teletype, Los Angeles to FBI director, 15 November 1978, FBI 183-701-125X; teletype, Los Angeles to FBI director, 15 February 1979, FBI 183-701-134; teletype, Los Angeles to FBI director, 21 February 1979, FBI 183-701-138; teletype, Los Angeles to FBI director, 23 May 1979, FBI 183-701-146x; teletype, Los Angeles to FBI headquarters, 12 October 1979, FBI 183-701-156X; teletype, Los Angeles to FIB director, 21 November 1979, FBI 183-701-157; airtel, SAC Los Angeles to FBI director, 12 February 1980, FBI 183-701-160; airtel, SAC Los Angeles to FBI director, 20 February 1980, FBI 183-701-161.

96. Teletype, Los Angeles to FBI headquarters, 19 March 1980, FBI 183-701-162.

97. Memo, Criminal Investigative Division, 19 May 1980, FBI 183-701-163; teletype, Los Angeles to FBI headquarters, 29 May 1980, FBI 183-701-164; teletype, Los Angeles to FBI director, 10 October 1980, FBI 183-701-170.

98. Teletype, Los Angeles to FBI director, 14 November 1980, FBI 183-701-178; "Five Accused of Mafia Ties Found Guilty of Conspiracy," *Washington Post*, 15 November 1980.

99. Teletype, Los Angeles to FBI director, 21 January 1981, FBI 183-701-185.

100. Teletype, Los Angeles to FBI director, [?] November 1980, FBI 183-701-183.

101. Ronald Koziol, "Californians: The Shame of the Mob," *Chicago Tribune,* 25 November 1980.

102. Airtel, SAC, WFO, to FBI director, 13 July 1981, FBI 145-6053-154X1; airtel, SAC, WFO, to FBI director, 25 February 1981, FBI 145-6053-50X.

103. Teletype, SAC, WFO, to FBI director, 4 May 1981, FBI 145-567-6; blind memo, FAST PLAY, 13 April 1982, FBI 145-6053-273.

104. Blind memo, FAST PLAY, 13 April 1982, FBI 145-6053-273.

105. Ibid.

106. Teletype, SAC, WFO, to FBI director, 30 September 1981, FBI 145-6053-194.

107. Airtel, SAC, WFO, to FBI director, 16 September 1981, FBI 145-6053-196.

108. Teletype, SAC, WFO, to FBI director, 24 December 1981, FBI 145-6053-2389; blind memo, FAST PLAY, 13 April 1982, FBI 145-6053-273.

109. Blind memo, FAST PLAY, 13 April 1982, FBI 145-6053-273.

6. The End of the Obscene File and the Temporary Revival of the FBI's Role in Adult Obscenity

1. Memo, [deleted] to [deleted], 8 September 1981, FBI 80-662-351; MBO write-up, [deleted] to [deleted], 12 February 1981, FBI 80-662-NR (not recorded); Ronald Kessler, *The FBI* (New York: Pocket Books, 1983), 117.

2. Memo and MBO write-up, [deleted] to [deleted], 4 January 1982, FBI 80-662-352; memo and MBO write-up, [deleted] to [deleted], 29 June 1982, FBI 80-662-354; memo and MBO write-up, [deleted] to [deleted], 30 December 1982, FBI 80-662-355.

3. Memo, [deleted] to [deleted], 3 July 1984, FBI 80-662-356.

4. Memo [SAC letter] no. 20-86, 8 July 1986, FBI 80-662-NR; Robert Pear, "Panel Calls on Citizens to Wage National Assault on Pornography," *New York Times,* 10 July 1986, A1.

5. Ronald Reagan, Message to the Congress Transmitting Proposed Legislation on Child Protection and Obscenity Enforcement, 10 November 1987, in John T. Woolley and Gerhard Peters, The American Presidency Project [online], hosted by the University of California–Santa Barbara, http://www.presidency.ucsb.edu/ws/?pid=33677.

6. Edwin Meese III, *With Reagan: The Inside Story* (Washington, DC: Regnery, 1992), 312–313.

7. Reagan, Message to Congress Transmitting Proposed Legislation on Child Protection and Obscenity Enforcement.

8. Memo [SAC letter] no. 20-86, 8 July 1986, FBI 80-662-NR; "Meese Names Panel to Study How to Control Pornography," *New York Times,* 21 May 1985, A21; "Obscenity Report Nears Completion," *New York Times,* 3 May 1986, 36; Pear, "Panel Calls on Citizens," A1.

9. Memo [SAC letter] no. 20-86, 8 July 1986, FBI 80-662-NR.

10. Ibid.

11. Ibid.

12. Ibid.

13. Ibid.

14. Memo, [deleted] to [deleted], 12 September 1986, FBI 80-662-357; memo, [deleted] to [deleted], 13 September 1986, FBI 80-662-358; memo, [deleted] to [deleted], 7 November 1986, FBI 80-662-359; Philip Shenon, "Justice Dept. to Form Team to Handle Obscenity Cases," *New York Times,* 18 October 1986, 6; Philip Shenon, "Meese, in a Move on Pornography, Creates Special Prosecution Team," *New York Times,* 23 October 1986, A21; Katherine Bishop, "Justice Dept. Team Leading Broad Effort on Obscenity," *New York Times,* 22 August 1987, 6.

15. Memo, [deleted] to [deleted], 7 November 1986, FBI 80-662-359.

16. Memo, R. T. Castonguay to [deleted], 14 November 1988, FBI 80-662-360.

17. Ibid.

18. Addendum: Legal Council Division, 27 February 1988 [*sic;* 1989], to memo, R. T. Castonguay to [deleted], 14 November 1988, FBI 80-662-360; memorandum of understanding between the USCS and FBI, 23 May 1989, Roger T. Castonguay, assistant director of FBI Laboratory Division and William P. Rosenblatt, assistant commissioner for enforcement, USCS, FBI 80-662-360.

19. Memo, Executive Correspondence, Director Smuggling Investigations Division, U.S. Customs Service to [deleted], FBI Special Photo Unit, 28 June 1989, FBI 80-662-361; memo, [deleted] to Castonguay, 18 July 1989, FBI 80-662-362; memo, [deleted] to Castonguay, 18 July 1989, FBI 80-662-363; custody receipt, U.S. Customs Service to FBI, 8 February 1990, FBI 80-662-364; custody receipt, U.S. Customs Service to FBI, 24 May 1990, FBI 80-662-365; inventory sheet, n.d., FBI 80-662-365; U.S. Customs Service to FBI, 24 May 1990, FBI 80-662-366; custody receipt, U.S. Customs Service to FBI, 20 March 1989, FBI [no file number].

20. FBI teletype, SAC Los Angeles to FBI director, 6 October 1989, FBI 157-35228-1.

21. Airtel, FBI Director Louis Freeh to All SACs, 5 March 1993, FBI 80-662-367.

22. Ibid.

23. Memo, Prosecutions under the Federal Obscenity Statutes, Deputy Attorney General Eric Holder to U.S. Attorneys, 10 June 1998, http://www.justice.gov/dag/readingroom/obscen.htm.

24. Whitney Strub, *Perversion for Profit: The Politics of Pornography and the Rise of the New Right* (New York: Columbia University Press, 2011), 281; "It's Curtains for Modesty Drapes," *New York Times,* 25 June 2005, 11; memo, Supervisory Special Agent [deleted], Violent Crimes and Major Offenders Section, Crimes Against Children Unit, CID to All Field Offices, 24 February 2004, FBI 66F-HQC1256307.

25. Memo, Supervisory Special Agent [deleted], Violent Crimes and Major Offenders Section, Crimes Against Children Unit, CID to All Field Offices, 24 February 2004, FBI 66F-HQC1256307.

26. Ibid.

27. Press release, Obscenity Prosecution Task Force Established to Investigate, Prosecute Purveyors of Obscene Materials, U.S. Department of Justice, 5 May 2005; memo, Supervisory Special Agent [deleted], Violent Crimes Section, Violent Crimes Unit of the CID to All Field Offices, 29 July 2005, FBI 319W-HQ-A1487699-CID; memo, Supervisory Special Agent [deleted], Violent Crimes Section, Violent Crimes Unit of the CID to Washington Field Office, 29 July 2005, FBI 319W-HQ-A1487699-CID; memo, Supervisory Special Agent [deleted], Violent Crimes Section, Violent Crimes Unit of the CID to All Field Offices, 5 September 2006, FBI 319W-HQ-A1487699-CID. See also Barton Gellman, "Recruits Sought for Porn Squad," *Washington Post,* 20 September 2005.

28. Press release, National Operator of Sexually Oriented Business Pleads Guilty to Federal Obscenity and Tax Charges, U.S. Department of Justice, 4 November 2005.

29. As quoted in Gellman, "Recruits Sought for Porn Squad."

30. Paul Krassner, "Meet an FBI Porn Squad Agent," *Huffington Post,* 22 January 2006, http://www.huffingtonpost.com.

31. Ibid.

32. Memo, Supervisory Special Agent [deleted], Violent Crimes Section, Violent Crimes Unit of the CID to All Field Offices, 29 July 2005, FBI 319W-HQ-A1487699-CID; memo, Supervisory Special Agent [deleted], Violent Crimes Section, Violent Crimes Unit of the CID to Washington Field Office, 29 July 2005, FBI 319W-HQ-A1487699-CID; memo, Supervisory Special Agent [deleted], Violent Crimes Section, Violent Crimes Unit of the CID to All Field Offices, 5 September 2006, FBI 319W-HQ-A1487699-CID; Krassner, "Meet an FBI Porn Squad Agent."

33. Memo, Supervisory Special Agent [deleted], Violent Crimes Section, Violent Crimes Unit of the CID to Washington Field Office, 29 July 2005, FBI 319W-HQ-A1487699-CID.

34. Congressional testimony, statement of James H. Burrus, deputy assistant director, Criminal Investigative Division, FBI, in U.S. Senate, *Protecting Children on the Internet, Hearing before the U.S. Senate Committee on Commerce, Science and Transportation,* 109th Cong., 2nd sess., 19 January 2006 (Washington, DC: U.S. Government Printing Office, 2006), 8–11.

35. Ibid.

36. United States Attorneys—Criminal Caseload Statistics, Obscenity Program Category Code, Fiscal Years 2001–2009, United States Department of Justice, Washington, DC (sent to the author by the Justice Department upon request).

37. Matt Canham, "Hatch Says Feds Should Expand Porn Prosecutions," *Salt Lake Tribune,* 15 April 2010.

38. Letter, Senator Orrin G. Hatch et al. to Attorney General Eric H. Holder Jr., 4 April 2011, http://www.politico.com.

39. Josh Gerstein, "Senators Ask Holder for More Pornography Prosecutions," 7 April 2011, http://www.politico.com/blogs/joshgerstein/0411/Senators_ask_Holder_for_more_pornography_prosecutions.html?showall.

40. Letter, Assistant Attorney General Ronald Weich to Senator Orrin Hatch, 15 April 2011, http://www.politico.com.

41. Josh Gerstein, "Holder Accused of Neglecting Porn," 16 April 2011, http://www.politico.com/news/stories/0411/53314.html.

SELECTED BIBLIOGRAPHY

Manuscript Sources

Federal Bureau of Investigation (Freedom of Information Act [FOIA])
ACT-UP file
Adult Obscenity Initiative files, 2005–2006
Alfred Kinsey file
Andy Warhol file
Bud Costello file
Cardinal Francis Spellman file
CLEAN STREETS file
FAST PLAY file
Gerard Damiano file (director of *Deep Throat*)
Lou Abbott file
Louie Louie file
Obscene File, administrative file
PORNEX file

Marquette University, Special Collections and University Archives, Milwaukee, WI
FBI Investigation and Surveillance Records
    Bureau Bulletins File
    Official & Confidential File of J. Edgar Hoover
    Official & Confidential File of Louis Nichols
    SAC Letters File

U.S. Department of Homeland Security: U.S. Customs Service
Report of Investigation, 18 September 1975 (FOIA)

National Archives and Records Administration, College Park, MD
Record Group 60, Department of Justice
    Correspondence Files of Kenneth Star
Richard Nixon Presidential Materials
    White House Central File
        Subject Categories
            FG 95 Pres. Commission on Obscenity and Pornography
            FG-17 Department of Justice
            FG 17–5 FBI
            PU 2–6 Publications: Pornographic & Obscene Literature
    White House Special Files
        Staff Member & Office Files
            Egil Krogh papers
            John Dean papers
            Pat Buchanan
            Alexander Butterfield

H. R. Haldeman
President's Personal File
President's Official File

U.S. Department of Justice, Washington, DC
Electronic Reading Room, http://www.justice.gov/dag/readingroom/obscen.htm
United States Attorneys—Criminal Caseload Statistics, Obscenity Program Category
   Code, Fiscal Years 2001–2009

Primary and Secondary Sources

Allen, Frederick Lewis. *Only Yesterday: An Informal History of the 1920s.* New York:
   Harper & Row, 1931.
Ambrose, Stephen. *Nixon: The Triumph of a Politician, 1962–1972.* New York: Simon &
   Schuster, 1989.
——, ed. *H. R. Haldeman Diaries: Inside the Nixon White House.* New York: G. P. Put-
   nam's Sons, 1994.
Baldwin, Fred D. "The Invisible Armor." *American Quarterly* 16 (Autumn 1964):
   432–444.
Boyer, Paul S. *Purity in Print: Book Censorship in America from the Gilded Age to the Com-
   puter Age.* 2nd ed. Madison: University of Wisconsin Press, 2002.
Brantley, Will. "The Surveillance of Georgia Writer and Civil Rights Activist Lillian
   Smith: Another Story from the Federal Bureau of Investigation." *Georgia Historical
   Quarterly* 85, 1 (Spring 2001): 59–82.
Burrough, Bryan. *Public Enemies: America's Greatest Crime Wave and the Birth of the
   FBI, 1933–34.* New York: Penguin Press, 2004.
Charles, Douglas M. "'Before the Colonel Arrived': Hoover, Donovan, Roosevelt, and
   the Origins of American Central Intelligence." *Intelligence and National Security* 20
   (Summer 2005): 225–237.
——. "From Subversion to Obscenity: The FBI's Investigations of the Early Homo-
   phile Movement in the United States, 1953–1958." *Journal of the History of Sexuality*
   19, 2 (May 2010): 262–287.
——. *J. Edgar Hoover and the Anti-interventionists: FBI Political Surveillance and the Rise
   of the Domestic Security State, 1939–45.* Columbus: Ohio State University Press, 2007.
Charns, Alexander. *Cloak and Gavel: FBI Wiretaps, Bugs, Informers, and the Supreme
   Court.* Urbana: University of Illinois Press, 1992.
Dean, John. *Blind Ambition.* New York: Pocket Books, 1977.
Dean, Robert. *Imperial Brotherhood: Gender and the Making of Cold War Foreign Policy.*
   Amherst: University of Massachusetts Press, 2001.
DeLoach, Cartha D. *Hoover's FBI: The Inside Story by Hoover's Trusted Lieutenant.* Wash-
   ington, DC: Regnery, 1995.
D'Emilio, John, and Estelle B. Freedman. *Intimate Matters: A History of Sexuality in
   America.* 2nd ed. Chicago: University of Chicago Press, 1997.
Dennis, Donna. *Licentious Gotham: Erotic Publishing and Its Prosecution in Nineteenth-
   Century New York.* Cambridge, MA: Harvard University Press, 2009.
——. "Obscenity Regulation, New York City, and the Creation of American Erotica,
   1820–1880." Ph.D. dissertation, Princeton University, 2005.

Dickson, Del, ed. *The Supreme Court in Conference, 1940–1985: The Private Discussions behind Nearly 300 Supreme Court Decisions.* New York: Oxford University Press, 2001.

Donovan, John. *Crusader in the Cold War: A Biography of Fr. John F. Cronin, S.S., 1908–1994.* New York: Peter Lang, 2005.

Eisenhower, Dwight D. Executive Order 10501. "Safeguarding Official Information in the Interests of the Defense of the United States." 18 *Federal Register* 7049 (5 November 1953).

Ferris, William R., Jr. "Racial Repertoires among Blues Performers." *Ethnomusicology* 14 (September 1970): 439–449.

Finch, Stanley. "The White Slave Traffic." In *Self Knowledge and Guide to Sex Instruction,* ed. Thomas W. Shannon. Marietta, OH: S. A. Mullikin, 1913.

———. "The White-Slave Traffic." In *White Slavery Today,* ed. Ernest A. Bell, 91–100. Chicago: Lincoln Walter, 1917.

Freeh, Louis J. *My FBI.* New York: St. Martin's Press, 2005.

Friedman, Andrea. *Prurient Interests: Gender, Democracy, and Obscenity in New York City, 1909–1945.* New York: Columbia University Press, 2000.

Gathorne-Hardy, Jonathan. *Sex, the Measure of All Things: A Life of Alfred C. Kinsey.* Bloomington: Indiana University Press, 1998.

Gertzman, Jay. "John Saxton Sumner of the New York Society for the Suppression of Vice: A Chief Smut-Eradicator of the Interwar Period." *Journal of American Culture* 17, 2 (Summer 1994): 41–47.

Gilbert, James. *A Cycle of Outrage: America's Reaction to the Juvenile Delinquent in the 1950s.* New York: Oxford University Press, 1986.

Haines, Gerald K., and David A. Langbart. *Unlocking the Files of the FBI: A Guide to Its Records and Classifications System.* Wilmington, DE: Scholarly Resources, 1993.

Haney, Robert W. *Comstockery in America: Patterns of Censorship and Control.* New York: DaCapo Press, 1974.

Harrison, Maureen, and Steve Gilbert, eds. *Utterly without Redeeming Social Value: Obscenity and Pornography Decisions of the United States Supreme Court.* Carlsbad, CA: Excellent Books, 2000.

Hixson, Richard F. *Pornography and the Justices: The Supreme Court and the Intractable Obscenity Problem.* Carbondale: Southern Illinois University Press, 1996.

Hoff, Joan. *Nixon Reconsidered.* New York: Basic Books, 1994.

Holt, Michael F. *The Rise and Fall of the American Whig Party: Jacksonian Politics and the Onset of the Civil War.* New York: Oxford University Press, 1999.

Hoover, J. Edgar. "Combating Merchants of Filth: The Role of the FBI." *University of Pittsburgh Law Review* 25, 3 (March 1964): 469–478.

———. *Masters of Deceit: The Story of Communism in America and How to Fight It.* New York: Henry Holt, 1958.

Horowitz, Helen Lefkowitz. "Victoria Woodhull, Anthony Comstock, and Conflict over Sex in the United States in the 1870s." *Journal of American History* 87, 2 (September 2000): 403–434.

Howe, Daniel Walker. *What Hath God Wrought: The Transformation of America, 1815–1848.* New York: Oxford University Press, 2007.

Hyde, Montgomery. *A History of Pornography.* London: Heinemann, 1963.

Jeffreys-Jones, Rhodri. *The FBI: A History.* New Haven, CT: Yale University Press, 2007.

Johnson, David K. *The Lavender Scare: The Cold War Persecution of Gays and Lesbians in the Federal Government.* Chicago: University of Chicago Press, 2004.

Jones, James H. *Alfred C. Kinsey: A Life.* New York: W. W. Norton, 1997.

Kessler, Ronald. *The Bureau: The Secret History of the FBI.* New York: St. Martin's Press, 2002.

Langum, David J. *Crossing over the Line: Legislating Morality and the Mann Act.* Chicago: University of Chicago Press, 1994.

Lukas, J. Anthony. *Nightmare: The Underside of the Nixon Years.* Athens: Ohio University Press, 1999.

Mason, Robert. *Richard Nixon and the Quest for a New Majority.* Chapel Hill: University of North Carolina Press, 2004.

McGarry, Molly. "Spectral Sexualities: Nineteenth-Century Spiritualism, Moral Panics, and the Making of U.S. Obscenity Law." *Journal of Women's History* 12, 2 (Summer 2000): 8–29.

McNeil, Leggs, and Jennifer Osborne. *The Other Hollywood: The Uncensored Oral History of the Porn Film Industry.* New York: HarperCollins, 2005.

Meese, Edwin, III. *With Reagan: The Inside Story.* Washington, DC: Regnery, 1992.

Murray, Robert K. *Red Scare: A Study in National Hysteria, 1919–1920.* Minneapolis: University of Minnesota Press, 1955.

O'Reilly, Kenneth. *Hoover and the Un-Americans: The FBI, HUAC, and the Red Menace.* Philadelphia: Temple University Press, 1983.

Patterson, James T. *Grand Expectations: The United States, 1945–1974.* New York: Oxford University Press, 1996.

Paul, James, and Murray Schwartz. *Federal Censorship: Obscenity in the Mail.* Westport, CT: Greenwood Press, 1961.

Perlstein, Rick. *Nixonland: The Rise of a President and the Fracturing of America.* New York: Scribner, 2008.

Powers, Richard Gid. *Broken: The Troubled Past and Uncertain Future of the FBI.* New York: Free Press, 2004.

———. *G-Men: Hoover's FBI in American Popular Culture.* Carbondale: Southern Illinois University Press, 1983.

———. *Secrecy and Power: The Life of J. Edgar Hoover.* New York: Free Press, 1987.

Preston, William, Jr. *Aliens and Dissenters: Federal Suppression of Radicals, 1903–33.* 2nd ed. Chicago: University of Illinois Press, 1994.

Reagan, Ronald. Message to the Congress Transmitting Proposed Legislation on Child Protection and Obscenity Enforcement. 10 November 1987. In John T. Woolley and Gerhard Peters, The American Presidency Project [online]. Hosted by the University of California–Santa Barbara. http://www.presidency.ucsb.edu/ws/?pid=33677.

Scammon, Richard M., and Ben J. Wattenberg. *The Real Majority.* 2nd ed. New York: Donald I. Fine, 1992.

Shannon, Thomas W. *Ethics of the Unmarried, or Spooning.* Cincinnati: S. A. Mullikin, 1913.

———. *Eugenics: Nature's Secrets Revealed, Scientific Knowledge of the Laws of Sex, Life, and Heredity or Know Thyself.* Marietta, OH: S. A. Mullikin, 1920.

———, ed. *Self Knowledge and Guide to Sex Instruction.* Marietta, OH: S. A. Mullikin, 1913.

Small, Melvin. *The Presidency of Richard Nixon.* Lawrence: University Press of Kansas, 1999.

Strub, Whitney. *Perversion for Profit: The Politics of Pornography and the Rise of the New Right.* New York: Columbia University Press, 2011.

Sullivan, William C. *The Bureau: My Thirty Years in Hoover's FBI.* New York: W. W. Norton, 1979.

Theoharis, Athan. *Abuse of Power: How Cold War Surveillance and Secrecy Policy Shaped the Response to 9/11.* Philadelphia: Temple University Press, 2011.

———. *Chasing Spies: How the FBI Failed in Counterintelligence But Promoted the Politics of McCarthyism in the Cold War Years.* Chicago: Ivan R. Dee, 2002.

———. *The FBI: An Annotated Bibliography and Research Guide.* New York: Garland Publishing, 1994.

———. *The FBI and American Democracy: A Brief Critical History.* Lawrence: University Press of Kansas, 2004.

———. *From the Secret Files of J. Edgar Hoover.* Chicago: Ivan R. Dee, 1991.

———. *J. Edgar Hoover, Sex, and Crime.* Chicago: Ivan R. Dee, 1995.

———. *The Quest for Absolute Security: The Failed Intelligence Relations among U.S. Intelligence Agencies.* Chicago: Ivan R. Dee, 2007.

———. "Secrecy and Power: Unanticipated Problems in Researching FBI File." *Political Science Quarterly* 119, 2 (2004): 271–290.

———. *Spying on Americans: Political Surveillance from Hoover to the Huston Plan.* Philadelphia: Temple University Press, 1978.

———, ed. *A Culture of Secrecy: The Government versus the People's Right to Know.* Lawrence: University Press of Kansas, 1998.

Theoharis, Athan, and John Stuart Cox. *The Boss: J. Edgar Hoover and the Great American Inquisition.* Philadelphia: Temple University Press, 1988.

Theoharis, Athan, et al., eds. *The FBI: A Comprehensive Reference Guide.* Phoenix: Oryx Press, 1999.

Unger, Sanford J. *FBI.* Boston: Little Brown, 1975.

U.S. Congress. "Congress Studies the Problem of Juvenile Delinquency." *Congressional Digest* 33 (December 1954): 289–310.

U.S. House of Representatives. Judiciary Committee Report, Transportation of Obscene Matters. Report No. 2017, 5 May 1950, 81st Congress, 2nd session.

U.S. Senate. Judiciary Committee Report. Transportation of Obscene Matters (Phonograph Records). Report No. 1305, 27 February 1950, 81st Congress, 2nd session.

U.S. Senate. *Protecting Children on the Internet. Hearing before the U.S. Senate Committee on Commerce, Science and Transportation.* 109th Congress, 2nd session, 19 January 2006. Washington, DC: U.S. Government Printing Office, 2006.

Wilentz, Sean. *The Age of Reagan: A History, 1974–2008.* New York: HarperCollins, 2008.